Concrete Critical Theory

Historical Materialism Book Series

The Historical Materialism Book Series is a major publishing initiative of the radical left. The capitalist crisis of the twenty-first century has been met by a resurgence of interest in critical Marxist theory. At the same time, the publishing institutions committed to Marxism have contracted markedly since the high point of the 1970s. The Historical Materialism Book Series is dedicated to addressing this situation by making available important works of Marxist theory. The aim of the series is to publish important theoretical contributions as the basis for vigorous intellectual debate and exchange on the left.

The peer-reviewed series publishes original monographs, translated texts, and reprints of classics across the bounds of academic disciplinary agendas and across the divisions of the left. The series is particularly concerned to encourage the internationalization of Marxist debate and aims to translate significant studies from beyond the English-speaking world.

For a full list of titles in the Historical Materialism Book Series available in paperback from Haymarket Books, visit: www.haymarketbooks.org/series_collections/1-historical-materialism.

Concrete Critical Theory

Althusser's Marxism

William S. Lewis

Haymarket Books
Chicago, IL

First published in 2021 by Brill Academic Publishers, The Netherlands
© 2021 Koninklijke Brill NV, Leiden, The Netherlands

Published in paperback in 2022 by
Haymarket Books
P.O. Box 180165
Chicago, IL 60618
773-583-7884
www.haymarketbooks.org

ISBN: 978-1-64259-789-9

Distributed to the trade in the US through Consortium Book Sales and
Distribution (www.cbsd.com) and internationally through Ingram
Publisher Services International (www.ingramcontent.com).

This book was published with the generous support of Lannan
Foundation and Wallace Action Fund.

Special discounts are available for bulk purchases by organizations and
institutions. Please call 773-583-7884 or email info@haymarketbooks.org
for more information.

Cover art and design by David Mabb. Cover art is a detail of *Utopia, after
May Morris*, paint on pillowcase mounted on canvas (2003).

Printed in the United States.

10 9 8 7 6 5 4 3 2 1

Library of Congress Cataloging-in-Publication data is available.

Contents

Acknowledgements

This book could not have been written without the steady support and encouragement of Sebastian Budgen, Danny Hayward, and the rest of the Historical Materialism Editorial Board. Concrete material support was provided by Skidmore College, Lili Zeller and Jacques Amsellem, as well as the équipe at the *Institut Mémoires de l'Edition Contemporaine*. I am likewise grateful to the editors and reviewers at the *VersoBlog*, *Décalages*, *International Studies in Philosophy* and *The Journal of Speculative Philosophy*, where versions of this material first appeared as:

Lewis, William S. 2007, 'Concrete Analysis and Pragmatic Social Theory (Notes Towards an Althusserian Critical Theory)', *International Studies in Philosophy*, 39 (2): 97–116.

Lewis, William S. 2008, 'War, Manipulation of Consent, and Deliberative Democracy', *The Journal of Speculative Philosophy*, 22 (4): 266–77.

Lewis, William S. 2016, 'Althusser's Scientism and Aleatory Materialism', *Décalages*, 2 (1).

Lewis, William S. 2017, 'A New 'International of Decent Feelings'? Cosmopolitanism and the Erasure of Class', in *Cosmopolitanism and Place*, edited by Jessica Wahman, John J. Stuhr, and José M. Medina, 264–79. Indianapolis, Ind.: Indiana University Press.

Lewis, William S. 2019, ' "But Didn't He Kill His Wife?" ', www.versobooks.com, 29 May 2019.

Introduction

1   Concrete Analysis and Frankfurt School Critical Theory

In an introduction to 'The Humanist Controversy (196X)', Louis Althusser wrote of a 'chance encounter' with Frankfurt School critical theory which failed to take hold. As he relates it, both the historical conjuncture and personal caroms occasioned this brief commingling. The first historical condition was met with the circulation of Althusser's arguments about there being a 'break' between a young, humanistic Marx and a later scientific thinker. Second, previous to and partially inciting Althusser's philosophical intervention, communist theorists and fellow travellers had begun disseminating and discussing Marx's pre-Manifesto philosophical writings. Out of these texts, and in contradistinction to NATO and Warsaw PACT styles of domination and division, this international cohort was in the process of developing a cosmopolitan philosophy and politics of 'Marxist Humanism'.[1]

An event at a friend's house in 1963 put Althusser in touch with one of these intellectuals: Adam Schaff. A philosopher and Polish Communist Party ideologue, Schaff had just returned from a lecture tour in the United States.[2] While there, the Polish semiotician had met with Erich Fromm, a first-generation member of the Institute for Social Research. Since fleeing Germany, Fromm had become known for his Freudo-Marxian analyses of political psychology. Flush with the success of a 1961 book presenting a Marxist philosophy of human nature alongside a new translation of the *1844 Manuscripts*, Fromm was busy soliciting contributions for a transnational collection of writings on the topic of 'Socialist Humanism'.[3] Aware of Althusser's opinion on the 'Young Marx' and on his heterodox humanism, Schaff recommended Althusser for inclusion.[4] Informed of this backstory by Schaff, Althusser realised that it was no caprice that he had received a letter from Fromm requesting his participation in the collection a few days before making Schaff's personal acquaintance.

---

1 Demaitre 1965.
2 Althusser does not mention in the introductory note that he had strongly criticised Schaff's work 'On the "Young Marx"' (1963), Althusser 2003c, p. 222; 2005b, pp. 54–60.
3 Marx and Fromm 1961.
4 Schaff 1970, p. 258 fn 22.

Sensing that his contribution would be unwelcome in a volume celebrating Marx's humanism and socialism (about both of which Althusser had serious theoretical misgivings), Althusser tried to forbear.[5] Schaff, however, per-
suaded Althusser with the following 'impeccable syllogism': "'Every Humanist
is a Liberal; Fromm is a Humanist; therefore, Fromm is a Liberal'".[6] By this
Schaff meant that, if Fromm believed in the essential freedom of human beings,
then he must also endorse this freedom's expression in the realm of ideas.
Therefore, Schaff reasoned, as a liberal and humanist, Fromm would publish
Althusser's contribution regardless of it being at odds with the general tenor of
the volume. Pushed into acquiescence by his own theory of the 'displacement
of the dominant' Althusser drafted a 'very short and too clear' essay and sent
it off to Fromm.[7] That which was deductively impeccable was however, practically impossible and Althusser received a rejection letter from Fromm a few
months later. Though recognising the value of Althusser's contribution, Fromm
wrote that its argument did not fit well with the other essays, just as Althusser
had originally suspected it would not.[8]

Notwithstanding a single, uncited reference to Horkheimer in the early 1970s
and the never-realised prospect of a meeting with Marcuse in 1969, this epis-
ode comprised Althusser's sole association with Frankfurt School theory or
theorists.[9] For someone interested in Althusser as a critical theorist, is there
anything to be gleaned from this reedy and singular encounter? From one perspective, there is not. After all, by 1963, Fromm had been away from Germany
for thirty years. Moreover, he had dissociated himself from the Institute for
Social Research a generation before editing *Socialist Humanism: An International Symposium*.[10] Additionally, however celebrated as a public intellectual,
empirical researcher, and clinician, Fromm had become a marginal or, better
put, marginalised figure in comparison with other theorists associated with
the Institute such as Adorno, Horkheimer, Marcuse, and Benjamin.[11] These
thinkers were, like Althusser, more archly philosophical in their approach to
critical research. Fromm, therefore, is somewhat of an unrepresentative fig-

5   Althusser 2003c, pp. 196, 223.
6   Althusser 2003c, p. 223.
7   Althusser 2003c, p. 223.
8   Althusser 2003c, p. 224; 1998b, p. 477.
9   'Dossier "Collège Hyppolite -Wolf" Concernant l'annulation Par Le Collège de France Du
      VIIème Congrès Hegel Prévu Les 8–12 Avril 1969 et Auquel Devaient Participer Louis
      Althusser et Herbert Marcuse.' 1969; Althusser 1999, p. 118; François Matheron 1999, pp. vi–
      ix.
10   Schmidt 2007, p. 53.
11   McLaughlin 2008, pp. 2–3.

ure and his choice to exclude Althusser may say more about his research programme than about Althusser's relation to critical theory.

Aside from Schaff's opinion that Fromm was a liberal and a humanist and apart from Fromm's rejection of Althusser's anti-humanism, from a certain vantage point there is little in this exchange to assist us in thinking about Althusser's relation to critical theory in general or to the Frankfurt School in particular. Of course, this is not the only option for considering Althusser as a critical theorist. In a manner not that unusual among intellectual historians and political theorists, one could arrange Althusser's arguments and opinions in all the areas where his thought intersects with those of Frankfurt School Critical Theorists. This exegesis accomplished, one could then show how, where, and to what extent their respective claims and conclusions overlap. As a political philosopher, one could even go a step further and demonstrate the superiority or inferiority of Althusser's positions compared to those of different Frankfurt School theorists. One could also argue for these positions' complementarity, utility, or veracity. In this regard, an eager reader could imagine fruitful comparisons across the topics of aesthetics, dialectic, science, social reproduction, ethics, ideology, state violence, psychoanalysis, historiography, subjectification, critique, praxis, and abstraction. Given the paucity of such studies and comparisons, this is a book or series of articles which deserves and needs to be written.[12] However, this volume developing Althusserian concrete analysis as a species of critical theory does not choose this option.

Returning to the missed encounter and also now beginning to articulate this book's premise and approach, there is another perspective which holds that elements of the exchange with Fromm do indeed tell us something about how the practice of concrete analysis outlined by Althusser in the mid-1970s relates to Frankfurt School Critical Theory. What we learn is that, when Althusser sketched out a theory of concrete analysis in such works as *Les Vaches noires* (1976) and *Que Faire* (1978), he took up many of the same problems in philosophy of social science as did the founding members of the Institute for Critical Research.[13] What we also find when we develop this theory is that there are salient differences between the two approaches to critical philosophy and to practical research. These differences can be appreciated not only in the luckless encounter with Fromm but also by Althusser's attitude to the 'urtext' of

---

12   In the last 30 years, there have been fewer than ten articles in English, French, German, Spanish or Portuguese which directly compare Althusser to Frankfurt School Critical Theorists or Theory. These include Cardella 2014; Catanzaro 2015; 2013; Grollios 2013; Méndez 2014; Pfeifer 2015; Parra 2014; Robles 2018; Trom 2008.

13   Adorno 1977; Horkheimer 1999.

critical theory: Marx's September 1843 'Letter to Arnold Ruge'. When we compare the contours of Althusser's 'concrete analysis' to the general criteria for a critical theory developed by Raymond Guess, these disparities are also visible.

Scrutinising the component claims of Schaff's decisive modus ponens, we find Althusser agreeing to the claim that there is a necessary relationship between being a humanist and being a liberal. The 'he will publish your contribution' conclusion Schaff and Althusser drew from this pairing relies on the implicit metaphysical-cum-normative claim that part of what it is to be human is to be free and that those who recognise this principle (i.e. liberals) have an obligation to respect this freedom. Notoriously, Althusser critiqued not only the classical liberal idea of what it is to be human but also its Hegelian Marxist reformulation as developed by Lukács, H. Lefebvre, Merleau-Ponty, Schaff, Garaudy, and other thinkers during the inter- and post-war periods.[14] In this regard, both the liberal conception which posits reasonableness, freedom, and equality as components of the human essence and the Marxist humanist alternative, which sees these principles as the outcome of a dialectical process in which 'man's' powers are first alienated, developed, and then restored to him in their full, social form, Althusser judged to be ideological.[15] These concepts which have the effect of supporting certain ways of life, institutions, and political projects are – and this was Althusser's big claim – unsuitable starting points from which to begin a scientific analysis of historical events or of the present political conjuncture. In fact, they foreclose such a theory.[16] According to Althusser, both liberal and Marxist humanisms prematurely answer the question which was to be posed by any materialist analysis: namely, what is the way in which human beings, by producing their means of subsistence, also produce themselves? In this sense, to say that humans are by nature free or that they are destined by nature to become so is to make the same anti-scientific, anti-materialist mistake.[17] In addition, as metaphysical concepts with normative ramifications, both philosophical anthropologies prematurely settle the question of what is to be done. For liberals and for Marxist humanists the answer is always: that which best allows man to achieve or to express his essence, an essence already decided upon and known in advance.

---

14   Althusser 1977a, pp. 149–60; W.S. Lewis 2005b, pp. 155–87.
15   Althusser 2003c, pp. 258–59, 266. The masculine pronoun, sometimes capitalised, as in the phrase 'Total Man', is used almost exclusively by these authors to denote humanity as a whole.
16   Althusser 2003c, p. 264.
17   W.S. Lewis 2007a, p. 147.

The contrasting takes on Marx's September 1843 open letter by Althusser and by Frankfurt School critical theorists (and their numerous chroniclers) further reflect the difference in each's conception of critical theory. At least in this regard, his reception of the Ruge letter shows Fromm to be in conformity with other members of the Institute for Social Research. Whereas Fromm, Adorno, Horkheimer, Habermas and other prominent contemporary critical theorists approvingly cite Marx's appeal to inaugurate the '*ruthless criticism of all the exists*' and read the *1844 Manuscripts* as this charge's necessary methodological elaboration, Althusser pauses.[18] Why does he hesitate? Not because he disagrees with Marx's claim that the 'construction of the future' demands critical philosophy. Nor does he find Marx's reciprocally formulated contention dubious that 'Tying our criticism ... to real struggles' is the effect of adopting a new political position and that this 'politics could bear within it theoretical consequences'.[19] What he doubts is whether or not Marx, before 1845, had sufficiently cast off Hegelian and Feuerbachian metaphysical frameworks such that the theoretical consequences of binding one's theory to political struggles could be recognised and appreciated.[20] Whereas the inaugural Frankfurt School theorists saw in these texts Marx's true philosophy of man revealed from underneath an obscuring layer of political economy, Althusser did not even appreciate these writings as the 'seeds' of Marx's mature theory.[21] That Marx identifies the 'ruthless criticism of all that exists' with a 'public confession by Humanity of Humanity's sins' demonstrates to Althusser that, in the early 1840s, Marx was still thinking of criticism as normative and as based upon a telic philosophical anthropology.[22] In this 'theoretical' history, the end and good of human beings is disalienation; the first step to achieving it politically is by translating 'religious and political problems into their self-conscious Human form'.[23]

Though it would remain unachieved until Marxist theory abandoned its stadial theory of history, according to Althusser, the methodological key enabling communists to link criticism to real struggles occurred with the *Theses on*

18   Bottomore 2002, pp. 71–2; Cook 2001, p. 4; Fraser 2013, p. 97; Habermas 2007, p. 51; Koechlin 2015; Marx and Fromm 1961, p. iv; Marcus and Tarr 1984, p. 31; Marx and Engels 1982, p. 142.
19   Althusser 2003c, p. 246.
20   Althusser 2003c, p. 246.
21   Althusser 2003c, pp. 246–7.
22   Althusser 2003c, p. 247; Lindner 2011, p. 129.
23   Althusser 2003c, p. 248; Marx et al. 1976, p. 346; Marx 1992, p. 209. Marx and Engels 1982 erroneously translates 'political' as 'philosophical' in this phrase.

Feuerbach and *The German Ideology* in 1845–6.[24] There and then, 'theoretical history' was superseded (albeit not definitively) by concrete, material histories where the subject became 'real, empirical individuals, endowed with certain forces, living in concrete sociohistorical, conditions, and producing ... in 'relations of mutual commerce' that with which to satisfy their own vital needs in their material-life-process'.[25] In summary then, Althusser did not object to linking criticism to political struggle, nor did he challenge the consciousness-raising and strategic value of such analysis; what he challenged was the idea that criticism should proceed from anthropologico-normative notions of what it is to be or to become a human being.[26] 'Held in advance' stories about man splitting himself into subject and object in order to, one day, overcome all contradictions and to realise himself in full human freedom with others were as ideological as the liberal idea that God endowed us with reason. As ideological notions, such schemas and their entailed norms were neither to be the basis of critique nor its goal. Rather, they were to be subjected to 'ruthless criticism' by materialist historical methods.

If we turn from the common thread of Marx's 'Letter to Ruge' to the diagnostic criteria developed by Raymond Geuss in his 1981 study *Habermas and the Frankfurt School*, we again uncover reasons why someone committed to Frankfurt School style critical theory would reject an essay by Althusser on the Young Marx.[27] What we also locate are the means by which we can clearly describe the main contours of Althusser's variety of critical theory, 'concrete analysis,' in its similarity and dissimilarity from that developed collectively by members of the Institute for Social Research. Surveying the Frankfurt School and developing criteria by which to characterise them, Geuss lists three theses and two sub-theses. With some little modification Althusser would accept all three theses as descriptive of his critical project. It is for this reason that we can label concrete analysis a 'critical theory' in a broad sense.[28] However, he would substantially reject both sub-postulates under the first thesis, which most prominently include the anthropologico-normative aspects of the theory. In order to describe the main contours of Althusser's critical project in terms of

---

24   Lindner 2011, p. 122. Goshgarian 2003, lvi points out that, while embroiled in 'The Humanist Controversy', Althusser had yet to break with his own philosophical idealism.

25   Althusser 2003c, p. 259; 2006a, p. 36.

26   Lindner 2011, p. 130.

27   Geuss 2010, pp. 1–2.

28   This use of 'broad' differs from the use Bohman 2019 makes of the distinction between Frankfurt School Critical Theory and 'critical theory in the broader sense'. 'Broad' here is more capacious in that it refers not only to explicitly liberatory social theories but to all Marxian, materialist modes of critical analysis.

its affinities and differences with Frankfurt School Critical Theory, it is perhaps easiest to work backwards from Geuss' third element of critical theory, describing in general terms the way in which concrete analysis is compatible with each criterion before detailing why Althusser would disagree with the normative elements associated with the first.

The third principle which Guess argues unites critical theories is: 'Critical theories differ epistemologically in essential ways from theories in the natural sciences. Theories in natural science are 'objectifying'; critical theories are 'reflective'. Chapters 3 and 4 of this book go into much more detail regarding Althusser's epistemology and how Marxian critical research differs from natural scientific investigation. That said, the main thrust of Althusser's critique of conventional philosophy of natural science, as well as of Marxist humanism, is that both are 'empiricisms'. The core belief characterising empiricism is that the essence of an object can come to be known, as it is, by a subject.[29] Inasmuch as positivist philosophies of science tend to emphasise the way in which appropriate methods of investigation produce facts (i.e., true knowledge of scientific objects), Althusser rejects them. Likewise, he criticises idealist and 'reflective' theories which stress the way subjective factors eventually result in the total understanding of objects both natural and social.[30] So then, insofar as a critical theory emphasises a 'reflexivity' wherein human subjects come to know their truly human self through critical research, enlightenment, and political action, Althusser would also accuse it of empiricism. That said, and as Chapter 4 and 5 of this volume elucidate, Althusser does not think that we should accept the results of scientific research unproblematically. Because both science and politics begin from ideological knowledge, he endorses critical self-reflection on a scientific study's presuppositions, methods, and results from a specific class position. Doing so, he claims, will help to purge a study of ideological notions and improve the chances that acting upon a study's findings will bring success. Therefore, so long as 'reflexivity' is taken broadly to mean a moment in the critical process when engaged inquirers, occupying a certain class position, scrutinise a science and its results for ideological notions, Althusser's critical theory is consonant with the entirety of Geuss' third principle.

The second principle enumerated by Geuss and its compatibility with Althusser's critical theory is more easily dealt with than the first, and with less nuance. This criterion is: 'Critical theories have cognitive content, i.e. they are forms of knowledge'.[31] Though this book endorses the philosophical framework

---

29   Althusser 1969b, pp. 12, 151; Peden 2014, p. 158.
30   Althusser 1969b, pp. 227–30.
31   Geuss 2010, p. 2.

associated with Althusser's post-'theoreticist' period, some terms and concepts
from his earlier and better known work from the first half of the 1960s help to
make this point.[32] Following Marx and Engels, Althusser conceives of human
life as necessarily organised around production and reproduction. Rather than
excluding intellectual work from other productive practices, Althusser includes
it. So then, alongside biological, economic, and political production, Althusser
lists three sorts of intellectual production: ideological, scientific, and philosophical.[33] For the same epistemological reasons that he rejects empiricism,
Althusser chooses to avoid the Cartesian concept of cognition and its repres-
entationalist connotations.[34] However, if cognition is understood liberally as
'the mechanisms by which [humans] acquire, process, store and act on information from the environment' or even conservatively as necessarily involving
concepts of which we are aware, then Althusser would agree that concrete analysis produces knowledge.[35] Further, and as Chapter 4 develops, it is the unique
combination of scientific and philosophical thinking involved in concrete analysis that produces better practical knowledge than do the ideological 'truths'
we find ready-to-mind.

At first glance, concrete analysis also appears to satisfy Geuss' first principle.
Like Frankfurt School critical studies, the results of concrete analyses 'have special standing as guides for human action'.[36] Specifically, a group which engages
in Concrete Analysis is more likely to act in such a way that their political goals
are realised. That said, this correspondence does not seem sufficient to indicate
an accord with the totality of the first thesis. As Geuss clarifies under a subhead-
ing: 'Critical Theories have special standing as guides for human action in that:
(a) they are aimed at producing enlightenment in the agents who hold them,
i.e. at enabling those agents to determine what their true interests are;' and '(b)
they are inherently emancipatory, i.e. they free agents from a kind of coercion
which is at least partly self-imposed, from self-frustration of conscious human
action'.[37] If the conjunction 'in that' marks a strong causal claim, then Althusser
would disagree with Geuss' two ancillary statements while agreeing with the
primary criterion. As our analysis of Geuss' second criterion for a critical theory has already shown, concrete analysis accords with the assertion to the left
of the semi-colon in sub-thesis (a): it is aimed at producing knowledge which is

---

32   Althusser 1990a, p. 211.
33   Althusser 1969b.
34   Althusser and Balibar 1970, pp. 56–67.
35   Althusser 2018c, p. 19; Bayne and Heyes 2019, pp. 609, 611; Shettleworth 2010, p. 4.
36   Geuss 2010, p. 2.
37   Geuss 2010, p. 2.

otherwise unavailable and that may guide human action. However, Althusser does not argue that a critical theory helps 'agents to determine what their true interests are', and for two reasons. First, because our interests are said to be wholly produced in and through our socio-economic relations, Althusser does not deem humans to have 'true' interests which can be determined irrespective of these existing and historically contingent relations. Second, the aim of concrete analysis is not to discover our interests but to understand ourselves and our social relations such that we can alter them. Though they may be somewhat transformed in the course of inquiry, objective interests precede and instigate analysis rather than follow from it.[38]

Further, and to address sub-thesis (b) of the first element, it is not clear that concrete analyses are 'inherently emancipatory'. For one, like any science, their results are fallible.[39] Second, Althusser rejects the idea of alienation referred to by the phrase 'a kind of coercion which is at least partly self-imposed'. Underlying this element is the philosophical anthropology referenced above. According to this metaphysics, human beings as a species are one individual and this individual's journey to enlightenment and emancipation *is history*. According to this Theory of Man, the fact that one portion of humanity now restricts the freedom and steals the labour and potential of another part reflects an internal contradiction within the historical development of the human species as a whole. Insofar as alienation and class struggle are something 'man' does to himself, it is self-imposed. For Althusser, rejecting this anthropology as well as the transcendental normativity associated with it also means denying the inherently emancipatory and enlightening potential of critical theory identified by Geuss as an essential elements of Frankfurt School thought. This does not mean that concrete analyses are no help to us in comprehending our situations or that they cannot assist us in achieving emancipatory and egalitarian political goals. However, the fruits of a concrete analysis will be judged according to the particular values of those who initiate inquiry into a given conjuncture's transformation.

The promise of Althusserian concrete analysis, and what makes it a 'special guide' is that it can produce knowledge of how a particular class of people, in a particular time, in a particular place, is dominated, oppressed, or exploited. Moreover, it can suggest potential political means for the alleviation of these conditions. Nothing about concrete analysis, however, speaks to or guarantees general enlightenment and emancipation. In fact, there is little reason that

---

38   Althusser 1978c, p. 36.
39   Baltas 1993, p. 651.

exploiters could not use the tools sketched by Althusser to understand an historical conjuncture with the goal of *better* exploiting or dominating already subjugated peoples. Althusser is optimistic in suggesting that, because the dominant class produces and benefits from the prevailing ideology, it is unlikely to engage in a concrete analysis which challenge these beliefs.[40] However, despite this block, there is an argument to be made that such analyses are precisely what capitalists engage in – albeit in a somewhat haphazard but ultimately effective fashion – when they research the effects of legislation on their industry or before proposing legislation themselves.

So then, these are the main contours of Althusser's practice of concrete analysis as it is developed, defended, and applied over the course of this book. First, though it embraces the results of the natural and social sciences and though it starts from ideological notions, concrete analysis accepts neither of these cognitive forms uncritically. Rather, through a self-consciously reflexive process, inquirers occupying a certain class position engage in the production of knowledge about a particular spatio-historical conjuncture and about the concrete roles they play in it as subjects and agents. Second, concrete analysis produces practical knowledge. That is, when performed well, it permits engaged inquirers to understand how the socio-economic world works such that they may influence and thereby direct their lives more fruitfully than they would otherwise be able. Finally, concrete analysis serves as a 'special guide' but not to emancipation and enlightenment for all of humanity. With no underlying normative notion of what it is to be human or of what we should enable humans to become, it cannot so serve. Beginning from an anti-humanist or, better put, an a-humanist position, enlightenment and emancipation are always relative and provisional; the judgment that they are achieved is based on the specific valuations of those who are compelled to initiate critical inquiry into their inegalitarian and unfree circumstances. John Dewey put this point better than Althusser ever did when he wrote in 1935 that 'nothing is clearer than that the conception of liberty is always relative to forces that at a given time and place are increasingly felt to be oppressive'. Using the term 'concrete' in ways strikingly similar to Althusser's employment of the term in 'concrete' analysis, Dewey adds: 'Liberty in the concrete signifies release from the impact of particular oppressive forces, emancipation from something once taken as a normal part of human life but now experienced as bondage'.[41]

---

40   Correspondingly, because the dominated class suffers by the prevailing ideology, they do have reasons to research and challenge these claims.

41   Dewey 2000, 54.

2   Methodology

As the quote from Dewey suggests, this book does not take as its goal the discovery or revelation of a suppressed or esoteric critical theory hiding within Althusser's published or unpublished writings. Rather, what it argues is that the rudiments for such a theory are present in Althusser's philosophy after 1966 and that these may fruitfully be developed and applied to present issues. However, because these suggestions are sketchy and as they include much that is contradictory, hyperbolic, or dated, they cannot stand on their own. In order to resolve these contradictions and to fill out Althusser's draft, this book makes extensive use of tools and arguments from contemporary value theory and philosophy of social science. More specifically, it relies upon contemporary Marxist, feminist, and pragmatist arguments regarding harm, class stratification, democracy, inequality, social kinds, historiography, scientific realism, methodological pluralism, anthropology, and cosmopolitanism. In the tradition of analytic political philosophy, it also employs relevant social scientific knowledge to make its points, but not unreflexively.[42] Reasoning that the history of an idea's employment tells us something about its contemporaneous correctness, this analytic approach is supplemented by a pragmatist-genealogical approach.[43] Finally, though it only pulls from the latter's work explicitly, the shape of this volume's argument was also influenced at a deep level by Allen's criticisms of the notion of progress in critical theory and by Jaeggi's 'thin' account of alienation and its associated normativity.[44]

3   Structure of the Book

While the purposes of this book are to construct an Althusserian critical theory and to show its applicability to certain problems in political philosophy and of social life, it does not begin with a direct consideration of concrete analysis. Cognisant of the present conjuncture, of the fact that this discussion is long overdue, and because the theoretical conclusions of Chapter 2 demand it, this volume leads with a discussion of how the harms associated with Althusser's 1980 killing of Hélène Rytmann-Légotien should affect the reception and use of his philosophical ideas. Manifestly, the conclusion is not that Althusser's work should be cancelled but, instead, that we should explicitly recognise and strive

42   McDermott 2008, pp. 23–4.
43   Althusser 2014a, pp. 227–8; Koopman 2011.
44   Allen 2016; Jaeggi 2016; 2014.

to mitigate the harms associated with letting this condemnable fact go unacknowledged and undiscussed.

Following Chapter 2's discussion of the ethics of reading Althusser and of employing his ideas, is a piece examining his scientism. The length of this chapter reflects the numerous purposes for which it is employed. For the reader perhaps little acquainted with Althusser's thought, it outlines the development of his understanding of philosophy, politics, ideology, science, and their interrelationships. As the book's elaboration of concrete analysis will pull extensively on these concepts, their definitions in this chapter constitutes a sort of prolegomena. As significant a task as informing new readers is the work of disabusing casual readers and those whose knowledge of Althusser comes chiefly through secondary sources presenting now ossified misconceptions regarding Althusser's philosophical trajectory. This chapter will demonstrate that, despite certain 'theoreticist' detours, Althusser's understanding of science and its role in political decision-making changed little throughout his career.

With the relations Althusser believes to exist between Marxist philosophy, science, ideology, and politics clarified, Chapter 4 begins the explicit development of an Althusserian critical theory. This chapter proceeds in three ways. First, it engages in a close reading of recently published texts from the mid-to-late 1970s in order to explicate Althusser's understanding of concrete analysis. It also provides the historical background necessary to understand why Althusser thought concrete analysis necessary for political strategy. Second, because much of what Althusser said about concrete analysis is contradictory, dated, or impracticable, its methodology is reconstructed and amended with the aid of contemporary political philosophy, philosophy of social science, and critical theory. Third, because contemporary critical theory has largely excluded historical materialism as a legitimate method of inquiry and because concrete analysis depends upon it, Chapter 4 concludes with an argument in its defence. This section simultaneously develops Althusser's heterodox form of historical materialism, which will be employed extensively in the book's later chapters.

Case in point: Chapter 5 builds on the previous chapter's claim that historical materialism is necessary for orienting and advancing critical theory. Along with a reconstructed understanding of historical materialism, this chapter argues that a recent conceptual advance in feminist philosophy can help revive the moribund Marxist concepts of 'class' and 'class struggle' in a way that is useful to social scientists studying class and its effects. The first section of this chapter explains the trait/norm covariance model of gender and gendered oppression as recently developed by Mikkola. After endorsing its superiority over competing social ontologies, the chapter shows how the model can help us to understand class and to target class oppression more effectively than competing Marxian theories.

The sixth chapter of the book forms a bridge between the part mostly concerned with developing a tenable theory of concrete analysis and that part which applies it to problems in political philosophy and social life. Theoretically, Chapter 6 develops the solution Althusser proposed in 1966 to the dilemma of how to separate ideological from scientific knowledge. It then argues that the same apparatus enabling the critical theorist to distinguish scientific concepts obscured by class prejudice from ideological notions is similarly applicable to the problem of how to separate racist ideology from racial science. The chapter concludes with an application of this critical tool to an egregious example of racist social science.

Chapter 7 applies the insights of Althusser's Marxism to contemporary political philosophy. In so doing, it provides examples of how concrete analysis works in practice to inform democratic deliberation. It also weighs in on the 'feasibility' debates within deliberative democratic theory. Perhaps surprisingly given the proceeding chapter's emphasis on separating out ideology, this chapter argues that ideology is the necessary starting point for any concrete analysis or democratic deliberation.

Chapter 8 returns to something like pure political philosophy and to the original anti-humanist, anti-normativist position which marks out the difference between Althusserian concrete analysis and Frankfurt School Critical Theory. Using one of Althusser's earliest essays, this chapter contends that the principal arguments for cosmopolitanism recently advanced are analogous to those of certain post-World II French philosophers and their calls for universal solidarity in the face of atomic destruction. The two value theories are comparable in their universalising tendencies and in their shared intention to provide moral and political order to a world historical situation that has undergone rapid change and where political and moral hegemony is ambiguous. It is argued that these philosophies' appeals to common ideals often results in the forgetting of class differences and in the paving over of particular, concrete class struggles. This ignorance makes it difficult to identify and solve the problems of exploitation, domination, and oppression associated with global, national, and local capitalisms.

CHAPTER 2

'But Didn't He Kill His Wife?'

There is a common reaction when people find out that the work of Louis Althusser significantly informs one's thinking.[1] If the person knows who Althusser is – and especially if the acquaintance identifies as female – one will often be met with a stunned silence, followed by the phrase: 'But didn't he kill his wife?' How to respond? The banal and facile reply is: 'Yes, but this fact doesn't matter philosophically'. However, given the frequency of this and similar reactions, to say that the killing does not matter at all is plainly wrong. For those of us who find Althusser's rethinking of Marxism of theoretical or practical relevance and particularly for those who write books like this one exploring and employing his ideas, a pressing moral and political question is, therefore, how can we continue to think with Althusser. Should we continue to employ Althusser's philosophical ideas theoretically and politically in light of this offence?

The ways in which theorists and activists have typically dealt with the uncomfortable fact that Althusser ended the life of his wife, the sociologist and *résistante* Hélène Rytmann-Légotien, have undoubtedly hindered the reception of Althusser's philosophy.[2] In preparation for a colloquium marking Althusser's centenary, a list of philosophers, political theorists, and social scientists whose work was significantly informed by Althusser's ideas was assembled. The male to female ratio of the persons on the list numbered eleven to one, making Althusser studies worse in terms of gender equity than academic philosophy as a whole – and probably much worse than political philosophy as a sub-discipline.[3] When the centenary colloquium was eventually held, twenty-nine of the presenters were men. Two were women.[4] That Marxism, socialism, and the far left have their own gender problems present con-

---

1   The author wishes to thank Banu Bargu, Arne de Boever, Fabio Bruschi, Thomas Carmichael, Caren Irr, Asad Haider, Alexander Gorman, Geoff Pfeifer, Hasana Sharp, and Panagiotis Sotiris, and the Verso Blog editor John Merrick for their comments on this chapter, most of which have been incorporated.

2   'Légotien' was the nom de guerre which Hélène Rytmann continued to use after the conflict. See: Moulier-Boutang 1992, p. 345 Various texts render her surname as Rytmann, Rittman, Rytman, Légotien as well as with the hyphenates Légotien-Rytmann and Rytmann-Légotien.

3   There is data to suggest that women gravitate to Value Theory rather then LEMM fields as well: Jennings 2016; Jennings and Schwitzgebel 2015; Schwitzgebel 2017.

4   Fabula 2018.

founding variables. But anyone having researched, conferenced, or correspon-
ded with folks interested in Althusser is aware that this subset of left theorists
and activists overwhelmingly identifies as male. Further, there is now debate in
graduate seminars and at conferences about whether one should teach, read, or
cite Althusser given this history. This chapter does not weigh in on the question
of whether Althusser's mental health in November of 1980 makes him culpable
of murder. The ultimate answer to this question is unknowable and the judi-
cial response has been rendered. Instead, it focuses on the consequences of
this act for contemporary theory and politics: areas where we can have knowledge and where we can make changes. Clearly, we have sufficient evidence
to suggest that Althusser killing his wife is off-putting for those who might
otherwise be interested in his thought and particularly so for women. It is therefore both timely and overdue that we consider Althusser's philosophical ideas
and the history of their reception in relation to this climate and to these reactions.

1   The Duty to Cite

If one made two stacks of the literature written about Althusser, the mound
that puts the killing of Rytmann-Légotien front and centre – the *externalist* or
biographical approach – would far outweigh the pile that exclusively treats of
Althusser's contributions to political philosophy.[5] That said, the latter, *philosophy first* or *internalist* approach, is the one taken by this volume and it is
therefore of paramount importance to examine the arguments on its behalf.
The internalist approach takes two forms: one for those interested in the *history of philosophy*, and another to those engaged in *political philosophy* in a
narrower sense. History of philosophy types consider Althusser's work in its
historical context and look to understand how it contributed to contemporaneous theoretical debates. Here, biographical claims only enter when they help
to explain things like the effect of philosophical formation on a work's production or reception. Political philosophers and theorists, by way of contrast, tend
to elaborate, reconstruct, criticise, apply, or reject the arguments and concepts
that Althusser developed in order to solve philosophical or political problems.
Therefore, they give even less attention to his biography than do those concerned with history of philosophy.

---

5 Kelley 2002, p. 3.

Despite differences in focus and methodology, the arguments for treating Althusser exclusively as a political philosopher are basically identical for history of philosophy and for contemporary political philosophy. The first argument is very rough and may be contestable given the definition of philosophy it includes. From the standpoint of history, it is that the history of philosophy consists of a history of ideas about ourselves, our universe, and about our place within it. Philosophy in this definition is about finding the truth of things or, better put, about developing concepts adequate to the conceptualisation of the universe that we inhabit and about deciding how we should live in it. Correspondingly, political philosophy is about creating, analysing, and defending adequate or true ideas about how we should live with others. Combining the former and the latter, history of political philosophy surveys, criticises, or applies ideas from the past regarding how we should live together and about who has legitimate power over others. For both, and regardless of whether we are doing straight political philosophy or history of political philosophy, it is the ideas and arguments that matter and – as with the development of other sciences – the biography of the thinker of the ideas and arguments is irrelevant to the utility, adequacy, or truth value produced by this practice.

The second argument for treating Althusser exclusively as a political philosopher, rather than just implying a duty to treat ideas in the abstract as the first, fleshes out why it matters that ideas are tied to a specific person. Brian Leiter makes the case for such reference succinctly in a 2018 essay for the *Chronicle of Higher Education* titled 'Academic Ethics: Should Scholars Avoid Citing the Work of Awful People?'[6] There, he argues that scholarship is about advancing knowledge within a discipline and that, within a discipline, scholarly citation has only two purposes. These are 'to acknowledge a prior contribution to knowledge on which your work depends' and 'to serve as an epistemic authority for a claim relevant to your own contribution to knowledge'. According to Leiter, failure to cite relevant knowledge is harmful because scholarship is thereby not advanced. Therefore, if an idea or argument is relevant to one's scholarship, then our duty as scholars is to cite it and to name the originator of that knowledge.

Combined, the first and second arguments suggest that not only must we do philosophy by reference to past ideas – even if awful people originate these notions – but also that we have a *duty* to explicitly reference these people. Notice, however, that these two arguments do not imply that we have a duty to skip over the wrongful deeds and characters of the originators of philosoph-

---

6   Leiter 2018.

ical concepts; merely that any such mention is extraneous to the purpose of scholarship, which is to advance knowledge on a specific topic in a specific discipline.

2 Countervailing Harms

As mentioned above, this book employs an internalist or philosophy-first approach. Its employment signals endorsement of the argument that concepts can fruitfully be considered in alienation from the persons and context in which they were produced and, further, that philosophy would be irremediably harmed if we were to expunge the ideas of vicious philosophers.[7] There is another, practical reason to employ this method: it more readily permits Althusser's ideas to be discussed and accepted within Anglophone analytic political philosophy. In this tradition, it is standard to discuss ideas irrespective of the context of their production. Thus, there is a convenient disciplinary norm where all three strikes (French, Marxist, murderer) against Althusser's ideas being entertained in the Anglosphere could be ignored and one could just focus on 'advancing political philosophy'.

Strategically convenient, yes, but the response obviously flees from the question this chapter poses: that of whether and how to employ Althusser's ideas in light of his killing of Rytmann-Légotien. In order to answer this question, we should seek a better understanding of what harms are associated with both the externalist and the internalist methods.

The approach outlined so far, which puts the content of the philosophy first, has three central problems. First, internalists ignore the direct interpersonal harms caused by Althusser's offence. Second, not only is it oblivious to the impersonal harm to the discipline of philosophy such ignorance may precipitate, this approach also ignores the damage to Marxist practice that occurs when people who may otherwise advance Marxist philosophy or practice are deterred by leftists discussing the ideas of vicious people in the same way that we discuss the ideas of virtuous ones. Third, and particularly apposite to the subject of this chapter, the philosophy first approach disregards the impersonal harms to society when we do not hold someone accountable for his or her crimes. Althusser was judged non-culpable and let off for the homicide due to his being mentally unstable at the time the killing was committed.[8] More than a few critics have argued that patriarchal dominance and structural misogyny

---

7 For more on this line of argument see Baggini 2018.
8 'Meurtrier de sa Femme' 1981. http://www.lemonde.fr/archives/article/1981/01/26/meurtrier

were the reasons for this verdict, that the victim herself was silenced (while Althusser kept on speaking) and that to continue to read Althusser is to contribute to women's ongoing oppression.[9]

2.1   *Direct Harms*

Of these three problems with the philosophy first approach, it is the impersonal wrongs – being widespread and persistent – that perhaps most deserve our consideration. As for direct harms, the person Althusser maltreated is deceased and so cannot be harmed any further. That those close to Rytmann-Légotien were directly robbed of her care and friendship is also true. However, lacking children and being born in 1910, the number of people who knew her is small. If there are friends and relations of Rytmann-Légotien still hurting because the killer of a loved one is discussed while his victim is forgotten, then this is a type of direct harm, albeit limited in scope and becoming ever more restricted. As for the wrong of profiting from one's notoriety, Althusser is dead and so he cannot be said to directly benefit in prestige or lucre from the harm he committed when one reads, discusses, or cites his work. Richard Seymour suggests that there is another source of direct injury in that, by shortening Rytmann-Légotien's life, we all lose the benefit of hearing her ideas.[10] Temporally, this is, indeed, a permanent loss. However, Rytmann-Légotien published and lectured little in her lifetime and there is no indication that, at the age of 70, her public career was about to accelerate.[11] Plus, and noted with shameful irony, it is almost certain that we know as much as we do of Rytmann-Légotien's life and ideas precisely because Althusser killed her and wrote a book about the murder. Without the autobiography and its sales, the couple's correspondence would most probably never have been published.[12] Further, it is indubitable that the success of the autobiography led to articles and investigations into the life and work of Rytmann-Légotien, studies which would not otherwise have been undertaken.[13]

-de-sa-femme-m-louis-althusser-beneficie-d-un-non-lieu-et-demeure-interne_3041332_1
819218.html.

9   Boyer 2014; Dupuis-Déri 2015; Finn 1996; Seymour 2017.
10   Seymour 2017.
11   Dupuis-Déri 2015, p. 99.
12   Althusser 2011.
13   Dupuis-Déri 2015; 2016; Seymour 2017.

2.2   *Indirect Harms*

In contrast to the direct harms, that, while serious, are limited in scope or time, the impersonal harms associated with ignoring the killing of Rytmann-Légotien and simply reading and using Althusser for his ideas are both persistent and grave. First among them, we should consider the injury to the discipline of philosophy and to political movements done by alienating those who might otherwise be interested in Althusser's thinking but who are put off by scholars' and activists' easy embrace of the internalist approach. Similarly, there is much to be said on behalf of the argument that failing to punish violence against women and continuing to ignore female victims of male violence by not discussing past harms reinforces patriarchy and contributes to women's ongoing oppression. Ignoring a victim of male violence who can no longer speak for herself as a result of that violence is perhaps the most egregious form of 'testimonial smothering'.[14] This silencing is compounded when theorists and activists seek to limit discussions to ideas and arguments and to bracket past misogynistic offenses as unrelated to present egalitarian political strategies and struggles. The 2018 Kavanaugh Supreme Court confirmation hearing in the United States Senate, where senators and pundits demanded that the yet-to-be appointed Justice be scrutinised only for his jurisprudential record should be exhibit 'A' in this regard.[15]

Consequently, if there be plausible impersonal harms to the discipline of philosophy, to women, and to an egalitarian future by ignoring the inconvenient facts of Althusser's biography, then it would seem that the externalist or biographical approach to Althusser's philosophy has merit. This is because those who consider Althusser's philosophy in relation to his life and his life in relation to his philosophy cannot be considered to have similarly ignored the female victim of male violence while celebrating the male's achievements. Moreover, rather than alienation by omission, externalist accounts invite those potentially interested in Althusser's philosophy to think of him as a whole person, embedded in history, with severe mental health problems, who manifested both virtues and vices, but who also had interesting ideas about ideology, causality, overdetermination, the state, and class struggle.

---

14   Dotson 2011, p. 244; Manne 2017, p. 17.
15   Rosenfeld 2018.

3   External and Internal Approaches

3.1   *Externalism*

As mentioned above, the scholarship on Althusser that takes the externalist approach is voluminous. Can one name another twentieth-century political philosopher who has had multiple volumes written about their inner life and television and radio documentaries similarly devoted to them?[16] For that matter, name another thinker who has had multiple dramatic pieces mounted exploring their dreams and inner monologues.[17] These are just the large pieces: there exist dozens of op-eds, essays in literary reviews, and book chapters relating Althusser's philosophy to the internal and external events of his life. Given the sheer amount of material, we may use this body of work to determine whether the biographical approach may plausibly diminish the harms associated with the philosophy first approach.

To aid us in this assessment, we might think a bit with the philosopher under consideration. Famously, Althusser maintained that the truth of a philosophy is in its effects.[18] If all of the pieces that attempt to understand Althusser's philosophy by his biography are themselves a type of externalist philosophy, then at this point in the game, their effect is quite noticeable. However, and again to follow with Althusser's ideas about overdetermination and uneven development, the effects of philosophical ideas are not always and everywhere the same and they do not happen at the same time.[19] In different countries, at different periods, externalist approaches have had different results.

In France, the obsession with Althusser's biography and especially with psychoanalytic explanations of his behaviour and ideas has largely occluded these ideas' philosophical consideration. As a once prominent intellectual and Marxist, Althusser is not alone in this occlusion: lingering romantic obsessions with madness and genius as well as French anti-communism have overdetermined the production and reception of externalist work. The result is that Althusser has been reduced to a caricature: the mad Marxist philosopher whom history passed by and who remains only of pathological, nostalgic, or dramatic interest. The result of this is an industry – the Althusser industry – where plays, documentaries, and staged readings compete with texts of dream narratives

---

16   Adler 2011; Althusser and Institut Mémoires de l'édition contemporaine 2015; Benedjaïzou 2015; Druelle 2018; Moulier-Boutang 1992; Pommier 1998; 2009; Van Reeth 2018; Yhuel 2018.

17   'Sami Frey lit: Lettres d'Althusser à Hélène 1/9' 2014; Billington 2002; '"Le Caïman", 'très proche' d'Althusser' 2006.

18   E. Balibar, Cohen, and Robbins 1994, pp. 157–8.

19   Althusser 1969a.

and personal letters for notices in *Le Monde littéraire*.[20] The most recent and perhaps most egregious in this regard was France Culture's 'La vie secrète des philosophes : Le procès Althusser', which dwelt almost wholly on murder and pathology and only tangentially on his importance as a philosopher.[21]

Unlike Greece, Turkey, Japan, Germany, Italy, and much of North and South America where the level of scholarship on Althusser is fairly high (and everywhere mostly male), this obsession with the past has stunted Althusser studies within the country of his birth. In France, Althusser scholarship seems stuck in 1978 and the same texts: the ISA essay, *For Marx*, *Reading Capital*, and the published 'Philosophy of the Encounter' texts are discussed *ad nauseum*. Too often these works are read sloppily, subjected to 'immanent' or 'psychoanalytic' critique or supplemented with inaccurate accounts of the theoretical, political, or biographical conjuncture that produced them. It is as if Althusser's ideas were hermetically sealed on the eve of Mitterand's election. There are exceptions to this quarantine, but these pieces and their authors are the exception and not the rule.[22]

In Anglophone countries, but particularly in the United Kingdom, the level of theoretical engagement outside of specialist circles has been even lower.[23] While novel interpretations and usages of Althusser's thought flourished among Analytic Marxists, Critical Realists, and Neo-Marxists in the 1970s and 1980s, these research programmes declined with Cold War budgets. Now, the most prominent English-language voices that 'deal with' Althusser are writers and historians like Sunil Khilnani, and Tony Judt. In essays like 'The Paris Strangler', such critics have constructed a faulty syllogism that functions as an *ad hominem* attack on Marxism.[24] It goes something like this:

- Althusser killed his wife.
- Killing is bad.
- Althusser was communist and Marxist.
- Communists also killed people
- ∴ Marxism and communism are bad.

When these scholars do a little research, they read so far as Althusser's autobiography and there discover self-incrimination: astonishingly, the most celebrated post-war Marxist philosopher declares in *The Future Lasts Forever* that

---

20   Sinard 2017.

21   'La vie secrète des philosophes (1/5)'.

22   Cf. Anthony Crèzegut, Pascale Gillot, G.M. Goshgarian, and Guillaume Silbertin-Blanc.

23   Specialist circles where very good Althusser scholarship is advanced and his ideas interestingly applied include *Viewpoint Magazine*, *Historical Materialism*, and *Décalages*.

24   Judt 1992; Khilnani 1993; Sturrock 1999, pp. 43–51.

he did not even read Marx![25] These writers never bother to check the archives
to see Althusser's meticulous notes. Neither do they bother reading any contemporary scholarship, research that makes a strong case for the continuing
relevance of his political philosophy. Unlike in France where the externalist
approach has ossified Althusser's reception, in the case of Anglophone extern-
alists, the biographical approach has rendered his philosophy invisible, if not
anathema.

Of course, part of the problem with both the Anglophone and Franco-
phone externalist approaches to Althusser's philosophy is that the biographical methods employed are reductivist and facile. The former is animated by
anti-communism and anti-intellectualism. The latter stems from fascination
with intellectual celebrity, armchair psychoanalysis, and notoriety. These deficiencies mean that we must suppose a methodologically rigorous biographical account in order to test if externalist accounts avoid the harms associated with externalism. Thorough biographical work would take seriously the
fact Althusser was a product of his times and that he also contributed to
them. They would look at the totality of available archival documents that
relate his biography to his philosophy and – in order to give the best possible
exposition of this philosophy – they would consider the relevant internalist
research. Finally, such accounts would distinguish as best they can between
a mentally well Althusser and one suffering from mental health issues, giving
primacy to the former when his philosophical ideas are discussed and elaborated.

Such methodological rigour would, no doubt, give us a much better idea of
how Althusser's ideas are the product of a socially and historically embedded
life. But would they solve the problems noted above as well as have the advantages that the internalist account offers for the due philosophical consideration
of Althusser's ideas? That is, would they or could they: (a) attract those who
might be interested in Althusser's ideas but who are alienated by internalist
approaches that do not acknowledge the killing; (b) work against the existing narrative that silences female victims and thereby contributes to women's
ongoing oppression; (c) adequately consider his work in its historical context,
showing how it contributed to debates of the time and shaped these debates,
such that his contributions to the history of Marxism and political philosophy
can be recognised; and (d) elaborate, reconstruct, criticise, and apply the arguments and concepts that he developed such that philosophers, activists, and
political strategists can make use of them?

---

25   Althusser 1995e, pp. 165–6, Boyer 2014.

If we set to one side questions of format and disciplinary norms such as those within Anglophone analytic philosophy, and further, if we suppose that authoring and publishing rigorous externalist accounts is possible, then the rough answer to these questions is that methodologically exacting externalist accounts could fulfil some of these desiderata but not others. Clearly, the condition that Althusser's work be considered in its historical context could be met. More specifically, sensitively written pieces that take the facts of Althusser's biography seriously may invite into the theoretical and practical conversation those put off by existing accounts. In their obsession with the homicide, current externalist work ends up making this one act the truth of Althusser's philosophy. It thereby replicates some of the impersonal harms catalogued above and compounds most of the direct ones. While a relationship between the murder and his thought may be uncovered, it is unquestionably true that Althusser's philosophy, the killing, his victim's status, the police response, and the French court's verdict were overdetermined by the masculine-dominated institutions and practices which formed, employed, and, eventually, judged him. The same true is for Althusser's posthumous reception. Thoroughgoing externalist approaches could elucidate these causal relations. Rigorous biographical approaches may also overcome the distantiation effect that externalist accounts trigger, as they do not ask the reader to dismiss the killing and to focus exclusively on Althusser's ideas and arguments. Further, in well-done externalist scholarship, Rytmann-Légotien would be given a voice and a history. Thereby, the tragedy of her demise would be felt and recognised independently of Althusser's and post-war Marxism's demise, two events under which it is facilely and all too frequently subsumed.

3.2   *Internalism*

Despite these benefits, the principal problem with rigorous externalist accounts is that, inevitably, the philosophy gets muddled with the history. The irony to Althusser's reception is that he worked diligently to extract and clarify Marxian philosophical concepts for the use of egalitarian political movements yet the facts of his life and his autobiography serve to occlude these notions from the circumstances for which they were intended.[26] A perhaps deeper irony is some of this work is not only deeply and presciently feminist but that feminist theorists have made interesting and productive use of Althusser's ideas.[27] Sometimes, as with Laura Mulvey's work on visual pleasure

---

26   Althusser and Balibar 1970, pp. 32–3.
27   Sharp 2000.

and Judith Butler's on gender, these applications have changed the direction of entire academic disciplines.[28]

Simply put, for philosophy and for political practice, there are certain times when we need to interrogate the assumptions and notions that undergird our analyses and our practices and there are other times when we simply need to focus on the construction of new strategies and concepts. Yes, Althusser probably would not have become a communist were he not imprisoned in a Stalag or if he never met Rytmann-Légotien. However, the adequacy and utility of his idea of communism as mutual relations of amity and respect under condition of non-domination and non-exploitation can be and sometimes need to be debated independently of these facts.[29] Linking biography with philosophy as intellectual historians often do tends to causally reduce the latter to the former. Internalist approaches, by way of contrast, allow us to elaborate, reconstruct, criticise, and apply the arguments and concepts Althusser developed in their autonomy. They then become tools whose usefulness to the movement can be assessed, applied, and then independently verified in terms of their helpfulness to philosophers, activists, and political strategists.

4   A Duty to Speak and to Respond

Fortunately, we are not stuck with a choice between philosophy first and biographical approaches to Althusser's political theory. There are publishing venues and discussion opportunities for both. Due to the horrific political conjuncture we now collectively face, these fora are multiplying. Both methods therefore can proliferate and both are useful; we can have internalist accounts which advance political theory and political strategy and we can produce sophisticated externalist accounts which do the same but which simultaneously redress the harms done by ignoring Rytmann-Légotien's death. Further, by incorporating mention of the uxoricide, internalist accounts can reduce the impersonal harms to women, left theory, and left strategy that are caused by ignoring it. Yes, inasmuch as Althusser advanced political philosophy and philosophy is about ideas, those concerned with refuting or reconstructing his ideas have a duty to cite him. However, we do not have to do so unreflectively. In time, by incorporating these changes, the damages to political philosophy and to left political movements by treating Althusser like any other philosopher might be

28   Butler 1997, 106–32; Mulvey 1975.
29   W.S. Lewis 2018.

reduced. Similarly, if these paths are pursued, it could no longer be said that those who study or use Althusser's ideas continue to ignore past and present female victims of male violence.

How though to address the challenge of the colleague or student who is potentially interested in Marxian political theory but who meets the seminar assignment of 'Contradiction and Overdetermination' with stunned silence or even with protest? What then, to do, when an activist calls out a comrade for using the concepts of ISA and RSA to explain racial disparities in sentencing and arrests? Will the combination and proliferation of rigorous externalist methods help here? It might, but only to a small extent. There will be some trickle-down as the scholarship improves and, perhaps, rebarbative or hostile receptions will become less frequent. However, the real work is and will only be accomplished when those of us who do find Althusser of theoretical and practical interest begin to take these moments seriously. Taking these moments in earnest means that we pause and that we listen to comrades, colleagues, and students when they express apprehension or reprobation about employing Althusser's ideas. After listening, we may dialogue together about the right way to proceed. Yes, concepts like Ideological State Apparatus, problematic, and overdetermination are theoretically and politically useful, and this volume puts them to use and demonstrates their efficacity. However, no one will engage with Althusser's philosophy if they are stuck wondering why someone would teach, research, or apply the thoughts of a man who killed his wife.

CHAPTER 3

Althusser's Scientism

Following the posthumous publication of the last philosophical writings of Louis Althusser on the subject of 'aleatory materialism' or, as the philosophy developed in these writings is also known, 'the materialism of the encounter', there has been a steady increase in the number of thinkers engaging with these texts. Most have done so either to explain them, to critique them, to apply them, or to compare them with other theories of revolutionary politics. Scholarly engagement with these writings possibly attained its apex with the publication of the collective volumes *Autour d'Althusser, Penser un matérialisme aléatoire* in 2012 and *Encountering Althusser: Politics and Materialism in Contemporary Thought* in 2013. A generation after their first appearance in French and more than a decade after their translation into English, there is now a large body of secondary literature on the subject of aleatory materialism and we can begin to categorise these responses. If we leave to one side the critiques of the later Althusser which begin from a clearly anti-Marxist perspective as well as those that search in Althusser's philosophy for a key to his biography (and in his biography a key to his philosophy) one can divide the responses which take Althusser's philosophy seriously into two categories. In the first are those readings which maintain that Althusser achieved something of importance with his classic works from the early 1960s and which also hold that there may be something of interest in Althusser's subsequent revision of these ideas and arguments. However, these readings also assert that – at a certain point – Althusser's thoughts become inconsistent, contradictory, and of little philosophical or political value.[1] This chapter challenges this position only indirectly, by suggesting that the difference between the Althusser of 1965 and that of 1985 is more a question of rhetorical style and of philosophical rigour than a question of philosophical content, depth, consistency, or applicability. In the second category can be placed those readings that take seriously Althusser's philosophical work from the late 1970s and 1980s, who try to explain it, to apply its insights to political questions, and who use ideas from these works to engage with other political philosophies. Within the responses of this type, there is another large division. On the one hand, there is a group of readings which maintain that the importance of the philosophy of the encounter is due somewhat to the fact

---

1   E. Balibar 1991; Cangiani 2013, 245; Elliott 2006a, pp. 255–300; 2006b, pp. 74–5; Garo 2012.

that, with this philosophy, Althusser rejected the scientistic aspect of his political philosophy and, instead, replaced it with a new ontology – a materialism of the encounter – that could explain and justify a renewed political practice.[2] On the other hand, there are responses which take seriously Althusser's philosophical work from the 1980s but which also maintain that there is a clear continuity between the Althusser of the 1970s – who strongly argued that it is only by the methods of the sciences and particularly by the methods of historical materialism that the political conjuncture could be understood and a correct political line identified – and the Althusser of the 1980s who seemed to hardly speak of these relations or of this need.

The readings of Althusser that emphasise the continuity of his thought between 1960 (or even earlier) and 1987 is fast becoming the accepted one.[3] However, within this consensus, the majority opinion is that, in his last works, Althusser denies, rejects, or simply abandons the theory of the relation he had previously specified as necessary between good scientific knowledge and effective political action (where 'effective' is defined as a political action that secures and maintains a desired good). This denial of the scientistic aspect of his project has had significant effects. The first consequence is that it has served to obscure the importance of Althusser's arguments and theoretical innovations from the first half of the 1960s as well as the significant revisions and developments these arguments and concepts underwent between 1966 and 1978. The second consequence of this reading is that it has helped establish an apparently clear connection between Althusser and certain contemporary philosophers who look to ontology in order to find a political direction and who tend to reject or minimise the role played by the sciences in such a process.[4] A third consequence is that it has encouraged or even justified the contemporary retreat of Marxism into political theory (where it mostly competes in theoretical space with other political theories) instead of into a scientific and practical engagement with the socio-economic-political world and its possibilities.

This chapter will not challenge the forging of a connection between Althusser and contemporary philosophers who look to ontology in order to discover a revolutionary possibility, nor will it analyse specific instances of this retreat into intramural theory. However, by demonstrating the correctness of

---

2 Badiou 2011, p. 304.
3 Boer 2007; Goshgarian 2013; Henninger 2007, p. 37.
4 Those who follow this tendency wholly or partially include: Bryant, Srnicek, and Harman 2011; Badiou 2011; Diefenbach 2013, pp. 179–80; Illas 2013, p. 3; Johnston 2013; Negri 1996; Toscano 2004; Vatter 2003.

the reading of Althusser which finds in his conception of the relations between science, philosophy, and politics a continuity, it will challenge those critics: (a) who wish to differentiate between an earlier, scientistic Althusser and a later, ontological one; (b) who want to forge a connection between Althusser and contemporary philosophers who look to ontology in order to suggest a political direction; and (c) who overestimate the role played by philosophy in understanding and encouraging revolutionary transitions.

In order to show that the reading of Althusser which finds a pronounced continuity in his conception of the relations among science, philosophy, and politics is the correct one, this chapter begins with an examination of Althusser's 'scientism'. The meaning of this term (one that differs slightly from contemporary usages) will be specified before showing how and in what way Althusser's political philosophy between 1960 and 1980 can be described as 'scientistic'. The next section will detail the important political role Althusser assigned to the sciences and particularly to the science of historical materialism during this period. This accomplished, the arguments of interpreters who emphasise the apparent difference in Althusser's attitude towards science before and after 1980 will be considered. Here, possible reasons for such a reading will be rehearsed. Next, with the support of posthumously published and archival documents, we engage in a close and comparative reading of Althusser's texts from the 1970s and 1980s that have as their subject the relations among philosophy, science, and politics. This survey will show the continuity in Althusser's position vis-à-vis the sciences: namely, that if we want good (i.e. desired) socio-politico-economic changes to result from our political actions, then it is necessary to engage in social scientific research or, at the very least, to consult such research and to use this knowledge in our political decision-making. All this serves to support the conclusion that Althusser's 'new' political philosophy from the 1980s is not really so new. On the contrary, his writings on the materialism of the encounter and aleatory materialism represent prolongations and elaborations of positions and ideas already developed in the 1960s and 1970s and that include a mostly consistent understanding of the relations between scientific knowledge and political action. This is true even if the rhetorical and philosophical style in which these ideas are put forth in the 1980s differs from the ways in which these ideas were introduced during the prior two decades.

1   Definition of Althusser's Scientism

It is well known and often remarked upon by his critics that Althusser's work from the early 1960s until the end of the 1970s is 'scientistic' or that he was guilty of something called 'scientism'.[5] Almost always, these remarks are pejorative.[6] Those who levy this charge do so to mark out Althusser as someone who reductively and wrongly appeals to the methods of the natural or social sciences (or the knowledge produced by these sciences) in order to understand an aspect of existence that the critic believes might better be understood by other means.[7] Sometimes, though, the charge of scientism is meant to convey a slightly older but still utilized sense of the term: namely, that Althusser holds the epistemological position that all questions of knowledge and action are best answered by the methods of the natural sciences and that the natural sciences on their own can explain any and all phenomena.[8]

Although Althusser certainly endorsed scientific practice during this period as the best and most reliable way to produce knowledge about the way our socio-economic relations are structured and intentionally transformed, he did not believe that all questions of knowledge and action are best answered by the methods of the natural sciences.[9] For instance, he also argued that artistic and philosophical practice can produce critical awareness of the world and that these practices may even occasion political transformation.[10] He also did not think that the natural sciences can explain or give the truth of any phenomenon or that the social world and its history can be explained wholly by appeal to the laws of the natural world.[11] He believed even less that the social sciences could give us the truth of ourselves, of our individual and collective natures, or of our future social and economic arrangements.[12] Therefore, his work does not exactly fit the definition of scientism, at least according to the two most common meanings of the term.

Despite the fact that Althusser's work exactly fits neither of the typical definitions of scientism, his philosophy was scientistic in this precise respect: Althusser consistently argued that science is the only human theoretical practice that allow us to reliably understand politico-socio-economic structures such that we might intentionally assist in their transformation. Science, and more specifically the Marxist science of history, historical materialism, can do so, he argued, because it allows us to understand the origin of our ideological notions about what is good for society and about what is to be done politically.

5 Dosse 1997, pp. 88–91; George 1971; Rancière 1973, p. 39; Wolin 2012, pp. 120–1.
6 An exception is Amariglio 1987, p. 163.
7 Schöttler 2013.
8 Haack 2012, p. 77.
9 Althusser 1990e, pp. 105–9.
10 Althusser 1995a; 1995c; Bargu 2012; Wilson 2010.
11 Resch 1992, pp. 195–201..
12 Althusser 2003a.

It also allows us to critique these notions and to replace them with scientific understandings (principles) of why we think and act the way we do. In turn, this knowledge allows us to develop new plans for political actions, ones based on a critical and scientific understanding of the actual processes at work in a particular historical conjuncture and of its possible transformation.[13] Unlike ideological practice, which tends to the reproduction of existing socio-economic relations, one of the most important things about historical materialism for Althusser is that, once inaugurated, its practice tends to replace existing ideas about our social and natural relations and to generate new and politically reliable knowledge about the world. This new awareness and this new knowledge of social relations is practical knowledge or knowledge for practice. Insofar as it is correct, it allows us to change ourselves and to change our world.

2   Althusser's (Mostly) Consistent Scientism: 1960–1980

Although it is part of the argument of this chapter that Althusser's scientism was consistent between 1960 and 1980, this contention has not yet been supported. It is important to provide an account of this position's consistency for three reasons. First, because this position is often neither well explained nor well understood. Second, because it is unlikely that someone who held such a position for two decades would suddenly renounce it, the demonstration of this position's longevity raises the burden of proof for those who would argue that Althusser dropped the scientistic aspects of his political philosophy in subsequent work. Third, detailing the consistency of Althusser's position over this time allows one to see the evolution in his thought regarding the relations among philosophy, science, and politics and, thereby, to better understand

---

13   All translations are by the author. All emphases (signified by *italics*) are Althusser's. Althusser 1966b, p. 12.

Cette révolution théorique a permis ce qui était interdit aux anciennes philosophies de l'histoire : la connaissance du type d'unité complexe existant entre une société et ses idéologies. La science de l'histoire marxiste est en effet une théorie qui rend compte de la *structure* d'une société, et donc en même temps des 'niveaux' ou 'instances' distincts qui constituent cette structure au niveau économique, mais aussi du niveau politique eu du niveau idéologique. C'est l'existence de cette théorie qui permet à la connaissance marxiste de courir à la fois la connaissance des fondements de la société existante, ce que le socialisme utopique, suspendu en aveugle aux principes idéologiques existants, est évidemment incapable de produire.

La théorie marxiste met ainsi en oeuvre ses principes scientifiques dans 1/ la connaissance critique de la société existante 2/ la définition des *fins* du socialisme 3/ la détermination des *moyens d'action* propres à faire la révolution.

any changes to his view of philosophy that may have precipitated a change in Althusser's attitude regarding the role of science in his political philosophy.

In an interview with the Mexican philosopher Fernanda Navarro that took place near the end of his career, Althusser provided a brief periodization of his thought. He distinguished these periods by the definition of Marxist philosophy that characterized each one. During the time that his most well-known or 'classic' works were published (1960–5), Althusser defined philosophy as 'the theory of theoretical practice'. Only a year or so after the appearance of *For Marx* and *Reading Capital* in 1965, he revised his opinion and began arguing that '[Marxist] philosophy represents politics with the sciences and scientificity with the practices'.[14] Then, about five years after this understanding of philosophy was promulgated (1972), Althusser replaced it with the pithier definition: 'philosophy is class struggle in theory'.

In the interview with Navarro, Althusser insisted that the characterization of philosophy as 'class struggle in theory' was definitive.[15] However, this neat periodization and the claim that this definition of philosophy was final is complicated by the fact that Althusser introduced at least five other definitions of Marxist philosophy during the course of his career, three of which were coined between 1976 and 1986. These include the definition of Marx's philosophy as 'void', as 'non-philosophy',[16] as the 'Marxist position *in* philosophy',[17] as 'hyper-materialism', as a 'materialism of the encounter' and as 'aleatory materialism'. Given these shifts, we might wonder whether the successive changes or variations to his definition of philosophy also meant changes to his understanding of science. If they did, then there is perhaps an argument to be made for the evolution of Althusser's scientism. If not, then we can argue that Althusser's view of science, of science's relation to philosophy, and the role of scientific knowledge in politics remains more or less consistent after 1965.

2.1   *Althusser's Scientism 1960–1965*

The most well-known of Althusser's positions on Marx's development, on Marxian philosophy, and on Marxist science were promulgated between 1960 and 1965, first in a series of articles and then in the books *For Marx* and *Reading Capital*. In addition to being original and heterodox, these positions had the virtues of being clean, simple, and formal. In these works, Althusser maintained that, sometime between 1845 and 1847, Marx broke with the idealist notions

14   Althusser 2006c, p. 240, 249fn27.
15   Althusser 2006c, p. 240.
16   Althusser 1994a, p. 177.
17   Althusser 2013, p. 375.

that characterized his early work and that he then inaugurated a philosophy (dialectical materialism) that allowed for the advancement of a critical materialist science of history (historical materialism).[18] Though Althusser also tried to show that Marx could not and did not always render explicit concepts such as mode of production, productive forces, relations of production, superstructure, contradiction, overdetermination, ideology, etc., that allowed this science to proceed, he argued that these and other concepts could be made so by a symptomatic reading of Marx's mature writings.[19]

Along with this revisionist reading of Marx and the analytic work on Marxist concepts, Althusser also undertook the complementary epistemological task of explaining how Marxist science went about producing true knowledge of the socioeconomic world and of how this knowledge differs from the spontaneous ideological understanding we have of it. According to Althusser, Marxist Science or 'historical materialism' differs from other social sciences. It does so both in terms of its object, the history of class struggle, and in terms of its method, which is synthetic and critical. Historical materialism is synthetic insofar as it employs the results of the social and natural sciences in its own demonstrations. It is critical insofar as it also sees fit to direct scientific research and to evaluate any specific science's results or methodology. However, historical materialism does not differ in terms of being a science. As a science, it makes use of a body of concepts and abstractive practices including experimentation, observation, and quantification to develop new knowledge about the real. This knowledge is verified by the criteria it has established in the formation of its proper concepts.[20] Historical materialism also recognises the knowledge that it produces as provisional, that is, as amenable or as able to be overturned through further scientific practice.[21]

The knowledge that scientific practice produces is seen in its openness and novelty to differ fundamentally from that other theoretical practice which Althusser habitually contrasts it with and from which it emerges: namely, ideological practice. Defined as that set of beliefs necessarily held by groups of individuals whose effect is to guarantee the reproduction of certain socioeconomic relations,[22] ideology always relates directly to the political and economic exigencies of the events that give birth to it and to which it is subjected. As Althusser notes, ideology is 'content to *reflect* the historical changes which it

---

18   Althusser 2005b; Resch 1992, pp. 169–70.
19   Althusser 1970; S. Solomon 2012.
20   Elliott 2006a, p. 82.
21   Elliott 2006a, p. 84.
22   Althusser 1972b, pp. 132–3.

is its mission to assimilate and master'.[23] Therefore, unlike science, which is potentially productive of new knowledge and remains open to revision, ideology 'is theoretically closed'.[24]

But how does one tell the difference between scientific knowledge and ideological knowledge? During this period, Althusser solved the problem of demarcation by bringing in Marxist philosophy as arbiter. Marxist philosophy, he maintained, is itself a science, but one that has as its object the rational critique of the scientific ideas established in the course of historical materialist research. Philosophy, he maintained, is the 'Theory of theoretical practices' and its job is to rationally differentiate between ideological notions and scientific concepts. By seeing if a theory accords with Marxist philosophical concepts, philosophy can rule on what constitutes a genuine addition to knowledge.[25] Without such an analysis, Althusser argued, it is impossible to differentiate between scientific and ideological knowledge. Further, and because correct action follows from correct knowledge, without historical materialist research, it is impossible to ensure correct political action.[26]

Clearly, Althusser's thinking about the relationship between scientific knowledge and successful political action between 1960 and 1966 was scientistic according to the definition of the term given above: historical materialism is said to be the only human theoretical practice which allow us to reliably understand existing socio-economic structures in their history, their existence, and in their possible transformation. However, it is also true that Althusser maintained during this period that Marxist science (historical materialism) had need of Marxist Philosophy (dialectical materialism) in order to certify its research and to monitor its progress.[27] Science, though crucial for political progress, was not represented as an autonomous practice that independently produces reliable results. Marxist philosophy was needed to modify its body of

---

23   Althusser and Balibar 1970, pp. 141–2.
24   Althusser and Balibar 1970, pp. 141–2.
25   To rehearse a simple example employed by Althusser, if some set of thinkers was to claim that the historical essence of human beings is to be engaged in creative acts that tend toward the overcoming of our own alienation, then a philosopher could use her stock of Marxist concepts to analyse and critique this claim. Is it scientifically warranted, this philosopher might ask, to believe that humans are fated to achieve the self-overcoming of their own alienation through creative acts? Which of Marx's scientific concepts are used in order to make such a claim? What historical materialist research supports such a claim? If no concepts are used and no support is given and yet such a belief persists and is promulgated, then the historical materialist has reason to suspect that the idea may be ideological and that it somehow reinforces existing socioeconomic relations. Althusser 2007.
26   Althusser 2007; Bruschi 2018, pp. 1–4.
27   Althusser 1990c, pp. 5–13, 34–42.

knowledge and its methods by separating out from the science any ideological contents. In this respect, philosophical practice guaranteed historical materialism's own scientificity.[28]

2.2   Althusser's Scientism 1966–1972

Despite fighting strongly for this position and for the political recommendation which followed from it – that the direction of the French Communist Party [PCF] be given over to philosophers or at least that philosophers' voices be given more weight in party decision-making – in 1966 Althusser began modifying his ideas about the definition of Marxist philosophy and about its relation to Marxist Science. He also weakened his claim about a clear break in Marx's work.[29] From this time on, he referred to this epistemological stance as 'theoreticist' and admitted his mistake in thinking that philosophical practice allowed one to clearly differentiate scientific from ideological knowledge.[30] While he did not give up on finding a method to differentiate between the two types of knowledges, he also no longer maintained that this could be done using solely rationalist criteria.

Though the transition was by no means sudden or entirely clean, by 1967 and certainly by the time he was preparing his lecture notes for the seminars that would eventually be published as *Philosophy and the Spontaneous Philosophy of the Scientists*, Althusser had revised his definition of philosophy.[31] Philosophy was no longer understood as the 'the theory of theoretical practices'. Instead, he now ventured the thesis that 'philosophy represents politics in the domain of theory, or to be more precise: *with the sciences* – and, *vice versa*, philosophy represents scientificity in politics'.[32]

In the early 1960s, philosophy was understood by Althusser to exist outside of both ideology and science; it was an independent theoretical practice that had its own rules and its own object. Now though, it was thought to exist only as a void, as a partisan and critical moment within the existing theoretical practices of ideology and science.[33] Within a specific science's body of theory, Althusser explained, philosophy acts in a partisan manner when it works against that science's tendency to embrace idealistic explanations of its

28   Althusser 1990c, pp. 38–40.
29   W.S. Lewis 2007a.
30   Althusser 1972c, pp. 182–6.
31   Goshgarian 2003, pp. xiii–xvi.
32   Macherey 2008.
33   Althusser 1972c, p. 65.

object.[34] It also acts critically when it calls a specific science's attention to its own ideological contents. The contents that it criticises may be ideological prejudices from the wider society that constitute part of the conceptual assumptions of the science or they may be biases that colour its results and their reception. Alternately, these ideological contents may consist in the importation of concepts proper to other sciences within a particular science's explanatory schema.[35] Within politics, Althusser maintains, philosophy acts by demanding that our accepted ideas about the world, about how it works, and about who inhabits it be subjected to scientific scrutiny or that they be informed by scientific results. Because scientific practice always and in the long run tends to the side of materialism, this act is also a partisan intervention against ideal explanation (and therefore against ideological support) of the socio-economic world and its contents.[36]

As the last paragraph suggests, Althusser did not argue after 1966 that the knowledge science produced was free from ideology or that philosophy could emancipate it and us from all ideological thinking. In fact, one of the main and lasting changes Althusser's epistemology underwent between mid-1966 and 1968 was his embrace of Foucault's insight that thought always functions in relation to politics or, better put, that all theory is political.[37] A correlate to this insight was Althusser's claim that science and ideology are always admixed, that there is no definitive method for their separation, and that ideological concepts always frame the production and reception of scientific results.[38] Despite this correlation, Althusser remained consistent in his belief that scientific practice tends to produce a more reliable understanding of the world (at least if we wish to change it) than does the preexisting conception of our world that we find ready-to-hand (and mind) in ideology. More specifically, Althusser persisted in his argument that all societies are class societies riven by class conflict, and that, on the basis of this discovery, Marx founded a science called historical materialism.[39] Further, he argued that it was only by the adoption of this science that the workers' movement could potentially find success.[40]

Not only was Althusser steady in this position, he developed it further in works like *Lenin and Philosophy* (1968) and in the 1968 interview 'Philosophy

---

34   Francois Matheron 1998, p. 28.
35   Althusser 1972c, p. 64.
36   Althusser 1974, pp. 96–8.
37   Garo 2013, p. 282.
38   Althusser 1974, pp. 132–4.
39   Althusser 1974, p. 256.
40   Althusser 1974, p. 130.

as a Revolutionary Weapon'. In texts from this phase in his career, Althusser argued that historical materialism produces a reliable form of socio-economic knowledge, one that can be used in the intentional transformation of human social and economic relationships. As a critical and overarching social scientific discipline, it makes use of the results from specific sciences while also engaging in their critique and in their synthesis.[41] Historical materialism's critical powers are derived from its understanding of historical necessities, of why we must think and act the way we do, and of the ways we might potentially think and act. They are not derived from any extra-scientific critical method, morality, or philosophical anthropology, although this is always a danger that must be guarded against.[42] Historical materialism allows us to understand our history, our present, and our future possibilities scientifically (that is, by way of abstractions from experience and then by demonstrations).[43] With this knowledge, philosophy can then argue in politics. It can demonstrate what ideas about the social world are ideological (including philosophical ones), explain why they exist, and it can suggest the correct actions to be taken if we want to change not only these ideas but also the social forces that produce and sustain them. The result of this intervention of philosophy into politics is better political practice; that is, a political practice more likely to generate the results desired.[44]

2.3   Althusser's Scientism 1972–1980

While most associate the definition of philosophy as 'class struggle in the field of theory' with Althusser's short work from 1972 titled 'A Reply to John Lewis', the approximate phrase appears already in the 1968 interview cited above. It is also strongly implied in the 1967 work *Philosophy and the Spontaneous Philosophy of the Scientists*.[45] However, it is in the polemic against John Lewis that Althusser introduces its definitive formulation: 'philosophy is, in

41   Althusser 2003b, p. 161.
42   As Althusser writes in the draft of a Communist Party manual in 1966 or early 1967:
      La critique de la société existante passe donc, dans le marxisme, par la critique de ses principes *idéologiques*. Mais alors la *critique* prend un nouveau sens : il ne s'agit plus de *juger* de la bonté ou de la malfaisance de telle société, au nom de 'valeurs' (morales ou juridiques) donc d'approuver et de condamner, – il s'agit d'abord de *connaître*, donc de *comprendre* la nécessité *à la fois* de la société existante et de ses principes idéologiques et de leur disparition. La critique n'est pas première, elle est seconde à la connaissance de la nécessité historique, elle ne lui est pas antérieure mais intérieure.
      Althusser 1966b.
43   Althusser 1966b; Goshgarian 2013, p. 105.
44   Althusser 2014b, p. 7; 1990e, p. 103.
45   Althusser 1990e, pp. 116–17; Aristides Baltas 1993, p. 655.

the last instance, class struggle in the field of theory'.[46] This new formulation marks more a simplification of the phrase 'philosophy represents politics in the domain of theory, or to be more precise: *with the sciences* – and, *vice versa*, philosophy represents scientificity in politics' than it does any significant change to its meaning. This is the case because, as Althusser explains in the 'Reply', philosophy is only able to affect these practices within theory itself. Philosophy does not march in the streets, call for a general strike, or bribe an official. However, it can be employed within politics to suggest that, based on a historical materialist analysis of the historical conjuncture, it may be a propitious time to do any one of the above.[47] Philosophy also does not experiment, observe phenomena, or reason deductively about natural or social processes. However, within science and from the point of view of class politics, it can move around in existing theory. Once there, it can critique the results of a science or suggest that there are problems with a science's presuppositions or with its reasoning. These criticisms may change the way a science is practised and how it understands its object or it might even inaugurate a new way of thinking about social processes and structures.[48]

Althusser's streamlining of his definition of philosophy in 1972 did little to change his understanding of the role of science in effective political decision-making. In fact, the first half of the 1970s saw Althusser refining this position as part and parcel of his enduring war on two fronts against Stalinism and Humanism within the Communist Party. The second half of the decade though saw him developing in some detail his theory of how science contributes to political change and how it influences philosophy. This development was occasioned by discussion within the PCF of whether or not it should drop from its platform the position that a dictatorship of the proletariat is necessary to affect a transition from capitalism to communism. Spurred on by these discussions and indignant that a sound historical materialist concept developed over the course of the workers' movement might be dropped, Althusser elaborated his points about how scientific knowledge must be harnessed so as to optimally inform communist political action.

The specifics of Althusser's plan to direct social scientific research and to employ it in party political decision-making is covered in Chapter 4 of this book and the political context is made clear in Goshgarian's 2006 intro-

---

46   Althusser 1976e, p. 37.
47   Althusser 1976e, p. 58; 2003b, p. 166.
48   Althusser 1976b, pp. 117–18; 2018b, pp. 107–18.

duction to *Philosophy of the Encounter: Later Writings 1978–87*.[49] Rather than rehearse these details, it may be more useful in this section to look at some texts from this period that evidence these elaborations but which also show Althusser's developing thoughts on the relationship between philosophy and science.

A few writings from this period that show the development in Althusser's ideas about how Marxist science can aid the workers' movement and which also show the relationship between philosophy, politics, and science are grouped together in Althusser's archives under the rubric 'Textes divers sur la philosophie'. Their argument is difficult to follow if one does not keep in mind that – by this point in his career – Althusser had largely stopped repeating the communist dogma that Marxist philosophy is identical with dialectical materialism. After trying for years to reconstruct dialectical materialism as a 'non-speculative, non-positivist' position in the public (and Communist Party) mind and failing, Althusser had by this point almost given up.[50] Instead, he began to label the philosophy inaugurated by Marx as, alternately: 'the philosophy of Marx', 'a Marxist position in philosophy' or, to better contrast it with the idealist philosophy of which dogmatic dialectical materialism had for him become a representative, 'anti-philosophy' or 'non-philosophy'.[51]

If we register this change in nomenclature, we can better follow Althusser's critique of the position that 'a science [and in particular the science of historical materialism] is an integral part of a philosophy [dialectical materialism.]'[52] This Stalinist formula, he notes, has historically deformed historical materialism; it has subordinated Marxist science to the 'philosophy' of dialectical materialism and to its laws. Why has this subordination occurred? Althusser suggests that one reason may be the influence of bourgeois ideology (in the form of bourgeois philosophy) on the communist movement. However, he does not believe it is simply this. The complementary reason he cites for historical materialism's subordination is the perennial need for philosophy and espe-

---

49   Goshgarian 2006; W.S. Lewis 2007b; Sotiris 2008, 148–49.

50   Althusser 1976a, 115.

51   Althusser 2006a, pp. 32–3. By the end of 1978, Althusser had given up trying to identify Marx's philosophy with dialectical materialism and crossed the term out from texts he was in the process of writing. He replaced it with the other terms mentioned above; see Althusser 2013, p. 375.

52   Althusser 1975.

      ... il est surprenant, du point du vue marxiste d'entendre affirmer qu'une science (le Matérialisme historique) est partie intégrante d'une philosophie (le Matérialisme dialectique).

cially for idealist philosophy to totalise, unify, and control all.[53] Against this tendency, Althusser continues, 'the sciences always present a certain danger to the established order ... they always have the smell of materialism and of liberty about them ...'[54]

Because they present this danger, Althusser explains, idealist philosophy working on behalf of the established order tries to control the sciences and, simultaneously, to provide them with their epistemological guarantee. In providing this guarantee and by placing dialectical materialism over and above historical materialism, an existing political situation can be justified or one can end up responding incorrectly to the actual political demands of a situation. When philosophy is placed in this dominate position it is charged with a huge number of strategic tasks, which it works on without the benefit of the sciences. Althusser's chief examples of these tasks are that of defining what is human or what is good for humanity and of deciding based on these understandings what are to be socialism's and communism's main goals. However, by appealing only to philosophy to make such definitions and to decide on its objectives, it sets up the Communist Party's direction (which has the power to dogmatically dictate Marxist philosophy) as the communist movement's sole authority.[55] Althusser concludes these texts with a warning, a wager, and a promise. The warning is that 'when scientific analyses are lacking, it is necessary that something else take their place. It is taken by philosophy'.[56] The wager is that

---

53 Althusser 1975.

C'est clair pour la fonction apologétique de la philosophie : si la philosophie se met au pouvoir sur les sciences, c'est pour leur extorquer l'aveu philosophique d'un sens dont elle a besoin pour boucler son système au service de l'idéologie dominante, contre le matérialisme. C'est clair aussi pour les fonctions de contrôle et de garantie, puisque dans les deux cas il s'agit d'orienter les sciences ou de les confiner dans un domine limité, pour bien s'assurer qu'elles se tiendront tranquille à la place que leur assigne l'idéologie dominante.

54 Althusser 1975.

... les sciences présentent toujours un certain danger pour l'ordre établi, ne serait-ce que parce qu'elles ont toujours une certaine odeur de matérialisme et de liberté?

55 Althusser 1975.

Et derrière cette justification, derrière cette mise au pouvoir de la philosophie sur la science marxiste-léniniste, se profilait une autre justification, où il était aussi question de pouvoir: la justification du dirigeant du Parti à dire le dernier mot sur toutes les questions, y compris les questions scientifiques, ce qui supposait non seulement une certaine conception du rapport entre la philosophie et les sciences, mais aussi une certaine conception du rapport entre le dirigeant et le Parti, le Parti et l'État, et le Parti et les masses, et aussi, bien entendu, une certaine conception de la lutte des classes.

56 Althusser 1975.

... lorsque les analyses scientifiques manquent, il faut bien que leur place soit prise: elle est prise par la philosophie.

'Marxist philosophy has everything to gain from the abandonment of all [philo-sophical] formulas' and that the Marxist movement 'has everything to gain from the correction of the practices which follow from adherence to these for-mulas'. The promise is that 'the worker's movement today ... has everything to gain by making use of scientific, theoretical, historical, and concrete analyses'.[57]

In this warning about the deformation of Marxist science and of Marxist political practice by the rationalising force of idealist philosophy, one can see Althusser's consistent idea that scientific knowledge is what the Marxist move-ment needs in order to correctly direct its political practice. In their condemna-tion of philosophy as being for the most part idealist and as serving bourgeois interests, one can also see in the *Textes divers sur la philosophie* the emergence of a position characteristic of Althusser's aleatory materialism. This is not sur-prising, as more than one observer has noted that many of the ideas that were to characterise the Materialism of the Encounter are clearly present in docu-ments from this period.[58]

The co-existence of recognizably Aleatory Materialist ideas with ideas that we have already labeled as scientistic is also found in a posthumously published manuscript from 1976. Titled 'Être marxiste en philosophie', this text begins with a critique of philosophies which try to totalise all entities and occurrences and which posit an origin as well as an end to the world. Part of this manuscript reads just like the criticism of idealist historiography that is found in writings from the 1980s.[59] In addition, it includes a discussion of the 'givenness' of the world (citing Heidegger positively) and lauds Epicurus for his idea of contin-gency and of the encounter. Further, it includes the idea of a *Kulturkampf* in philosophy between materialist and idealist camps.[60]

Notwithstanding the thematic similarities to Althusser's Aleatory Material-ist writings, at a certain point there is a clear shift to science and a justification of Marxist scientific practice that the published writings associated with the

---

57   Althusser 1975.

      Pour tout dire, la philosophie marxiste n'a rien à perdre, mais tout à gagner, en aban-donnant les formules dont la fonction d'apologétique, de contrôle et de garantie sont évidentes. Et si, comme c'est à parier, ces fonctions ont des effets pratiques réels, les marx-istes ont tout à gagner à la rectification de ces pratiques. Oui, tout à gagner. Et pour me limiter à un seul point, je dirais que le Mouvement ouvrier a tout à gagner aujourd'hui à disposer des analyses scientifiques, théoriques, historiques et concrètes, qui lui manquent cruellement: je ne parle pas d'analyses d'inspiration philosophique, mais des analyses sci-entifiques....

58   Goshgarian 2006, pp. xvi–xvii, xlv–xlviii; 2013, pp. 89–90; Beaulieu 2003, pp. 162–3.

59   Althusser 2015, pp. 77–82.

60   Althusser 2015, pp. 103–4, 118, 233–9.

materialism of the encounter do not make as clearly. In fact, there is a long and rather surprising section in 'Être marxiste en philosophie' where Althusser points out his agreement with Karl Popper on the criterion for distinguishing a scientific theory from other types of ideas. Though he does not agree with Popper that we can say in advance whether a scientific theory is falsifiable, he does concur with Popper's point that hypotheses that cannot be invalidated by experience are not scientific.[61]

If historical materialism is a science, Althusser maintains, it must be able to be validated. If this is so, then in what way are it results confirmed? Historical materialism, Althusser explains, like mathematics and psychoanalysis, presents a special case among the sciences because its results are not experimentally reproducible. Mathematics is distinct because the objects that it studies are not material; rather, it has for its object the results of its prior practices. Its demonstrations therefore do not consist of experimental proofs, but in a logical reordering or analysis of its objects.[62] Psychoanalysis and historical materialism are unique as well, Althusser maintains, because, in contrast to the natural sciences which study the material real and whose findings (as theoretical representations of universal elements) are or should be infinitely reproducible, they have for their object complex historical singularities or 'conjunctures'. Unlike the universal elements that natural science studies, the moment of the class struggle studied by historical materialism or the moment in a subject's psyche analysed by depth psychology 'is singular and only defines and describes itself *progressively* in the course of the analysis or of the struggle itself.'[63] This does not mean that these science's findings cannot be confirmed, only that they are confirmed by experience but not by 'experiment'.[64] In this sense, the proof of historical materialism's and psychoanalysis' truth is 'inseparable from the direct transformation of their object[s]'.

The rudiments of such a practical transformation and therefore of such a validation are spelled out in more detail in a book written by Althusser between 1976 and 1978 (but only edited and published in 2015) titled *Initiation à la philosophie pour les non-philosophes*. In a chapter devoted to 'Philosophy and the Science of Class Struggle', Althusser imagines how and under what conditions such a transformation (and thereby confirmation) is possible. He supposes that the conditions for such a transformation are the following. First, that the members of a non-exploitative class become unified in their understanding

---

61   Althusser 2015, pp. 93–4.
62   Althusser 2015, pp. 93–6.
63   Althusser 2015, pp. 96–7.
64   Althusser 2015, pp. 96–7.

of themselves as exploited subjects and that they do so by subscribing to a philosophy that facilitates this unification. Then, if that class 'arms itself with a scientific theory of class struggle, the conditions of that philosophy's elaboration will change completely'. This philosophy will change from a 'blind' and subjective class ideology expressing and ensuring that class's relation to the dominant mode of production to an objective and 'conscious determination, assured by scientific knowledge of [that relation's] conditions, of its forms, of its laws'.[65]

This philosophy (just like all philosophies) will then be deployed politically. It will suggest to politicians, or at least to those who can direct the expression of political power, the reasons and objective means for the transformation of these relations. From this will follow a political line.[66] As Althusser strongly maintains in another document from the same period, if this philosophy does not include objective, social scientific knowledge of existing relations – of that which produces and sustains them and of what tendencies in them might allow for their transformation – and if the philosophy does not grow and change from lessons learned in the course of its implementation, then there is no hope of choosing the correct line and for the transformation of existing relations.[67] Without this knowledge, the philosophy expressed by the non-exploitative class and the political choices that follow from it are easily influenced and countered not only by the dominant ideology, but also by the repressive state apparatuses (army, state, police, laws, courts, etc.),[68] which guarantee the reproduction of the conditions of the proletariat's exploitation.[69]

In the spring of 1980, Althusser gave an interview to his friend and Italian journalist Giorgio Fanti.[70] In it, he answered wide-ranging queries about present political issues, about the difference between Italian and French communist parties, about the current crisis in the communist movement, and about how to resolve it. He also reflected on his career as a whole and offered up some reflections on the relations between philosophy, science, and politics. Regarding Marxist philosophy, Althusser stated in no uncertain terms his judgment that 'dialectical materialism' as it had been historically formulated through the course of the Marxist movement is 'absolutely indefensible' and

---

65   Althusser 2013, pp. 364–5.
66   Althusser 2013, pp. 364–5.
67   Althusser 2018c, pp. 37–50.
68   Althusser 2014b, pp. 65–6.
69   Althusser 2013, p. 362.
70   Althusser 1980.

that it has nothing to do with Marx's philosophy.[71] Though less detailed than the balance sheet provided in the 1978 essay 'Marx in his Limits', Althusser supported this contention by tallying up the idealistic philosophical mistakes committed not only by Marx's interpreters, but also by Marx himself.[72]

When asked by Fanti whether his rejection of dialectical materialism for a version of Marx's position in philosophy that Althusser now referred to as '*sur-matérialisme*' or '*hyper-matérialisme*' meant a change to his position regarding the Marxist science of historical materialism, Althusser offered a detailed and passionate reply. He began by saying that his core argument had not changed and that 'we must defend in the trenches the idea that Marxism is a revolutionary science'.[73] Further, though he continued to disavow his earlier position that there is a definitive break in Marx's philosophy when Marx rejects idealist philosophy and becomes scientific, Althusser told his interviewer that that there remains a discernible difference between Marx's scientific ideas (which are sound and potentially transformative) and his philosophical ideas (which were mostly bourgeois and ideological).[74] When Fanti asked a follow-up question about whether or not Althusser had said in 1973 that dialectical materialism was the undeniable core to Marx's thought,[75] Althusser replied:

No, no. On the contrary, for me, [this core] is historical materialism ... If this word designated something, it was that there was something scientific in Marx. It remains to be seen if the extent of the scientific ground opened by Marx was effectively as big as we had believed it to be, as Marx believed, etc. What I have always defended is the idea that there is something scientific in Marx, and I will defend that always.[76]

71 Althusser 1980, pp. 51–2.
72 Althusser 2006a, pp. 26–61.
73 Althusser 1980, p. 52.
   J'ai dit alors qu'il fallait défendre dans la tranchée l'idée que le marxisme est une science révolutionnaire.
74 Althusser 1980, pp. 50–1.
75 Fanti is probably misremembering the line from Althusser 1976a, p. 117 where Althusser states: 'Yes, it is quite correct for us to speak of an unimpeachable and undeniable scientific core in Marxism, that of historical materialism'.
76 Althusser 1980, pp. 51–2.
   Non, non. Pour moi le matérialisme historique, contrairement! Justement Si ce mot désignait quelque chose, c'était ce qu'il pouvait y avoir de scientifique dans Marx. Quitte à voir, si effectivement, l'extension du domaine scientifique ouvert par Marx était aussi grande qu'on avait pu le croire, que Marx le croyait, etc.... Ce que j'ai toujours défendu c'est l'idée qu'il y avait quelque chose de scientifique dans Marx, et ça je le défends toujours.

3   Althusser 1982–1987: Marxist Philosophy without Marxist Science?

The 1980 interview with Giorgio Fanti contains Althusser's last recorded and edited thoughts on the relations between philosophy, science, and politics prior to the two-year philosophical caesura occasioned by Althusser's murder of his wife, Hélène Rytmann-Légotien, on 16 November 1980. Some readers have argued that Althusser's thought underwent a change during this interval or that a change begun in 1975 or 1976 was solidified. These analysts maintain that when Althusser began writing again in the summer of 1982 it was with a profoundly changed view of the relation between Marxist philosophy, Marxist science, and Marxist politics. In this new assessment, Marxist science was dismissed while ontology and politics were foregrounded. Exploring neither the plausibility of this claim nor its possible external political and philosophical motivations,[77] this section will briefly explore how some readers have argued that there was such a modification in Althusser's attitude towards science in his idea of philosophy after 1980.

Within Althusser scholarship, there is a divide between those who emphasise a continuist reading of his work and those who emphasise its breaks. The 'breakist' understanding, which underscores the changes or ruptures in his thought, was in the majority in the 1990s and remains a popular interpretive rubric. Almost all who hold this position argue that Althusser renounced his scientism in his last works.[78] However, among those scholars who have worked extensively with archival or posthumously published materials and who have tried to comprehend the arc of his career, a continuist consensus has emerged over the last decade that focuses on the permanence of certain themes in Althusser's work. These themes include the primacy of relations, the idea of the conjuncture, the claim that history is a process without a subject, and the idea of philosophy as a void.[79] Even amongst the continuists, however, a significant majority explicitly holds the position that Althusser gave up his scientism in the 1980s or else supports this position implicitly by emphasising only the political and philosophical aspects of Althusser's thought from this period.[80] Despite a

---

77   Garo 2012. In this essay Garo offers a comprehensive assessment of the political and philo-
      sophical climate that may have encouraged the foregrounding of ontology and politics in
      Althusser's work in the mid-1980s.

78   Bargu 2012; Bensaïd 1999, p. 253; Diefenbach 2013; Elliott 2006b; Garo 2012; Haider and
      Mohandesi 2012; Navarro 1998, 96; Thomas 2013; Williams 2013, pp. 73–4.

79   Morfino 2005; Goshgarian 2013; Francois Matheron 1998.

80   Beaulieu 2003; Boer 2007; Del Lucchese tr. Warren Montag 2010; Gillot 2012; Ichida and
      Matheron 2005; Illas 2013; Lahtinen 2009, p. 87; Francois Matheron 1998; Moulier-Boutang
      2005; Fernández Liria 2002; Thomas 2013, p. 148.

near consensus among his readers that Althusser gave up his scientism in the 1980s, there is a contingent of continuists who argue that Althusser's scientism remains consistent throughout his career.[81] One purpose of the present chapter is to provide more and better evidence of this consistency.

The next few paragraphs will summarise the accounts of a few representative readers who explicitly maintain that Althusser gave up his scientism in the 1980s. This survey will begin with one interpreter who accentuates the break from Althusser's earlier philosophical positions with the advent of aleatory materialism. It will then review the readings of two representative continuists, both of whom maintain that – despite the deep continuities discernible in Althusser's philosophy as a whole – his later philosophy lacks the scientistic element that had previously marked his thought. Following this review, the form, presentation, and content of Althusser's posthumously published work on the materialism of the encounter will be examined in order to show why, based on these texts, there are perhaps good reasons for thinking that Althusser altered his position on the role of science in his political philosophy as a whole. In addition to a close and comparative reading of Althusser's published and unpublished texts from the late 1970s and 80s, the final section makes use of one 'continuist non-breakist' reading of aleatory materialism to support its contention that Althusser's writings include a mostly consistent understanding of the relations between scientific knowledge and political action.

3.1   Althusser's Scientism Abandoned?

The best-known identifier of a break in Althusser's thought is Antonio Negri. In a frequently cited essay that appeared only two years after the collections that contained the bulk of Althusser's reflections on aleatory materialism (*Sur la philosophie* and *Ecrits philosophiques et politiques, Tome 1*) were published, Negri argues that Althusser's last writings evidence a profound *Kehre* or turn in his thought. Negri pegs the beginning of this turn to Althusser's rereading of Machiavelli in 1978. At this time, Negri maintains, 'the structural framework of Althusser's previous theoretical analysis is completely reversed: theory does not show the convergences and consequences, in a structural and systemic manner; on the contrary, it shows ruptures, paradoxes, voids and points of crisis'.[82] This structural change, Negri argues, firmly took hold by the early 1980s. At this time and in the works comprising the corpus of aleatory materialism, Althusser developed 'an ontological conception of crisis as key to an

81   Goshgarian 2006, p. 95; Haider and Mohandesi 2012; Kirn 2013, pp. 346–7; Sotiris 2008, p. 170; Suchting 2004; Tosel 2013, p. 15.
82   Negri 1996, p. 54.

understanding of the historical process and as motor of the transformation of the real'.[83] In this ateleological universe constituted solely of discrete materials bound and sundered only by 'chance and event', a revolutionary struggle can happen anywhere and at any time. No longer burdened by a 'distinction between ideological and non-ideological thinking,'[84] or by the need to scientifically analyse the conditions of a revolution, any subject 'in the open freedom of the surface' can assert an aleatory revolutionary thesis ('a revolutionary truth unacceptable to the given conditions'),[85] which may have the possibility of overturning current theoretical practices. At least as Negri interprets Althusser, aleatory materialism includes a denial of the difference between ideological and scientific knowledge and, therefore, of the practical efficacy of scientific knowledge in politics. Because, according to Negri, any given condition is subject to change by an unexpected event, it is simultaneously an affirmation of the supremacy of philosophy (which may operate in the void beyond current theoretical practices) in politics.[86]

Negri's position on aleatory materialism is extremely loose and schematic and it takes many liberties in its citations, interpretations, and overall argumentation. Probably not coincidentally, the aleatory materialism described by Negri anticipates and prophetically justifies many of the positions that Negri was simultaneously asserting in his own work.[87] However, even among those readers who are not so obviously involved in acts of creative appropriation, who read Althusser carefully, and who take an overall continuist view of his work, the thesis that aleatory materialism includes a renunciation of Althusser's philosophy's scientistic elements remains an influential interpretation.

Among the proponents of the view that aleatory materialism – despite its fundamental continuity with the rest of his oeuvre – includes a renunciation of his political philosophy's scientistic element is Althusser's biographer, Yann Moulier-Boutang. In a 1997 article that is mostly concerned with the relation between Althusser's biography and his contradictory philosophical claims, Moulier-Boutang states that the theoretical crisis brought on by Althusser's relinquishment of dialectical materialism led around 1975 or 1976 to the 'abandonment of historical materialism' and its 'apparatus of scientific laws of history ... in favor of a logic of the singular situation, of the pure political practice

83   Negri 1996, p. 59.
84   Negri 1996, p. 63.
85   Negri 1996, p. 54.
86   Negri 1996, p. 62.
87   Day 2011; Read 2013.

of the aleatory encounter'.[88] The details of this abandonment are provided by Moulier-Boutang in a 2005 essay titled 'Le matérialisme comme politique aléatoire'. In this paper, Moulier-Boutang connects aleatory materialism with the logic of overdetermination developed by Althusser in the early 1960s.[89] In addition to persuasively forging this connection, Moulier-Boutang argues that, with the materialism of the encounter, Althusser gave up on the idea of using Marx's historical materialist scientific tools to engage in 'the concrete analysis of the concrete situation'.[90] As he sees it, Althusser abandoned this idea in his later works because he grasped that 'revolution is an irreducible, unpredictable, "overdetermined" event' and because the idea of univocal causality and the assumption of continuity in nature cannot explain such revolutionary occurrences.[91] With this realisation, Moulier-Boutang maintains, Althusser put to one side his older supposition that historical change happens in an orderly and predictable way as well as the corresponding idea that, because of this orderliness, scientific analysis of the present conjuncture will allow one to understand how to occasion revolutionary change. The prior ontological assumption of orderliness was replaced with the supposition of 'the absolutely arbitrary character of existence'.[92] Further, the idea of the usefulness of concrete analysis for first understanding and then precipitating revolutionary change gave way in Althusser's late thought to the idea that an aleatory materialist ontology demands that we think of revolutionary politics as an art rather than as a science.[93] As a practitioner of this art of revolution, Moulier-Boutang explains, the aleatory materialist philosopher stops looking at what was and what is in order to see what can be changed in the future; he does so because he recognises that the relation between present patterns and future possibilities is always uncer-

---

88   Moulier-Boutang 1997.
      'La solution théorique vers laquelle Althusser se dirige à partir de 1975–76 est l'abandon du matérialisme historique, avec la crise du marxisme: l'appareil scientifique des lois de l'histoire (mode de productions, succession, transition), conjurateur de l'angoisse, est désinvesti, au profit d'une logique du cas singulier, de la pratique politique pure (Machiavel et nous) de la rencontre aléatoire.'

89   Moulier-Boutang 2005, p. 163.

90   Moulier-Boutang 2005, p. 162.

91   Moulier-Boutang 2005, p. 163.
      'La révolution est un événement irréductible, imprévisible, « surdéterminé ». La causalité univoque, la continuité ne sont d'aucune utilité.'

92   Moulier-Boutang 2005, p. 163.
      'La... caractère absolument aléatoire de l'existence n'apparaît pas comme thème philosophique chez Louis Althusser avant la rencontre avec Machiavel'.

93   Moulier-Boutang 2005, p. 163.

tain.[94] Akin to and inspired by Machiavelli, such a philosopher instead steps into an existing situation and attempts to found an absolutely new political regime where one has not before existed. To do so, he or she must 'think of politics as the meeting of the conditions of becoming, of that which is not still, of that which is otherwise missed'.[95]

Like Moulier-Boutang in 2005 but in much more detail, Lahtinen in his 2008 book *Politics and philosophy: Niccolo Machiavelli and Louis Althusser's aleatory materialism* attempts to show what Althusser's late thinking on the materialism of the encounter owes to his reading(s) of Machiavelli. As with Moulier-Boutang, this account includes the thesis that aleatory materialism includes a renunciation of the scientistic elements of Althusser's political philosophy. Along with many others, Lahtinen is critical of the scientism in Althusser's work prior to 1980. He correctly recognises that between 1960 and 1965 Althusser sought to position Marxism 'as a high-standard science able to withstand critique'.[96] He also rightly notices that later, during the period of his self-criticism, Althusser became less optimistic about the possibility of separating science from ideology (even as Althusser still insisted that critical science was essential to the revolutionary movement).[97] When the book comes to its interpretation of Althusser's aleatory materialism, however, Lahtinen contends that the idea of science did not play an important role in Althusser's late political philosophy. With aleatory materialism, Lahtinen maintains, Althusser renounced even the epistemically modest idea, which dated from the period of his self-criticism, that Marxism should be thought of as a critical science perpetually on guard against its idealist contents and suppositions. He replaced it, Lahtinen argues, with a 'philosophy for Marxism', which understands itself as a non-scientific critical political practice. Lahtinen traces the reason for this change to Althusser's reflections on Machiavelli. Through these sustained (if intermittent) readings, Lahtinen argues, Althusser developed an increasingly subjectivist epistemological position, one of whose consequences was a changed understanding of the relationship between politics and philosophy.

The basic argument of Lahtinen runs like this. From his sustained reading of Machiavelli, Althusser learned that an objective standpoint on politics is impossible and that 'the effects of coincidences and exceptions on human life'

---

94   Moulier-Boutang 2005, p. 162.
95   Moulier-Boutang 2005, p. 164.
         '... il pense la politique comme la réunion des conditions de l'avènement de ce qui
         n'est pas encore, qui a d'ailleurs raté'.
96   Lahtinen 2009, p. 74.
97   Lahtinen 2009, pp. 77, 81.

as well as the perspectival nature of all political knowledge made a 'general theory about human life or *praxis* in general' likewise unrealisable.[98] This new awareness excluded the possibility of an objective, universal, 'modern' political science upon which a revolutionary science of politics might be based.[99] However, according to Lahtinen, Althusser also absorbed from Machiavelli the lesson that the subjective knowledge of a particular political situation from a particular perspective is not the sole type of knowledge available to the aleatory materialist philosopher but that this practical knowledge is desirable for the philosopher who wishes to encourage revolutionary change. Because politics is not predictable in the same way as physics, knowledge of a conjuncture (of a particular socio-economic-historical arrangement) cannot come from an understanding of the general laws of social organisation or from laboratory-like experiments on persons or on social groupings.[100] Rather, in order to be effective, the aleatory materialist philosopher or political actor must study 'the constants repeated from one case to another, knowledge of which *may* be useful for the political actor planning a strategy of action'. This actor must also be sensitive to the workings of chance and to the specifics of his or her situation[101] Unlike Moulier-Boutang, who goes from the identification of an aleatory materialist ontology to the requirement that we think of revolutionary politics as an art rather than as a science and also unlike Negri, who goes from ontology to rhetoric, for Lahtinen, the ontological portion of Althusser's aleatory materialism appears as secondary or instrumental. According to this reading, the primary reason for Althusser abandoning any claim to the scientificity in Marxism in his later works is the realisation, taken from Machiavelli, that as participants we can have no objective knowledge of laws animating our social life and that radical changes to our social life always appear as a surprise, without knowable antecedent cause or causes.

3.2   Internalist Explanation of the Abandonment Thesis

In contrast to Negri's reading, the accounts of Moulier-Boutang and Lahtinen are well sourced and take few liberties with the posthumously published texts on aleatory materialism. However, irrespective of the quality of the analysis or whether or not their author is a continuist or a breakist, the majority of scholars who have engaged with Althusser's late works have come to the conclusion that, in them, Althusser abandons the scientism that was hitherto a constant

---

98   Lahtinen 2009, p. 123.
99   Lahtinen 2009, p. 117.
100   Lahtinen 2009, pp. 162–3, 238.
101   Lahtinen 2009, pp. 309–10.

in his political philosophy. As this chapter argues in its final section that this is not the case and that aleatory materialism represents a prolongation and elaboration of positions and ideas already developed in the 1960s and 1970s, we should perhaps seek an explanation for why so many readers believe that aleatory materialism represents a change from Althusser's previous endorsement of scientism.

Even if we avoid referencing the personal, political and philosophical circumstances of their writing, by looking at the selection and editorial presentation of the works constituting the aleatory materialism corpus we can find sufficient internal explanation for the preponderance of the interpretation that Althusser abandons scientism in his work from the 1980s. Indeed, given the content of the available texts, their presentation, and their immediate reception, the conclusion that Althusser dropped his scientism appears somewhat warranted. The next two paragraphs will examine explicit statements from these texts that tend to support such a conclusion. The paragraph that follows them will look at a few relatively clear editorial inclusions as a factor in this work's reception as anti- or non-scientistic.

In both their French and English editions, the philosophical essays on aleatory materialism are accompanied by letters which Althusser wrote to friends and collaborators and with an interview whose status is somewhere between that of original work and collaboration.[102] The letters in particular provide an account of Althusser's mental state at the time of the project. They also set out its philosophical and political intent as well its historical and biographical context. Clearly present in many of these epistles, is Althusser's desire to synthesise and present in an accessible form ideas that had been percolating for years and to construct a 'philosophy for Marxism'.[103] As this philosophy was presented as 'new' or as a break from Althusser's previous work it is little wonder that people have looked to see how this work differs from the previous philosophy.[104] One can add to this the fact that a few of the letters and interviews included passages where Althusser seems to denigrate or question his prior work and to problematise its account of the sciences.

Two letters and two interview responses stand out in particular for the way in which they seem to show Althusser in the process of rejecting his earlier scientism. In the first, a 1978 letter addressed to the Georgian philosopher Merab Mardashvili, Althusser announces himself as being in a period of transition and hints at the gestation of the materialism of the encounter (no doubt the reason

102   Althusser 2006c, pp. 1–6, 208–51; 1994b, pp. 81–137; Goshgarian 2006, p. xvi.
103   Althusser 2006c, pp. 258–9.
104   Elliott 2006b, p. 366; Navarro 1998, p. 94.

this letter is included).[105] He also reflects on his previous work and its relation to the sciences, writing: 'I see clear as day that what I did fifteen years ago was to fabricate a little, typically French justification, in a neat little rationalism bolstered with a few references (Cavaillès, Bachelard, Canguilhem, and, behind them, a bit of the Spinoza-Hegel tradition), for Marxism's (historical materialism's) pretension to being a science'.[106] In another letter, this one from April of 1986 and addressed to Fernanda Navarro, Althusser instructs his collaborator on how to edit and improve the text of the interview she was conducting with him, writing: 'I'd like you to drop the passage about "lines of demarcation" in the sciences, particularly the demarcation between the scientific and the ideological, as well as everything pertaining to the difference between ideology and the ideological'.[107]

In the published interviews, we see two more responses that seem to show Althusser in the process of rejecting his earlier scientism. In the first, Althusser responds to a question posed by Navarro about the distinctive features a materialist philosophy might be said to display with the reply, '... it does not claim to be autonomous or to ground its own origin and its own power. Nor does it consider itself to be a science, and still less the Science of sciences'.[108] In the second, Althusser replies to a question about the nature of history by stating that the objects of Marxism and psychoanalysis 'belong not to accomplished history but to *Geschichte*, to living history, which is made of, and wells up out of, aleatory tendencies and the unconscious. This is a history whose forms have nothing to do with the determinism of physical laws'.[109]

In addition to statements and passages like these which seem to imply that Althusser was in the process of rethinking the position that Marxism is a science or even that he was engaged in this position's active denigration and renunciation, there are also the unfinished 1978 essay 'Marx in his limits' and the likewise fragmentary 'Machiavelli and Us'. The former was published with the aleatory materialist writings while the latter appeared in French and English editions during the 1990s alongside prefaces that suggested the connection between Althusser's reading of Machiavelli and the materialism of the encounter.[110] As has been noted above, one source of the claim that Althusser renounces his scientism are the passages in his writing on Machiavelli where

---

105   Althusser 2006c, p. 5.
106   Althusser 2006c, p. 3.
107   Althusser 2006c, p. 287.
108   Althusser 2006c, p. 274.
109   Althusser 2006c, p. 264.
110   Althusser 1995b, p. 40; Elliott 1999.

Althusser says that he is not interested in Machiavelli as a founder of political science but only as a philosopher of the contingent event.[111] That this may have been a conscious choice of Althusser's to concentrate on the relation between philosophy and politics rather than a dismissal of political science *tout court*, however, seems to have been missed.[112]

A similar interpretation appears to have been made in the case of 'Marx in his Limits' as well as the other 'texts of the crisis': 'Marxism Today (1978)' and 'The Transformation of Philosophy (1976)'. Each speaks extensively of science and of Marxist science.[113] However, each does so almost exclusively in pejorative terms, enumerating the problems that have resulted in the workers' movement due to its adoptions of certain 'Marxist scientific' concepts about the material nature of the world, concepts that are, in reality, merely idealist philosophical notions.[114] The lack of any mention of Marxist theory of science in positive terms, as well as the diagnosis of a 'crisis in Marxism' caused in part by Marxism's erroneous scientific claims, might lead one to conclude that, during the late 1970s' 'crisis of Marxism', Althusser abandoned his longstanding claim that Marxism is a science, that this science is historical materialism, and that its object is the history of class struggle. Indeed, some read these texts as announcing this repudiation. For example, one of Althusser's best readers, Gregory Elliott, was moved to interpret these texts in this way. In a post-script and intellectual balance sheet included with the second edition of *The Detour of Theory* (2006) he wrote:

> Around 1976, a new period [of Althusser's work] begins, which is one not of the auto-critique, but of the auto-deconstruction – even self-destruction – of Althusserianism and the radical problematisation of the scientificity of Marxism itself. It is most dramatically attested to in the 1977 talk 'The Crisis of Marxism' and the 1978 encyclopaedia article 'Marxism Today' – texts whose content overlaps with that of the abandoned manuscript on 'Marx in His Limits'. Writings of *a break*, they can also be regarded as in some sense *transitional* works, paving the way for a final period of Althusserian production.[115]

---

111   Lahtinen 2009, pp. 117–18; Elliott 1999, p. xvii.
112   Althusser 1999, p. 11.
113   Althusser 2006a; 1990b; 1994a.
114   Cavazzini 2009.
115   Elliott 2006b, p. 366.

4   An Aleatory Materialism Consistent with Marxist Science?

In the preceding section we have suggested why, given the form, presentation, and content of the published texts, readers of Althusser might come to hold the position that he gave up his scientism in the 1980s. Nonetheless, given the manifest consistency of his scientism prior to 1980 (as detailed in section 2 and summarised again below), we have reason to be suspicious of this inference. Another reason to mistrust this conclusion is that the information that it is based upon is partial: the majority of Althusser's writings having to do with the materialism of the encounter and its gestation remain unpublished.[116] In addition, the principal texts which develop this philosophy have been subject to marked editorial interventions. For instance, in order to compose the essay 'The Underground Current of the Materialism of the Encounter', the introductory chapters of the book provisionally entitled *J'écris ce livre en octobre 1982* were cut. These chapters include an evaluation of the present conjuncture and specific recommendations for political action.[117] Rather than presenting *J'écris ce livre en octobre 1982* as Althusser unambiguously intended – as an attempt to think the (then) present conjuncture 'otherwise' – this omission gives the appearance that, in one of the two major principal texts on aleatory materialism, Althusser was exclusively involved in the development (exhumation?) of a politico-ontological philosophical tradition.[118] In addition to debatable rearrangements, comparable omissions mark that other principal aleatory materialism text, 'Philosophy and Marxism, Interviews with Fernanda Navarro'. Also missing from consideration or, in the case of *Initiation à la philosophie pour les non-philosophes*, only recently considerable, are numerous texts from the 1970s (some of them book-length) which clearly contain aleatory materialist arguments and concepts and that may or may not corroborate the thesis that Althusser was in the process of abandoning his scientism or that this abandonment went along with aleatory materialism's development.[119]

---

116   Althusser 1982c; 1982a; 1982b; 1985a; 1985b; 1986a.
117   Althusser 2006c, p. 164; 1982b, pp. 17–30 According to its editors, these sections of the book were omitted because they consisted of:

   exchanges of opinion, of dubious value because they are not justified, not defended, not supported by textual citations or convincing examples.' However, given their misleading and erroneous citations, the dubious interpretations of philosophers both modern and contemporary, and the quality of argumentation, the sections that were included in the book fall under the same criticisms.

118   Althusser 1982b.
119   Althusser 2013; 2015; 2016; 2018b; 2018c.

Except for one instance where Althusser gave specific permission that a text be edited and published posthumously (and that only in Latin America), there is little reason to privilege the published texts over those still held in the archive.[120] Therefore, in trying to make the judgment of whether or not, in his later works, Althusser abandoned his scientism, it is both licit and important to consider the unpublished writings. To the end of making such a determination, the next section examines relevant passages from the posthumous collections of Althusser's writings as well as some texts from the period 1982–7 that remain unpublished. In so doing, it will provide a counter-reading to those accounts which argue that Althusser gave up his scientism in the late 1970s as well as to those which claim that Althusser's thought emerged in 1982 cleansed of its previous scientism. The primary goals of this counter-reading will be to demonstrate that Althusser did not abandon his scientism and to show how it appears in his later work as a continuous and important part of his Marxist theory. A secondary objective will be to account for the seemingly anti-scientistic statements detailed above.

4.1   An Alternative to the Abandonment Thesis

If one wants to build the argument that Althusser rejected the scientistic aspect of his thought in his later works, the claim that he emerged in the summer of 1982 after two years marked by trauma, by severe mental illness, by institutionalisation, and by little access to philosophical materials with a profoundly changed view of Marxist thought appears psychologically implausible. As it explains the origin of such a change in the context of a profound theoretical and political struggle in which Althusser rejected his well-known claims about the scientificity of Marxism, the theory that marks the origin of this rejection in the texts from the 'crisis of Marxism' period appears the much more likely account. However, based on the sum of available evidence, is it the best reading of what was happening in Althusser's philosophy during the late 1970s and is it the best explanation for the genesis of his work from the 1980s?

When Althusser's published and unpublished writings from 1972–80 were scrutinised in section 2.3, it did not appear that he was in the process of reconsidering the position that Marxism is a science or that he was modifying the corresponding assertion that there is a necessary relationship between correct scientific knowledge and effective political action. On the contrary, the majority of the texts from this period insist on this relation. They also show Althusser attempting to work out the practical details of how Marxist science

---

120   Althusser 2006c, pp. 249–50 fn30.

should be pursued and then integrated into political decision-making. Though some of the published materials display little of this effort, *Initiation à la philosophie pour les non-philosophes* (1978/2013) includes an extensive discussion of the relations among Marxist philosophy, Marxist science, and Marxist politics as well as a clear endorsement of Marxist science.[121] In short, this book, as well as many other lengthy texts published in that last decade show Althusser developing the argument in philosophical, practical, and polemical terms that intentional political change is best enabled by scientific analyses of the political conjuncture.[122]

If it is the case that Althusser did not dismantle his claims about the scientificity of Marxism in the late 1970s, then what was he up to in works like 'Marx in his Limits' and 'Marxism Today' that are singled out by some critics as evidence of this undoing and which gave rise to this confusion? As we have argued, the explanation that fits the available evidence is that Althusser was in the process of doing with Marxist science something very similar to that which he was simultaneously trying to do with Marxist philosophy. Specifically, he was attempting to purge it of its ideological components and, therefore, of its idealist content and inheritance.

Rather than condemning Marxist science as a whole, the Marxist science that Althusser ruthlessly critiqued between 1975 and 1980 is the version of historical materialism that has historically been twinned with Marxist philosophy and that is known as 'dialectical materialism'. Understood as 'an integral part of dialectical materialism' or as a 'result of the application of dialectical materialism to history', this version of Marxist science has historically been dominated and defined by its dyadic relation with an idealist metaphysics of history and of nature.[123] That the historical pairing of historical materialism and dialectical materialism has had deleterious consequences for the workers' movement, Althusser often marks as obvious between 1976 and 1980.[124] Nevertheless, it does not follow from Althusser's simultaneous dismantling of historical materialism and of dialectical materialism that 'the core of Marxist thought' is not scientific. After all, simultaneous to these critiques, Althusser was in the process of working out what a scientific analysis of the present socioeconomic and

---

121   Althusser 2013, chapters 4, 9,10, 17–19.

122   Althusser 1975; 2018c; 2016; 2018b.

123   Althusser 1975.

        On trouve en effet de nos jours constamment, sous la plume d' auteurs marxistes autorisés, la formule suivant : *'le matérialisme est partie intégrante du matérialisme dialectique.'*.

124   Althusser 2006a, pp. 18–33; 1990b, pp. 10–12; 1990d, p. 262.

political conjuncture should include.[125] He was also arguing that, in order for political action to be successful, the Party must engage in critical social scientific analyses of the present conjuncture.[126] Further, and as evidenced by the Fanti interview and many other texts from this period, Althusser did not shy away from calling this analysis 'historical materialist'. Seen in this context, Althusser's criticism of historical materialism in the late 1970s appears as deeply complementary to his simultaneous elaboration of a renewed materialist approach to Marxist science and to Marxist philosophy in which both are stripped of their relations to idealist metaphysics.

As with his critique of Marxist philosophy but to a greater extent, the problem of nomenclature arises with this elaboration. In the case of Marxist philosophy, Althusser marked the difference between the historical iterations of Marxist philosophy that he was trying to dismantle and the philosophy for Marxism that he was in the course of developing in the late 70s by labelling the historical iteration 'dialectical materialism' and his reconstructed materialism variously as 'non-philosophy', 'anti-philosophy', and 'philosophy for Marxism'. In the 80s, the designations for this reconstructed Marxist philosophy grew to include 'aleatory materialism' and 'materialism of the encounter'. Though Althusser was not always consistent in his use of these expressions and often employed the generic 'Marxist philosophy' to refer both to the idealist version of Marxism he rejected and to the materialist philosophy he was in the course of developing, the distinction had at least been made. Further, the type of Marxist philosophy Althusser meant to denote was usually clearly signalled by context.[127] In contrast, whether Althusser referred to the concept of Marxist science as historically dominated by dialectical materialism or to his revised version of the concept stripped of its relations to an idealistic metaphysics, he habitually referred to each by the same names: 'Marxist science' and 'historical materialism'.

That Althusser was in the late 1970s critical of historical materialism and that he argued for an alternative understanding of Marxist science, for this alternative science's pursuit, and for its use in political decision-making should have been made clear in Section 2.3. What has not been made explicit though is exactly of what this reconstructed understanding of historical materialism consisted. Negatively, we know from Althusser's critique of the relation of Marxist science to dialectical materialism that it is an idealist mistake to think that:

---

125   W.S. Lewis 2007b, pp. 97–105.

126   Althusser 2016, pp. 81–90.

127   Althusser 2006c, pp. 173–4, 188–9.

(a) there are general laws of history and (b) that social relations are determined in the manner that physical relations are determined.[128] We also know from our scrutiny of texts written between 1975 and 1978 that, in Althusser's reconstruction, historical materialism has the following positive characteristics. First, it is a science that has for its object of study the existing forms of class struggle and that has as its goal the transformation of its object of study. Because of this goal and the changing structures of its object, it defines and describes itself *progressively* in the course of the struggle itself. Second, the characteristics of its object of study delimit the type of knowledge that it is possible for it to acquire. Unlike the natural sciences which study the material real and whose findings (as theoretical representations of universal elements) are or should be infinitely reproducible, reconstructed historical materialism has as its object complex historical singularities or 'conjunctures'. Under analysis, these structures reveal tendencies or patterns of relation that endure over time and which can be said to differentially order and structure these conjunctures in terms of the way in which a tendency is (or is not) expressed in relation to the other tendencies that constitute a singular conjuncture.[129] In order to gain knowledge of a specific conjuncture, this version of historical materialism synthesises the findings of the other (non-critical) social sciences that it judges to be relevant to understanding the conjuncture and initiates inquiry into those areas where it finds knowledge lacking. In order to help weed-out the influence of bourgeois ideology on these sciences' assumptions, methodology, and conclusions, it also subjects this knowledge to critical scrutiny.[130] The result of all of this labour is a synthetic analysis of the present conjuncture and a concrete political recommendation for how to transform it. Reflecting the goal and object of the science, the validity of this result can only be confirmed practically by the transformation of the very object that it has studied: the existing forms of the class struggle.[131]

---

128 Dumenil 1977.
129 Although Althusser used this word frequently in his previous work, it is clear that by 1978 (and probably by Althusser 2015) it had taken on this particular meaning in the context of historical materialist analysis. For instance in Althusser 2018c, 16 Althusser writes:

Tout dépend alors de 'l'analyse concrète' de la 'situation concrète', de la tendance actuelle de la lutte de classe ouvrière et populaire dan sons antagonisme avec la lutte de classe bourgeoise, donc de l'analyse concrète de cet *antagonisme* qui constitue à la fois la classe bourgeoise en classe dominante et exploiteuse et la classe ouvrière en classe dominée et exploitée.

130 Althusser 2016, pp. 88–9.
131 Althusser 1990d, pp. 265–6.

In the last few paragraphs we have summarised the available materials in order to detail Althusser's understanding and endorsement of a reconstructed historical materialism in the five years prior to 1980. In so doing, we have shown why any analysis that marks out 1975–80 as a period of transition away from scientism in Althusser's thought is incorrect. Not only do most of the writings from this period evidence an explicit endorsement of historical materialism, they also position it as a science separate from any dialectical materialist underpinnings. Though Althusser's understanding and endorsement of historical materialism between 1975–80 differs in some of its details from its earlier conceptualisation (and particularly that of 1960–65), his overall position is still recognizably scientistic in that he continues to mark out science and particularly the Marxist science of historical materialism as the only human theoretical practice that allows us to reliably understand socio-economic structures such that we might intentionally assist in their transformation.

If this summary accurately represents Althusser's reconstructed understanding of historical materialism right before the two-year break in philosophical activity which began in the spring of 1980, then the burden of proof is yet higher if one hopes to maintain that the 1980s writings on aleatory materialism are marked by their sudden rejection of scientism. This is the case as many of the ideas that are associated with Althusser's reconstruction of historical materialism clearly appear in the aleatory materialist writings. We also know that the development of a reconstructed historical materialism and the beginnings of Althusser's radical revisions to Marxist philosophy were simultaneous and that the two projects were conceptually linked. Therefore, in addition to needing to show that the positive endorsement of historical materialism disappears in the 80s, one would also need to show how and why a set of concepts and practices that were once described by Althusser as constituting a Marxist science complementary to a reconstructed Marxist philosophy are no longer so described.

4.2   The Explicit Endorsement of Scientism in Althusser's Later Works

As we have seen, due to the lack of positive mentions of Marxist science in the published texts from the 80s and owing to certain statements where Althusser wrote negatively about his attempts in the early 1960s to make Marxist philosophy scientific, a case can be made that Althusser was in the process of developing a non- or even anti-scientistic Marxist political philosophy. However, if we look at these writings against the background of the mid-to-late 70s reconstruction of Marxist science and Marxist philosophy and if we include the additional context provided by Althusser's writings between 1982 and 1987 that remain unpublished, we will see that Althusser never abandoned his scientism and that the endorsement of scientific practice appears in these works as a continuous and important part of his political philosophy.

In order to make these points, this sub-section will examine selected passages from Althusser's unpublished writings between 1982–7 that clearly contradict the theory that he forsook his scientism. Aware that the mere statement of Althusser's continued endorsement of Marxist science does not constitute proof that he remained steadfast in his belief that science is the only human theoretical practice that allows us to reliably understand socioeconomic structures such that we might intentionally assist in their transformation, the subsection that follows this one will turn to a reading of published and unpublished writings that illustrates how the scientific aspect of Althusser's late thought relates to its philosophical and political aspects. This illustration will challenge our preliminary account of how the published materials can be read as evidencing an abandonment of Althusser's advocacy of scientific practice for the workers' movement. It will do so by giving an explanation for the apparent negative references to science in these texts.

In the archives at IMEC there are multiple texts from the 1980s in which Althusser indicates his endorsement of scientific practice and declares scientific knowledge's privileged relationship to political change. These texts also detail the relation of scientific practice to Marxist philosophy. Included among these texts are unpublished sections of the Interviews with Fernanda Navarro as well as two long drafts from 1985 and 1986–7 titled 'Qu'y faire? Que faire?' and 'Thèses de juin'. The latter two are not only unambiguous in their endorsement of science and in their assessment of its efficacy; they also connect this affirmation to the project of aleatory materialism.[132] This connection, along with the less clear-cut but still evident endorsement of science found in the Navarro interviews, will be explored after citing these texts' explicit scientistic statements.

Following the model set by Lenin in 1901, both 'Qu'y faire? Que faire?' and 'Thèses de juin' resemble a slew of un- or recently published texts from the 1970s and 1980s in which Althusser reflects on 'What is to Be Done' in order to advance communism's goals. Just as the complete text of J'écris ce livre en octobre 1982 contains an evaluation of the present conjuncture along with specific recommendations for political action, so too does the unfinished book

---

132   The omission of these texts does not so much appear to reflect an active intent on the part of Althusser's posthumous editors to erase his scientism as it does an attempt on their part to emphasise the philosophical content of his work and to downplay the often hallucinatory or prophetic aspects of these texts, aspects which become prominent when Althusser speaks of current events and their concrete analyses.

from which the essay 'The Underground Current of the Materialism of the Encounter' is culled. Consistently, these 'stocktaking' sorts of pieces are comprised of historical and philosophical reflections, socio-economic analyses, and strategic recommendations. These exercises also habitually express Althusser's judgment that historical materialism is a science, that it has for its object the class struggle, and that this science must be pursued if one wishes to arrive at an effective political strategy. For example, in the introductory section of 1985's 'Qu'y faire? Que faire?', Althusser states that a successful long-term political strategy 'can only rest on objective ... scientific knowledge' of the present 'economic, political, and ideological conjuncture'. He further stresses that, 'in order to achieve this knowledge' which is, 'in the last resort, the analysis of the relations and forms of class struggle in the present conjuncture and its contradictory tendencies and its conflicts' we need to have 'at our disposal a scientific theory, one capable of furnishing the abstract-general concepts' that will allow us to understand the whole of the present conjuncture. Without such a theory, he maintains, 'we remain blind and we fall into political error'.[133]

Written in the summer and edited a few times during the autumn or winter of 1986, 'Thèses de juin' may be the last philosophical text to which Althusser touched a pen. It is certainly his ultimate sustained reflection on the relation between philosophy, politics, and science. Even at this late date and in a text that is disarmingly prophetic, Althusser's endorsement of scientific knowledge for correct political practice rings clear. In its first section, Althusser introduces 'Thèses de juin' as a piece intended to 'provide a couple of observations that might increase the awareness of men engaged in the struggle or of those who are waiting for "a different politics"'.[134] He then poses a methodological ques-

---

133   Althusser 1985b, p. 2.
       Cette stratégie ne peut, en bons principes marxistes et léninistes, reposer *que* sur la connaissance objective, c'est-a-dire scientifique (c'est l'expression même de Lénine sur l'analyse concrète de la situation «concrète» qui est pour Lénine l'essence du marxisme).
       Cette analyse concrète de la conjoncture économique politique et l'idéologique, c'est-à-dire en dernier ressort *l'analyse des rapports et formes des luttes de classes* dans la conjoncture actuelle et des tendances contradictoires de ces conflits, ne peut s'effectuer *que* si on dispose d'une *théorie scientifique* ... capable de fournir les concepts abstraits-généraux d'ensemble de l'évolution, non-évolution ou répression de la situation actuelle, de la conjoncture actuelle. Sans ces concepts aucune «analyse concrète de la situation concrète» n'est possible. ... sans théorie on reste dans l'aveuglement et on tombe dans l'erreur politique.
134   Althusser 1986a, p. 1.
       Voici néanmoins quelques observations générales qui pourront peut-être aider à la prise de conscience des hommes engagés dans la lutte... comme des hommes non engagés dans la lutte mais qui attendent une «autre politique».

tion about how to proceed to this knowledge, asking whether or not one should begin with 'the concrete analysis of the *concrete situation* of some country or even of the world; or, the examination and correction of the *theoretical instruments* that permit this analysis'. Because he believes that 'the second [path] will be more difficult but more sure', Althusser begins the critical section of the text with some detailed remarks on Marxist philosophy and Marxist science. After finishing this methodological portion, he then proceeds to what he labels a markedly 'less assured' concrete analysis of the contemporary political-economic-ideological situation.[135] We will return to the preliminary methodological remarks on Marxist philosophy and Marxist science below. However, it is important to note here that, in the theoretical section of one of his last texts, Althusser continues to insist that it is only 'historical materialism' and its body of 'scientific concepts' that 'permits a concrete analysis of the concrete situation'.[136]

4.3   *Aleatory Materialism and Marxist Science: Theory for Marxism*

As mentioned above, 'Qu'y faire? Que faire?' and 'Thèses de juin' as well as unpublished sections of the Interviews with Fernanda Navarro are doubly remarkable. These texts do not merely endorse Marxist science and link its practice directly to political efficacy; all three also contain explicit passages detailing the relation among aleatory materialist philosophy, scientific practice, and political practice. As supplements and corrections to the published materials, these writings make it clear that aleatory materialism in the 1980s

---

135   Althusser 1986a, p. 2. A charitable reader of this analysis would recognise it as the musings of a shut-in who has access to a television and to some newspapers but not to scientific materials. An uncharitable reader might label it hallucinatory, paranoid, and overly optimistic.

Ici, deux voies s'ouvrent devant nous :
– ou bien *l'analyse concrète* de la situation concrète de tel pays ou même du monde
– ou bien l'examen et la rectification des *instruments théoriques* permettant cette analyse.

La première voie serait plus facile mais moins assurée. La seconde voie sera plus difficile mais plus sûre. Je choisis donc la deuxième voie.

136   Althusser 1986a, p. 2.

A Marx nous devons des concepts scientifiques irremplaçables, comme les concepts de mode de production, de forces productives, de rapport de production, de marchandise, d'échange, de consommation, de capital fixe, de capital variable, d'exploitation économique, de dictature d'Etat, des vues sur l'action révolutionnaire des masses, sur l'avenir inéluctable du communisme etc. etc.

Ce sont là – et je ne cite que les principaux – des *concepts scientifiques* relevant de ce que la tradition marxiste désigne sous le nom de *matérialisme historique*, corpus de concepts permettant une analyse concrète de la situation concrète.

represents the positive side to the critical project of the mid-to-late 1970s when Althusser endeavored to purge Marxist philosophy and historical materialism of idealist elements. Indeed, Althusser unambiguously confirms this reading of the project in an unpublished section of the Navarro interview where he states that the aleatory materialist conceptions of philosophy and of scientific practice represent 'precisions' of his earlier ideas rather than their rejection.[137] In the next few paragraphs, we will explain what Althusser meant by precisions and how these refinements relate to his earlier work. We will also clear up any lingering misconception that Althusser renounced his scientism in his later work.

It is easier to understand the precisions made to Althusser's Marxist theory in the 1980s if one takes into account his consistent and overarching understanding of Marxism as well as the impetus for these adjustments. Fundamentally, Althusser saw Marxism as a political movement whose goal is the revolutionary transformation of existing socio-economic practices into communist ones. As a philosopher and committed Marxist, he put much effort into working out exactly how theoretical and political practices should be related in order to achieve the goals of the Marxist movement.[138] This focus comes through in most of the published work after 1966 and it is pronounced in the 'Marxist manuals' authored between 1966 and 1978 and of which *Initiation à la philosophie pour les non-philosophes* is a late example. Althusser's consistent effort to relate theory and practice in such a way as to attain the goals of the Marxist movement is also unmistakable in the series of stock-taking pieces from the 1970s and 1980s mentioned above where he goes from philosophical reflections on Marxist philosophy and Marxist science to methodological and procedural recommendations for party policies that will best allow it to analyse the contemporary 'concrete situation' and to politically act successfully in relation to this knowledge.

Stated simply, the impetus for most of Althusser's political philosophical output is his consistent belief that correct practice flows from correct theory.[139] If Marxist practice is not doing well in a specific conjuncture and if Marxist practice flows from Marxist theory, then it follows from this belief and this

---

137   Althusser 1986b, p. 47.
       ... je parie que la même méprise va se reproduire avec les précisions radicales que j'apporte maintenant, toujours dans la même ligne, à mes thèses anciennes. [*J*]*e n'ai jamais changé de ligne théorique et politique*, même si j'ai rectifié, en les affinant, quelques formules, provisoirement définitive.
138   Althusser 2014b, p. 51.
139   Althusser 1976b, pp. 111–12; 2003c, p. 297; 1986b, p. 48.

judgment that a new theorisation of how the socioeconomic world works and how to change it is a pressing problem for the Marxist movement. Given this basic supposition, one way to make sense of Althusser's career is as a series of reactions to practical (and, therefore, theoretical) crises in the Marxist movement. First there is the crisis of Stalinism, then that of Humanism, then that of Eurocommunism. Finally, after 1981, there is the problem of the rapid decline of the French Communist Party as a political power. During each crisis, Althusser worked to develop an alternative understanding of Marxist theory that he believed to be materialist and correct. As a body, this theory included positions on Marxist philosophy, Marxist science, and Marxist organisation. Taking stock of the philosophical, political, ideological, economic, and theoretical conjuncture at each moment of crisis, Althusser positioned this reconstructed theory in contradistinction to a hegemonic or nascent Marxist theory that he believed to be incorrect and idealist.

If we acknowledge Althusser's overall understanding of Marxism as well as the impetus for his successive interventions into Marxist theory, it is clear that the common thread which links the Marxist manuals, balance sheets, and many of the published works is that all represent criticisms of and revisions to existing Marxist theory that are written in order to better enable Marxist practice to achieve Marxist goals. If we then connect Althusser's consistent belief that correct practice flows from correct theory with these ideas about theory and especially with his understanding of philosophy as a perpetual battle between materialist and idealist tendencies, then we can better see what Althusser was up to the with his critique of dialectical materialism and his reconstruction of historical materialism in the late 1970s.[140] More directly and for the purposes of this section, we can also better understand Althusser's development of a new Marxist philosophy, aleatory materialism, in the 1980s. In this light, the 'texts of the crisis', 'Marx in his Limits' and 'Marxism Today', can be recognised as attempts to weed out those elements in Marx's or Marxism's philosophy that are idealist and to distinguish these elements from the materialist ones. Similarly illuminated by these connections, 'The Underground Current of the Materialism of the Encounter', and 'Philosophy and Marxism' can be seen as attempts to reconstruct a Marxist philosophy without or with fewer idealist elements and for the then-present conjuncture.[141] As we have shown above, this 'new' or unearthed materialist philosophy does not include a rejection of Marxist science. Instead, it is specifically proposed as a philosophy for

---

140   Althusser 1972c, p. 18; 1990a; 1990b; 1990d;1990e; 2005a, p. 184.
141   Althusser 2006a, p. 166.

a Marxist theory that, at its inauguration, lacked a philosophy and 'was basically scientific in nature'.[142] It was also meant to critique and replace that other
'Marxist philosophy', dialectical materialism, which had filled in the gaps in
Marx's theory with idealist concepts and whose adoption and development
had led to such unfortunate results for the Marxist movement.[143] Finally, it
was meant as a philosophy for the Marxist movement during a time in which
the communist political movement was in decline in France and in Europe but
where smaller communist movements showed promise in other areas.[144]

4.4   *The Relation between Aleatory Materialism and Marxist Science*

This section argues that the materialism of the encounter meets the goal that
Althusser set for it of being a philosophy that can successfully battle the idealist notions of dialectical materialism and replace them with a set of theses
about the world and its relations that, if adopted, might better allow for the
success of the global Marxist movement. Like Bourdin, Sotiris, Suchting, and
Tosel, we think that aleatory materialism contains some interesting ideas and
that it is worth exploring and developing.[145] However, we also agree with these
and other commentators that much of this work is sloppy and often delirious,
that it is rife with paradoxes and contradictory claims, and that the misreadings
of the philosophers it brings in to support its ideas detract from its virtues.[146]
This sub-section will also not try to correct these faults, to explain these shortcomings, or to give an account of aleatory materialism's contents. Instead, it
will merely try to suggest what Althusser meant when he argued in his later
writings that Marxism is a science and to show how this science relates to the
philosophy of aleatory materialism. Its thesis is this: aleatory materialism is
the philosophical part of a body of Marxist theory that also includes ideological, philosophical, political, and scientific components. As the philosophical
component of Marxist theory, it is not meant to replace Marxist science but
to complement it. It complements this movement as a whole by seeking to
remove from Marxist philosophy the idealist notions that prevent the Marxist movement from having access to scientific knowledge about the world and

---

142   Althusser 2006b, p. 257.
143   Althusser 2006b, p. 254.
144   Althusser 1985b, p. 22.

    Quoi donc nous attend ? Eh bien comme les petits dieux d'Epicure dans les «inter-
stices» des sociétés antiques, ce qui nous attend ce sont des *« interstices de communisme »*
dans les pores de nôtres propre société capitaliste-impérialiste-interimpérialiste mon-
diale.

145   Bourdin 2010; Sotiris 2008; Suchting 2004; Tosel 2005.
146   Bourdin 2012, p. 59; Tosel 2013; Sotiris 2006.

to replace them with concepts that facilitate the gathering of such knowledge. Althusser's hope was that this knowledge could allow the Marxist movement to overcome ideological notions about what is to be done and to develop a correct political line, a line which allows for the world's and that movement's own practical transformation.

As we have seen, the relationship between the Marxist philosophy of aleatory materialism and the Marxist science of historical materialism is obscured by the editorial choices made during the publication of Althusser's posthumous works. Despite not being especially visible in the published work, the nature of the relationship between the materialism of the encounter and Marxist science was nevertheless clear to at least one attentive reader, Jean-Claude Bourdin. In a 2012 book chapter titled 'Ce que fait la rencontre aléatoire au matérialisme', Bourdin notices that Althusser describes aleatory materialism as an 'assiette', as a serving plate on which correct (i.e. politically efficacious) ideas about philosophy, science and politics can be constructed.[147] In this understanding, aleatory materialism is not presented primarily as the launching of new political ontology, one which establishes the ever-present possibility of an aleatory reconfiguration of politics. Instead, aleatory materialism is recognised by Bourdin as 'a group of general categories, the most general, which are independent of experience and of all experimental proof, and which state some proposition on the structure and the becoming of the world (or of nature) and on the form that thought must take to arrive at these statements'.[148] Just as we have argued above, Bourdin contends that this set of categories is meant to replace the Dialectical Materialist assumptions that have failed both Marxist science and Marxist politics. As such, these categories are offered as a basic set of propositions about the world that might enable the Marxist movement to understand the historical conjuncture such that it can direct its transformation.[149] These propositions are not meant to directly replace scientific concepts (though they may end up suggesting that certain 'scientific concepts' are not scientific). Instead, they are offered as general categories upon which scientific investigations may be based, ones that will allow the Marxist movement to understand new conjunctures and unexpected conditions.[150]

---

147 Bourdin 2012, p. 63.

    ... on dira qu' une «assiette» représente un ensemble de catégories les plus générales, indépendantes de l'expérience de toute preuve expérimentale, qui énonce des propositions sur la structure et le devenir du monde (ou de la nature) et sur la forme que doit prendre la pensée pour parvenir à ces énoncés.

148 Bourdin 2012, p. 65.

149 Bourdin 2012, pp. 54–5.

150 Bourdin 2012, p. 82.

Bourdin builds up his case for this understanding of aleatory materialism in a compelling manner: first by showing how the ontological and voluntarist readings of the materialism of the encounter are problematic and then by linking Althusser's description of aleatory materialism as an 'assiette' to his insistence that aleatory materialism is a materialist philosophy for Marxism and not a materialist philosophy or ontology.[151] However compelling, this reading has the disadvantage of being mostly speculative and of departing from a few suggestions dropped by Althusser in the published texts. Fortunately, the texts that corroborate this assertion were written and they exist in Althusser's archive. As we have noted above, 'Qu'y faire? Que faire?' and 'Thèses de juin' as well as sections of the Interviews with Fernanda Navarro include specific endorsements of Marxist science and of historical materialism. In addition, in more or less lucid fashion, each provides confirmation of Bourdin's assertion that aleatory materialism is intended as an instrumentalist ontology that can ground Marxist science and thereby ground Marxist practice in the particular historical conjuncture that was the early 1980s. This Marxist philosophy can be said to be 'true' or more correct than dialectical materialism insofar as its ideas about the political world in its constitution and disintegration inform and allow Marxist science to proceed in such a way that Marxist strategy can be successful.

Let's start with 'Qu'y faire? Que faire?' as an example of a text which corroborates Bourdin's assertion that aleatory materialism is a materialist philosophy for Marxism, one that enables the Marxist movement to understand the historical conjuncture such that it might direct its transformation. After beginning this strategic piece with an impassioned call for a historical materialist analysis of the contemporary situation, Althusser then proceeds to bemoan the fact that 'no one in the world is capable of providing the least "concrete analysis" of the conjuncture' or 'of conceiving any strategy'.[152] He attributes this incapacity to the

> general abandonment of Marxist theory, the only [theory] in history which has given itself the means for the analysis of an economico-politico-ideological conjuncture and its aleatory becoming. There exists no *comprehensive theory* of the world capable of trying to *think* the actual

---

151   Bourdin 2012, pp. 70–1.
152   Althusser 1985b, p. 13.
            Et comme personne au monde n'est en état de fournir la moindre « analyse concrète »
            de la conjoncture, personne au monde, même les tout-puissants USA et leurs dirigeant,
            n'est capable de concevoir la moindre stratégie.

conjuncture *and* not only the long-term tendencies but even the medium and short term 'evolution' or regression of this conjuncture.[153]

In this grievance and in Althusser's explanation of the situation that led to this impasse we see marked out the relation between philosophy, science, and political strategy. At its most general, this quote tells us, Marxist theory provides or provided us with a '*comprehensive theory* of the world'. This theory renders us 'capable of trying to *think* the actual conjuncture' and its tendencies and it permits a historical materialist analysis of the present economico-politico-ideological situation and the possibilities for this situation's transformation.

In a more confrontational tone, the relationship within Marxist theory between philosophy and science is also concisely described in 'Thèses de juin' and 'Philosophy and Marxism'. In the interview, Althusser concludes a response to a question about his anti-humanism and the reasons for this position with the statement 'we at last understand why it is indispensable to know, and know *scientifically* what the ideological class struggle is in order to at last understand what ideology is. And if one has followed me, one will also have understood in what manner materialist philosophy is indispensable for understanding the ideological struggle'.[154] In this summary statement Althusser signals that Marxist philosophy is a comprehensive theory of the world, a theory that is not identical to scientific knowledge. Short of being identical to it, this philosophy is that part of Marxist theory that provides the conceptual categories that allow us to pursue scientific studies.

What is this 'center for theoretical thought and therefore the possibility of explaining the conjuncture and its evolutionary tendencies'?[155] Well, after ask-

---

153   Althusser 1985b, pp. 13–14.

   ... depuis l'abandon généralisé de la théorie marxiste, la seule qui se soit donné dans l'histoire les moyens de l'analyse d'une conjoncture économico-politico-idéologique et de son *devenir aléatoire*, [???] il n'existe aucune *théorie d'ensemble* au monde capable de tenter de *penser* la conjoncture actuelle *et* la (ou les) tendances non pas à long termes mais même à moyen et court terme d'«évolution» ou de régression de cette conjoncture.

154   Althusser 1986b, p. 48.

   Je m'arrête, – mais pour réponde à la question posée, on comprend enfin pourquoi il est indispensable de bien savoir, et d'un savoir *scientifique* ce qu'est la lutte de classe idéologique, pour enfin comprendre ce qu'est *l'idéologie*. Et on m'a bien suivi, on aura aussi compris en quoi la philosophie matérialiste est indispensable pour comprendre la lutte idéologique.

155   Althusser 1985b, p. 14.

   Nous nous trouvons donc exactement dans la situation que Machiavel décrit à propos de l'Italie : les moyennes humaines et matériels sont là des hommes capables à l'infini innombrables intelligents et vivants, n'attendant qu'une stratégie pour s'y engager, mais

ing a similar question in 'Thèses de juin' about 'what theoretical instruments
are at our disposition for the analysis of a concrete historical situation, either in
one country or in the world', Althusser first entertains the idea that the 'bourgeois theory of society' can provide such a centre. He rejects this possibility,
however, because 'the weakness of these theoretical elements is their being
rooted in a bad philosophy, whether it be subjectivist-idealist, positivist, or
structuralist ...'[156] With Marx though, Althusser opines, 'we owe irreplaceable
scientific concepts ... falling within what the Marxist tradition designates under
the name *historical materialism,* a corpus of concepts permitting a concrete
analysis of the concrete situation'.[157] Does this mean that historical materialism is this centre, the 'assiette', on which correct ideas can be constructed? No,
on the contrary and despite the recognition of historical materialism's necessity and power, Althusser does not recommend historical materialist concepts
as the centre for theoretical thought. Instead, he explains that these 'scientific
concepts are only valuable on the foundation of a *correct philosophy* and that
... we can only make use of them under the correct orientation that this *correct* philosophy confers'.[158] What is this philosophy? A few paragraphs later,
Althusser writes, 'the true materialism that is suitable to Marxism is aleatory
materialism'.[159]

4.5   *Making Sense of Late Anti-Scientistic Statements*

If by this survey of Althusser's published and unpublished texts from the 1980s
we have demonstrated that Althusser did not abandon his scientism and that
this belief appears in his later work as a continuous and important part of his

---

il leur manque un centre de *pensée théorique* donc de possibilité d'explication de la conjoncture et de ses tendances évolutives.

156   Althusser 1986a, p. 2
Il y a beaucoup de concepts intéressants à emprunter à la théorie bourgeoise de la société. On pourra les examiner en une autre occasion. La faiblesse de ces éléments théoriques
est leur enracinement dans une mauvaise philosophie, soit subjectivistes-idéalistes, soit
positivistes, soit structuralistes.

157   Althusser 1986a, p. 2.
A Marx nous devons des concepts scientifiques irremplaçables... Ce sont là – et je ne
cite que les principaux – des *concepts scientifiques* relevant de ce que la tradition marxiste désigne sous le nom de *matérialisme historique,* corpus de concepts permettant une
analyse concrète de la situation concrète.

158   Althusser 1986a, pp. 2–3.
... des concepts scientifiques ne sont valables que sur le fond d'une *philosophie juste* et
que d'une certaine manière on ne peut les utiliser que sous la juste orientation que leur
confère cette philosophie *juste*».

159   Althusser 1986a, p. 4.

philosophy then we have yet to account for the seemingly anti-scientistic statements in the published work on the materialism of the encounter. Based on
what we have established though, this accounting should not be hard to do.
We can now take it as established that Althusser never abandoned Marxist
science but that he did engage in its reconstruction in the 1970s. Further, we
know that this reconstruction was directly related to a thoroughgoing critique
of dialectical materialism and to the positive development of a new version
of Marxist philosophy, a philosophy that eventually came to be called aleatory materialism or the materialism of the encounter. In addition, we know
that choices made by Althusser's editors resulted in the expurgation of most
of the comments where Althusser clearly indicates the necessity of scientific
practice for political transformation.[160] If we acknowledge all this, then we
can see Althusser's admission in the letter to Merab Mardashvili that he had
in the early 1960s 'fabricated a little, typically French justification ... for Marxism's ... pretension to being a science'[161] as a critique of the *justification* for
Marxism's pretension to being a science rather than as a disavowal of the belief
that 'something in Marxism is scientific'. What has changed by the late 1970s
is not the belief that historical materialism is a science but the justification for
why Althusser understood it to be so. Whereas formerly Althusser had believed
there was a rationalist justification for Marxism's pretensions, by 1978 and the
writing of the letter to Mardashvili, the justification for Marxism's status as a science had become practical or pragmatic in the technical sense of the term.[162]

This change in the justification of Althusser's belief that an important part
of Marxist theory is scientific also explains Althusser's statement from the Navarro interview that materialist philosophy '... does not claim to be autonomous
or to ground its own origin and its own power. Nor does it consider itself to be
a science, and still less the Science of sciences'.[163] As we have seen, Althusser
did not consider materialist philosophy to be autonomous because its status as

---

160 In the editorial remarks that accompany the publication of 'Of Marxist Thought' (1982),
      Haider and Mohandesi notice this absent presence, remarking:
      The vocabulary we have come to associate with Althusser is nowhere to be found:
      science, ideology, problematic, epistemological rupture, materialism, and so forth are all
      terms which are either entirely absent or thoroughly emptied of their former theoretical
      connotations. But while the language in which it is told has certainly changed, the object-
      ive of the story seems to be the same: to discover what must be brought to life from the
      tortuous history of the thought of Marx and Engels.
      See: Haider and Mohandesi 2012.
161 Althusser 2006c, p. 3.
162 Baltas 1993, p. 655.
163 Althusser 2006c, p. 274.

a materialism depends on how it relates to other philosophies competing for theoretical space at a particular historical conjuncture; its contents are therefore historically contingent. Similarly, it is neither itself a science nor can it be the Theoretical Science that polices the other sciences. Instead, materialist philosophy in Althusser's aleatory materialist reconstruction is presented as a set of general judgments about the world that allow the sciences and particularly the science of historical materialism to proceed and to constitute itself. Materialist philosophy is not science nor is materialist science a philosophy of the encounter. Both, however, are complementary parts of a larger Marxist theory.[164] In a similar fashion, the larger context we have provided in our account allows us to understand that the editorial advice given by Althusser in a letter to Navarro in 1986 to drop the bits about science and ideology from the interview cannot possibly be motivated by a denial of the possibility of making a distinction between the two types of theory or by an abandonment of Marxist science. Instead, we should take Althusser at his word that '[t]hat section is not ready yet, and ought to be rewritten'.[165]

Of the seemingly anti-scientistic statements made by Althusser, there remains the Navarro interview where Althusser stated that the objects of Marxism and psychoanalysis 'belong not to accomplished history but to *Geschichte*, to living history, which is made of, and wells up out of, aleatory tendencies and the unconscious. This is a history whose forms have nothing to do with the determinism of physical laws'.[166] Though there is not space to go into a full explanation of this statement here, we should note that Althusser does not write that there cannot be a science of history, only that the objects of history do not act in a deterministic manner, as do physical objects. This recognition does not mean that there is no science of history; just that history cannot be a science of objects characterised by their adherence to certain invariable, deterministic laws. Indeed, as we have argued in another essay, to go from the statement that history does not work according to the determinism of physical laws to the assertion that Althusser rejects a science of history, can only be done by ignoring the consistent contrast Althusser makes between natural laws and the social scientific laws of which historical laws are a subset. One can also only make such an assertion if one ignores Althusser's decades long campaign against dialectical materialism for its insistence that historical laws and physical laws are identical in terms of there both being

---

164   Althusser 2006b, p. 22.
165   Althusser 2006c, p. 287.
166   Althusser 2006c, p. 264.

instances of the fundamental dialectical law of nature.[167] In short, this quote does not so much reveal the abandonment of Marxist science as it does the fruits of historical materialism's reconstruction as a non-teleological science that examines existing historical tendencies in the complexity of their contingent interactions and for the possibility of their adjustment or transformation.

5   Conclusion

Using both published and unpublished texts, this chapter has provided a diachronic examination of Althusser's understanding of Marxist theory and of the relations among philosophy, science, ideology and political change at different periods of his career. It has shown that, even with all the changes, precisions, and reconstructions to this theory's component parts and to his thoughts about these parts' interrelations, Althusser has consistently maintained that scientific practice tends to replace existing ideas about the social and natural word and to generate new knowledge about these interactions which, insofar as it is correct, conduces to these relations' transformation. By demonstrating that the reading of Althusser which finds in his conception of the relations between science, philosophy, and politics a pronounced continuity as well as pronounced scientism, it has also challenged those who insist upon a differentiation between an earlier, scientistic Althusser and a later, ontological one. A corollary to this finding is that it is now more difficult to forge a connection between Althusser and certain contemporary political philosophers who abandon historical materialism and the social sciences and who look to ontology in order to suggest the possibility of political transformation. In addition, the correction of the misunderstanding that Althusser abandoned his scientism in his later works allows us to view this later philosophy in a more charitable light. No longer is it necessary to assess aleatory materialism against other, more sophisticated, less contradictory, and more fully realised ontologies. Now, we can judge the materialism of the encounter as Althusser seems to have intended, pragmatically, in terms of how well it works with Marxist science to produce practical knowledge advantageous to our political transformation. Finally, if one agrees with Althusser about the relation between aleatory materialism and Marxist science, it becomes less easy to overestimate the role played by philosophy

---

167   W.S. Lewis 2013, p. 39.

in understanding and encouraging revolutionary transitions. It should also encourage us to return to the scientific study of our socio-economico-political conjuncture, its tendencies, and of how we can intervene so as to transform these conditions and relations.

CHAPTER 4

Historical Materialism and Concrete Analysis

... la théorie marxiste est hantée, dans son dispositif même, par un
certain rapport à la pratique, qui est à la fois une pratique existante,
et en même temps une pratique transformée, la politique.

LOUIS ALTHUSSER, 'Marx et l'Histoire', May 5, 1975[1]

..
.

In 1965, Louis Althusser argued that, for the success of the workers' movement, everything depended on theory.[2] By 1976, however, he had abandoned this call to theory and had begun to argue that 'everything ... depends on the "concrete analysis of the concrete situation"'.[3] The reasons for this change of emphasis are complex and have to do with revisions that Althusser made to his understandings of philosophy, science, politics, and ideology after his call for the French Communist Party [PCF] to be guided by theoreticians was rejected in 1966 and after he had come to the conclusion that his original schematisation of material practices was flawed.[4] These revisions included a rethinking of historical materialism's relation to philosophy, a disavowal of his previous claim for the conceptual unity of Marxist philosophy, and a radical revision of the ontological and epistemological claims he had advanced in *For Marx* and *Reading Capital*.[5] Though all of these revisions factor into and motivate Althusser's demand for concrete analysis, the most relevant are probably the alterations made to his ontology and to his epistemology. In regard to the former, Althusser modified his claim that the material practices of economy, politics, philosophy, ideology, and science develop in parallel and that they are conceptually and practically distinct. This claim was replaced with an assertion that, though we may analytically distinguish among them, these types of social production are always mixed and interrelated. In line with this revision,

---

1 Althusser 2018a, p. 264.
2 Goshgarian 2003, pp. xi–xii; Althusser 1990e, pp. 37–42.
3 Althusser 2018c, p. 16.
4 Goshgarian 2003.
5 Althusser 1998a; 1978b.

his epistemic claims that scientific practice produces truth and that philosophy guarantees the internal coherency of a science were replaced with a theory of inquiry which held that scientific practice – though always compromised by ideology – tends in the long run to produce correct results due to its interaction with the material real.[6] Now understood as a critical practice rather than as a truth guaranteeing or legitimating practice, post-revisions, Althusser argued that philosophy's role was to help science with this excision, separating that which was ideological and incorrect from that which was scientific and correct.[7] In line with this change, historical materialism was marked out as an overarching and critical social science which investigates the 'conditions and forms of class struggle'.[8]

Taking as a starting point the assumption that Louis Althusser's revisions to his original re-reading of Marx were necessary corrections and that the method of concrete analysis and understanding of historical materialism advanced out of these corrections is not only of bygone interest but that it also has something to offer political theory and democratic politics, this chapter provides an exposition of Althusser's understanding of concrete analysis as the practice was developed between 1976 and 1978.[9] Chapter 3 make the points that this understanding of the role that scientific inquiry should play in political practice continued with and was compatible or a part of the aleatory materialist philosophy explicitly developed in the 1980s. However, as Althusser himself only ever partially developed concrete analysis and because what he did say about it and its promise seemingly contradicts that which he simultaneously maintained about the ability of social science to overcome ideological biases, this exposition cannot be a simple one.

In order to supplement Althusser's unfinished work on concrete analysis as well as to illuminate and overcome some of its contradictions, this chapter draws upon recent work in the philosophy of the social sciences and particularly on pragmatic critical social theory. With this reconstruction, the hope is that the practice's usefulness to democratic decision-making processes and to the realisation of public ideals will be suggested. In line with this intention, this chapter will end with the claim that, if everything – up to and including the successful transition to a post-capitalist future – depends on concrete analysis, then that which democracy depends upon is a Critical Social Theory

---

6 Althusser and Balibar 1970, p. 42.
7 Althusser 1990c, p. 103.
8 Althusser 2018c, p. 81.
9 W.S. Lewis 2005a; E. Balibar, Cohen, and Robbins 1994, pp. 157–88 Some, including Elliott 2006a, p. 270 disagree and argue for his early work.

self-consciously advanced from a specific class position. Such a reconstructed critical theory must draw upon the best work in the social sciences to
make its arguments. Its success, however, will be judged by its effectiveness in
encouraging and enabling the transformation of exploitative, unsustainable,
and oppressive socio-economic relationships into more egalitarian, durable,
and rich associations.

1   The Theoretical and Political Context for Concrete Analysis

In 1976, when Althusser began demanding that the French Communist Party
practice concrete analysis, the Party was still trying rid itself of Stalin-era ideas
and practices. Facing unfavourable comparisons with 'westernised' or western-
ising communist parties in Spain and Italy and embarrassed by yet another
round of revelations regarding Soviet Gulags and other atrocities whose existence it had previously willfully overlooked, the PCF was desirous of shedding
radical and ostensibly anachronistic positions. These included its long-held
insistence on the necessity of the Dictatorship of the Proletariat as well as its
fealty to the Soviet Union. Not for the first time in its history was the PCF in a
directional crisis. At the time, and for its political survival, the Party was obliged
to decide between continued loyalty to the Soviet Union and to certain tradi-
tionally accepted tenets of Marxism-Leninism or to pursuing a path that would
make it more palatable to the broader French Left as well as more in step with
the practices of 'euro-communism'. Althusser's call for concrete analysis was
motivated by many of these same concerns and by his feeling that the PCF and
the global communist movement were in crisis.[10] However, instead of seeing
these problems as merely political, he also believed that they were epistemological and methodological: if the PCF was to survive this crisis and to realise its
goals, it needed to be certain of what the right moves were for it to make both
in terms of dealing with its past and in terms of deciding future actions.

With a 1976 introduction to Dominique Lecourt's *Lyssenko: histoire réelle
d'une science prolétarienne*, Althusser began to deal with the past in a fashion
that was also indicative of the way in which he would soon argue that Marxists
should settle questions about present possibilities. Specifically, he argued that
Marxists must come to terms with the past and with the present in a Marxian
fashion, that is, by providing a thorough historical materialist account of why
certain events occurred and why certain structures were now in place. Second-

---

10   Althusser 1979; 2017; 1998a.

ing Lecourt's work on Lyssenkism as a move in the right direction, Althusser argued that historical materialism must account for why Stalin and Stalinism took place in Russia. This type of explanation, he argued, was precisely the business and responsibility of Marxists.[11]

Shortly after making these claims about the ability and responsibility of Marxists to use the resources of historical materialism to account for past events, Althusser began to argue that – given sufficient analysis of the contemporary situation and of the historical events leading up to it – historical materialism also had the power to indicate and to affect what events might be possible. So then, in an attempt to (yet again) save the Party from thoughtless 'revisionisms' based on ideological notions about human nature and political possibilities as well as in an attempt to short-circuit its reflexive Stalinism, Althusser advanced the claim that, for the Party to realise its goals and to emerge from its crisis, 'everything ... depends on "the concrete analysis of the concrete situation"'.

Though manifestly an argument for pursuing a critical theoretic approach to social scientific investigation, this call was not motivated by an intellectual affinity with the Frankfurt School (of which his knowledge remained limited) but by Lenin's oft-repeated dictum that correct politics depends on the 'concrete analysis of the concrete situation'.[12] After Lenin, concrete analysis was promoted by Althusser as a social scientific programme of research that would be able to explain why certain events had occurred and to suggest what events are now possible.[13] More than this, in its critical function, it would have the power to explain the existence of, and correct for, the faulty notions held by the proletariat and bourgeoisie about the nature of the world and about 'what is to be done' politically. On the bourgeois side of the class struggle, these false ideas or 'spontaneous philosophies' naturalised the status quo, making the norms that direct and validate bourgeois actions seem intuitive. Done well, concrete analysis was intended to de-naturalise these norms, showing how changes in the mode of production occasion specific beliefs and how such values allow the capitalist mode of production to function. In contrast to Stalin, Althusser also maintained that those on the exploited end of the class struggle (as well as those directing then politically) held false beliefs. As this 'spontaneous ideology' all too often betrayed their actual self-interest, compelling exploited peoples to look towards existing institutions and to dominant

---

11   Althusser 1998a, pp. 9–19; 1977b.
12   Althusser 2003b, pp. 222–5; Goshgarian 2003, p. 298, fn 2–5.
13   Lenin 1965; Whitehall 2016.

notions of justice, freedom, and equality and the 'human spirit' as the ideals and means necessary to the realisation of their goals, it too needed to be critiqued.

As Althusser envisioned it, concrete analysis was meant to describe socio-economic relations, to explain why certain ideologies existed, to correct for these ideologies, and to thereby allow for less distorted political judgments by the Party. As a summary of the Leninist theory that inspired Althusser's call for concrete analysis puts it

> The specific objective of party theoretical work is to analyze economic and political conditions sufficiently concretely to provide the basis for an effective political line. The ability to carry out concrete analysis is the fundamental precondition for a Leninist political practice. If inflexible organisational and political formulae are substituted for conclusions arrived at by concrete analysis, then the practice of the party is reduced to just one more random element within a political process which is not understood by those acting in it.[14]

For Lenin in 1901, as with Althusser in 1976, the only hope for an effective political programme – one that truly advanced communist goals – was one guided by a Party aware of historical possibilities and self-consciously reflective about its historical role.[15]

Unlike Lenin, whose polemics on behalf of concrete analysis were intended to reinforce the authority of a Party elite, Althusser's appeals were made in the context of a critique of PCF leadership for its failure to follow the 'democratic' part of democratic centralism.[16] In work from 1976 and 1977 that would soon find its most stinging form in the pamphlet *Ce qui ne peut plus durer dans le Parti communiste* (1978), Althusser argued that the lack of democratic discussion within the Party allowed for and encouraged the pursuit of ill-considered political projects such as the abandonment of the Dictatorship of the Proletariat and opportunistic alliances with the Socialists.[17] These projects and alliances relied upon the isolated, spontaneous ideological decisions of individuals rather than upon judgments based on concrete analyses and following

---

14 'The Distinguishing Features of Leninist Political Practice' 1977.

15 Shandro 2014, pp. 116–17.

16 Althusser 1978a; 2016, pp. 323–4; Elliott 2006a, 294, 304–5.

17 Goshgarian 2006, pp. xvi–xxvii; Althusser 1978a; 1978c; 2016, pp. 124–49. In Althusser 1976d, Althusser diagrams the relations among Democratic Centralism, concrete analysis, and the Dictatorship of the Proletariat.

from public discussion of the results of these analyses.[18] Such analyses, he contended, were necessary to inform democratic debate within the Party and to
allow for correct political decision making.

In one of these works, *Les Vaches noires* (1976/2016), Althusser recorded his
discontent with Party practices in the wake of the PCF's 22nd Congress. In a
tone of palpable frustration, he noted that it was entirely possible for PCF con-
gresses to be filled with debates but that these were too often squelched by
calls for unity.[19] Of those things that should have been debated (but were not)
he lists four. The first were resolutions on the Party's direction for the immediate future, the second were the theses that define the proper usage of terms
in Marxist political theory, and the third was the Party's position in regards to
governmental participation. The fourth thing that should have been debated
(would that it had existed) was a 'concrete analysis of the concrete situation'.[20]

Though mentioned last, it is apparent from the attention paid in *Les Vaches
noires* to concrete analysis' delineation that Althusser believed these investigations to be of primary importance. Such work, he maintained, was the only
thing that would allow for correct resolutions to be adopted, for terms to be
defined properly, and for the Party's strategic relationship to the state to be
discerned. Not only were concrete analyses essential to informed democratic
debate, Althusser insisted that they were also necessary if the Party wanted
to resist its spontaneous impulses towards the adoption of certain platforms
that could be deleterious to the movement as a whole. As he wrote: 'Nothing
about all of this [concrete analysis] is simple: but it is exactly because reality
is complicated and highly contradictory *that its analysis is necessary*'.[21] In the
end, it was only the practice of concrete analysis that would allow individuals
to participate in an informed debate and to come to a collective, correct, and
democratic decision about what programmes to pass and what line to adopt.
Such analyses, Althusser argued, were infinitely preferable to the spontaneous
judgments made by Central Committee members that, if they were not made
for 'pragmatic' reasons, were based on 'Marxist principles' believed to be known
in advance of any proper analysis.[22]

---

18   Althusser 2016, p. 90.
19   Althusser 2016, pp. 85–9, 342–4.
20   Althusser 2016, pp. 85–6.
21   Althusser 2016, p. 90.
22   Althusser 2016, pp. 332–3; 2018c, pp. 46–7.

2   Althusser's Original Formulation of Concrete Analysis

Thus far, this chapter has focused on why Althusser believed that concrete analysis was necessary for the workers' movement and for democratic practice and it has also specified what he believed it to be capable of doing. To sum up: concrete analysis was necessary because it allowed political judgments to be made and to be debated which better allowed the Party to realise its goals and because it corrected for ideological distortions that would otherwise compromise these judgments. Obviously, if any analysis could achieve these things, it would be worth pursuing. The clear question, though, is what practice is capable of advancing an analysis that is able to overcome ideological beliefs in order to correctly describe a historical situation and its possibilities?

Though Althusser argues in Spontaneous Philosophy of the Scientists that every scientific practice filters out ideology, it will surprise no one that the science Althusser judges capable of correctly describing a historical situation and its possibilities is historical materialism. Unlike 'vulgar' sociology and economics (which study social and economic formations in their isolation and largely synchronically), Althusser believes that historical materialism can achieve these results because it takes the socio-economic whole to be constituted in and through history as a series of antagonistic class relations that are always in flux.[23] If all that existed was change there would, of course, be no regularities and the social sciences would have nothing to analyse. Modes of production, however, present themselves as relatively stable. What historical materialism studies, therefore, are the relatively stable structures or tendencies (norms, technologies, modes of exchange, etc.) that allow societies to reproduce themselves as well as the class struggles that not only allow this reproduction but that drive the change of these relatively stable formations into different formations marked by different struggles.[24]

Though historical materialism does not pretend to be a comprehensive science, Althusser certainly intended that, for the part of it that generates and contributes to politically useful knowledge (i.e., concrete analysis), it be understood as a multi-disciplinary pursuit marked by critical reflections on its results. That this is Althusser's understanding of concrete analysis is shown not only by his longstanding insistence that sciences produce knowledge of the real but also by his argument that the sciences need to be subject to self and external criticism.[25] Indeed, this understanding is apparent in his delineation of con-

---

23   Althusser 2016, p. 85; 2018c, p. 16.
24   Althusser 2018c, pp. 54–7.
25   See Chapter 6 on race.

crete analysis' necessary components in *Les Vaches noires*. In this description, he states that, if concrete analysis is intended 'to examine, from the class positions of the proletariat, at least the larger forms of actual class struggles', then the analysis it makes must be both comprehensive and critical.[26]

For Althusser, comprehensiveness includes quite a few things. First, concrete analysis must provide a description of the actual forms of imperialism, of the resistances that imperialism faces from the third world, of the actual forms of struggle undertaken by workers in the developed nations, and of the possibilities for real convergences and contradictions between these resistances. Second, it must provide an analysis of the effects of these contradictions on political struggles at both national and international levels and as these are affected by changes to capital's economic strategy. Third, a full analysis must include a study of the effects of this economic and political class struggle on the ideological forms of the class struggle.[27] Fourth and finally, a comprehensive concrete analysis must include an examination of the political effects, and even the electoral effects, of this ideological struggle such that the Party might understand why, in certain instances, it has lost votes and why, in other situations and at other times, it has gained them.[28]

Given Althusser's description of its method and what it needs to be comprehensive, every concrete analysis would have to involve a team of scientists and critics. At the very least, this would include historians, sociologists, psychologists, economists, and statisticians, not to mention numerous sub-specialists who would study such things as labour relations, the politics of developing nations, and the persuasive techniques of modern business and politics. Despite its size, this legion of scientists could only perform the necessary preliminary studies. In order to be sufficient to the task set for it, concrete analysis would also have to include a critical element. That is, the relations between its objects of study would have to be accounted for and an explanation given for why these forms of the class struggle indicate certain political possibilities and rule out others. Some group of critical theorists would also have to correct for the scientists' ideological biases, prejudices that influence their empirical studies and that effect these studies' results.[29] But this is only the beginning of concrete analysis' critical task. It would not be finished until an account is provided of why certain political actions and certain goals are thought by certain groups to be desirable when, in reality, they are not in their best interest.

---

26   Althusser 2016, pp. 85–6.
27   Althusser 2016, p. 86.
28   Althusser 2016, pp. 88–9.
29   Althusser 1990c, p. 133.

Thus, a concrete analysis sufficient to provide direction and to overcome ideological biases needs to explain such things as why labour shortages lead to the increased acceptance of workers' demands for shorter days and benefits in some countries but not in others and also why some workers feel compelled to make this demand and others do not feel so compelled. It must then relate all of these various conditions or 'forms of the class struggle' back to every other relevant instance such that individuals and groups might know when the political conjuncture is capable of being moved to satisfy a specific demand and also whether it is really in that group's or individual's best interest to make such a demand. Succinctly put, concrete analysis must provide an analysis of 'whole' situations where the whole is understood to include all relevant ideological, political, economic, and scientific practices (or forms of class struggle), as well as the history of class struggles, that have led up to a given political situation.

In a text on Gramsci and Machiavelli from 1978, Althusser attempted such an analysis. However, it is pursued in a less than rigorous manner. In this 'concrete analysis of the concrete situation', he bases his conclusion that Italian auto workers should not engage in revolutionary struggles (even though many of these workers 'know' this to be the best course of action) on loose speculation about the relationship between local factory conditions, Italian workers' ideology, Fordism, national production, and global capital flow. All of the data used to justify this conclusion and to suggest the utility of concrete analysis is gathered by Althusser from a single television documentary.[30]

3 Critique of Concrete Analysis

Obviously, this 'couch potato' critical theory does not represent the best attempt at performing a concrete analysis. Nonetheless, even given enormous scientific and critical resources, there is good reason to suspect that an analysis which takes into account all relevant historical and present forms of the class struggle bearing on a certain conjuncture could never be achieved. Indeed, when Althusser shared his argument for concrete analysis with two thinkers who often shared his political commitments, their responses were that he should abandon his demand that the Party pursue such studies. One of them, the sociologist Michel Verret, argued that concrete analysis' scope was too broad, that it seems to include everything, and that it does not limit itself to any definite historical period. Because its scale is so big, Verret suggested,

---

30   Althusser 2018c, pp. 20–47.

there will inevitably be component parts of the critique that are judged by specialists to be incorrect. These mistakes, he advised, would permit the dismissal of the study as a whole before it was ever thoroughly examined.[31] Like Verret, the philosopher Étienne Balibar also communicated to Althusser that he feared the contradictions, inevitable lacunae, and dead-ends which would inevitably accompany any such study would be used to invalidate it. He then advised Althusser to not be in a position of 'preaching for concrete analysis without ever furnishing it'.[32]

No doubt, any person who is even moderately conversant with contemporary philosophy of social science could single out flaws in Althusser's delineation of concrete analysis in addition to those pointed out by Verret and Balibar. Perhaps chief among these would be Althusser's assumption that, correctly done, concrete analysis will allow us to know in advance the correct political action to pursue. In this claim, Althusser seems to imply that, even though it is arrived at critically, the knowledge that concrete analysis establishes is somehow positive, objective, and predictive. Given the general consensus regarding social scientific knowledge – that it is conditional and historical, that people might and do change their practices and their self-understandings such that yesterday's truth about their beliefs and behaviours may today no longer be so – this last feature may be particularly surprising. To anyone familiar with the history of Althusser's thoughts on the relationship between ideology, science and politics, the other two features seem equally strange. From his juvenilia on through to his last remarks on the materialism of the encounter, Althusser repeated his criticism of 'empiricism' and never argued that science established positive knowledge of facts.[33] What's more, after 1967, he repeated the claim over and over again that all knowledges are contaminated with ideology and that every knowledge claim advances a class position.[34] Consistent with this position, he does indicate in *Les Vaches noires* that concrete analysis is always done from the class position of the proletariat and that historical materialism is the Marxist science of history. However, his argument as a whole suggests that the knowledge which results from this analysis is one mostly purged of both bourgeois and proletarian ideology. It is potentially more useful to the emancipatory interest of the proletariat than to the bourgeoisie only because the latter has no interest in escaping from its class ideology.

---

31   Verret 1976.
32   Balibar 1976.
33   Elliott 2006a, pp. 77–8; Maruzzella 2019, pp. 181–2; François Matheron 2004, p. 508.
34   See especially Althusser 1973.

Given all of the criticisms to which concrete analysis is vulnerable, it is no wonder that Althusser took Verret's advice and did not publish his work on the subject (though he continued to develop concrete analysis in private and published theoretical work propaedeutic to it on Marxist methodology).[35] To a certain reading of Althusser, one that sees him as advancing progressively weaker claims about the power of historical materialism to explain history, it would be easy to argue that Althusser himself gave up on his grand ambitions for concrete analysis and that those interested in reconstructing such a flawed project should do so as well. However, Althusser himself never gave up on historical materialist forms of explanation and, despite concrete analysis' manifest failings, there are very good reasons to attempt to preserve and reconstruct this method.[36] This is the case because a concrete analysis advancing much more modest claims may still have some pretension to scientific status and might still be very useful politically. This is especially the case if one champions a concrete analysis that, unlike Althusser's original formulation, is consistent with his larger claims about the relationships between philosophy, science, ideology, and politics.

It is these contentions that will be fleshed out in the remainder of this chapter. However, so that we know what needs reconstructing, it might be best to single out some of the holes, dead-ends and contradictions in Althusser's incomplete theorisation of concrete analysis. First, it is apparent that Althusser did not sufficiently work out the link between the empirical practice of gathering information about social, political, economic, and ideological formations and the critical function that it must also perform. The question of how one legitimately goes from empirical analyses and ideological critique to policy recommendations was thus never answered. A related question to the one about ideological critique that Althusser did address, albeit partially, is that of how concrete analysis is able to correct for the ideological distortion caused by the perspective of individual scientists.[37] There are also the problems of scope of analysis and of choice of method. Why, for instance, should one pick out a specific historical period as that which is relevant to a given question of political action? Also, why should some sciences be deemed relevant in a study (for instance: history, economics, and sociology) while others (such as biology) are

---

35   'Que faire' Althusser 2018c being the primary example of the work unpublished in his lifetime and Althusser 1998a 'Avant-Propos du livre de G. Duménil' a good example of the methodeutic.

36   Althusser 2006c, pp. 194, 264.

37   See Chapter 3 for how Althusser suggests that this be done at the level of the critique of scientific theory.

deemed irrelevant? Further, why are some effects seen as more important than others and why are some causes given priority over others in what are always-already overdetermined socio-economic formations? Historical materialism has usually privileged economic practices but Althusser himself has argued that this should not always to be the case.[38] How then do Concrete Analysts decide whether or not religion or the economy dominates peoples' relations in a certain conjuncture and how do they describe these relations? Finally, there is the problem of verification of the claims made by concrete analysis. Althusser does suggest one means of verification: the prosecution of a successful transition to communism via the Dictatorship of the Proletariat. However, short of this ultimate end being realised, how does one know that the judgment about the correct political line to take arrived at by concrete analysis and democratic debate is better than that provided spontaneously, by ideology?

4   Reconstructing Concrete Analysis

Though cases can be made for them, two understandings of social scientific practice can be rejected outright for the reconstruction of Althusserian concrete analysis. This is due to the fact that their ontological and epistemological assumptions differ so radically from Althusser's as to be inassimilable. The first of these is the classical realist understanding of social science which holds that there exist social scientific laws that are external to the knower and that can be discovered by the proper methods of investigation and description. Though in the rhetoric surrounding concrete analysis Althusser sometimes suggests that it is capable of achieving these kinds of positive results, it is apparent from the bulk of his theoretical work on the subject that he rejects this sort of discovery as a possibility. The second school of thought in the social sciences that is inassimilable to Althusser's is that which has variously been labelled the 'postmodern', 'discursivist', or 'neo-pragmatist', perspective on the social sciences. While the naïve realist position suffers from excess positivism, these explanations of scientific knowledge suffer from undue conventionalism and would be rejected by Althusser for not accepting the Marxian premise that there is a distinction between our 'real relation' and our 'imaginary' or 'lived' relationship with the world.[39] For Althusser, it is this difference that science uncovers and

---

38   Althusser 1969b, pp. 103–7.
39   See Chapter 6, section 1.

it is able to do so by the formulation of rules about the world that are testable and subject to revision. This is not the case with ideological principles.[40]

Currently, there are two schools of thought in contemporary philosophy of social science that offer resources towards concrete analysis' reconstruction. Like Althusser's philosophy of science, they combine methodological naturalism with hermeneutic scepticism. These two theories are the Critical Realist understanding of social science pioneered by Roy Bhaskar in the mid-1970s and the pragmatist perspective developed by James Bohman beginning in the early 1990s.[41] Both tendencies strike a happy balance between naïve realist and discursivist understandings of social scientific practice. In that both also suggest that social scientific analysis and reflection upon its results is capable of performing the empirical and critical tasks which concrete analysis demands, both also share certain affinities with Althusser's critical theory as a whole.

Not a few commentators have suggested that Critical Realism is the logical heir to the Althusserian critical project.[42] Because it seems to share the bulk of Althusser's ontological commitments, including that to causal realism, it does seem a likely choice to fill in concrete analysis' holes and to overcome some of its contradictions. However, Critical Realism's insistence that social science is dependent upon the pre-existence of social regularities is hard to jibe with Althusser's claim that social scientific laws are particular and that they are realised rather than discovered.[43] This is especially true of the 'transcendental realist' position as originally formulated by Bhaskar. It is also mostly true of those who more recently have tried to argue for a Critical Realism that does not rely upon transcendental argumentation.[44] Further, those theories that are most successful in ridding Critical Realism of its reliance upon transcendental justification get closer and closer to advancing a pragmatist understanding of social science.[45] As that branch of Critical Realism that is most compatible with Althusser's tends towards pragmatism anyway, it may be simpler and more efficacious to bracket Critical Realism's discussion and to skip directly to the consideration of a philosophy of social science that seems most immediately compatible: namely, pragmatic critical social theory.

As mentioned above, the critical social theory that has constructive affinities with Althusser's understanding of the relationship between philosophy,

---

40   W.S. Lewis 2005a, p. 467.
41   Manicas 2015 also develops a compatible theory.
42   Bhaskar 1989, pp. 187–8; Collier 1996, pp. ix–x; Heisler 2001.
43   Althusser 1978b, p. 9.
44   Kemp 2005.
45   P. Lewis 2000; Kaidesoja 2005; Wuisman 2005.

politics, science, and ideology is the pragmatist one developed over the last decade, principally by James Bohman but also and more recently by Patrick Baert, Osmo Kivinen and Tero Piiroinen.[46] Recognising an explicit debt to the Deweyan understanding of social science as the best means by which useful knowledge about our social relations is discovered and emphasising the utility of social scientific knowledge to democratic will formation and to its satisfaction, this understanding of social science does not immediately announce itself as compatible with a programme like Althusser's, which is predicated upon the existence of class struggle and which endorses a non-democratic mode of transition to communism.[47] As Dewey argued vehemently against class reductionism, this endorsement of historical materialism is not even self-evidently compatible with the weaker, methodologically pluralist claim advanced by this book as a whole that some sociological phenomena are best understood in terms of inter-class relation and that, as a form of standpoint theory, historical materialist analyses therefore can usefully supplement and inform methodologically individualist as well as holistic analyses of social behaviour.[48] However, when one looks at its features more closely, pragmatic critical social theory not only shares many features with concrete analysis, it also corrects for some of concrete analysis' shortcomings and renders its theory and method more compatible with Althusser's statements between 1967 and 1978 about the relationship between economics, politics, science and ideology.

As Bohman developed the theory over the last two decades, pragmatic critical social theory is designed to function politically much like Althusser's concrete analysis. By drawing on the best resources of contemporary social science and employing them in a deliberative context, pragmatic critical social theory is presented as capable of ideological critique and of supplying knowledge about human social relations that may effectively be put to practical use. However, unlike Althusser's description of concrete analysis in *Les Vaches noires*, which puts the critic in a position of epistemic authority, Bohman maintains that every scientist, every critic, and indeed, every person is socially embedded and that their evaluative frameworks are influenced by this position.[49] In addition to identifying the latent objectivism in Althusser's formulation of concrete analysis, it also solves the problem of the necessary scope of concrete analysis' research. By dint of their subject positions, any researcher or group of researchers will pick out certain problems as worthy of investiga-

---

46   Baert 2005; Kivine and Piiroinen 2004; 2006.
47   Manicas 1998; Goshgarian 2015, pp. 28, 36–40.
48   Dewey 1939; 2008b; 2008a, pp. 132–35.
49   Bohman 2008, pp. 96–8; 1999a, pp. 593, 605.

tion and they will pick out certain domains of scientific investigation whose objects seem related to the political problem at hand.[50] For example, concerns about public health and the spread of HIV could motivate a study of conspiracy theories among African-Americans regarding the virus and about how beliefs surrounding its origin and transmission function in a specific community.[51] Such a study could then be combined with historical, epidemiological, political scientific, economic, and psychological studies to indicate how, in what way, and to what extent attitudes and behaviours might be altered such that the virus be better contained or such that the conditions which gave rise to these beliefs and disproportionate impacts might be alleviated.[52] Setting a scope for research does not mean that a particular investigation cannot be expanded when eras, practices, institutions, sentiments, norms, or events that at first did not seem relevant now appear related. It also and especially does not mean that the analytic purview cannot be re-examined or expanded after the investigation is completed. If, in democratic dialogue between groups and individuals about the results of an inquiry, it is pointed out that a concrete analysis missed considering relevant practices or beliefs, then the analyst has a duty to go back and investigate these phenomena.[53]

Not only is the recognition that any specific concrete analysis will be limned by an individual's or group's subject position a more reasonable assumption (as well as one seconded by much feminist philosophy of science), it also is more Althusserian in that it accords with his theories of ideology and overdetermination.[54] This does not mean for Bohman or for Althusser that scientific knowledge and ideological knowledge are easily distinguishable. However, both would maintain that those who engage in sincere social scientific inquiry are more apt to manage their lives and to direct politics, economics, and society to desired conclusions than those who do not. Both would also maintain that the most useful knowledge does not result from solitary scientific investigation. Rather, as indicated by Althusser's inventory of the social scientific and critical work needed to give a useful picture of the relations between various class struggles in *Les Vaches noires* and as stated explicitly by Bohman in his article

---

50   Bohman 1999b, p. 472. Dahms 2017; 2008 criticises the comparative-historical analysis outlined in Streeck 2015 for its objectivism. Similar to Althusser, Dahm argues for a reconstructed or 'radical' critical theory to renew and ground the social sciences, one which recognises the classed subject positions which give rise to research questions in the social sciences.

51   Bohnert and Latkin 2009; Gilbert 2003, pp. 14–16; Simmons and Parsons 2005.

52   Bohman 2008, pp. 98–9.

53   Bohman 1999b, p. 478.

54   Jaggar 1989; Longino 1990, pp. 62–82.

'Theories, Practices and Pluralism', critical social theories rely on a plurality of investigators inquiring into many domains of human conduct.[55]

Not only are there many affinities between Althusser's and Bohman's views on the constitution of political or ideological subjects and of the relation of these subjects to scientific research, but there are also marked similarities between concrete analysis and pragmatic critical social theory in their understandings of what criticism does and of when and how the knowledge that criticism produces can be judged to be correct. Bohman assigns the scientifically informed pragmatic critic the role of calling to peoples' attention when their self-conceptions and their conceptions about the behaviour of others does not jibe with scientific knowledge.[56] He also charges them with providing possible explanations based on critical analysis of why these beliefs do not match.[57] This role is very similar to that assigned to the figure of the philosopher by Althusser during his course on the Spontaneous Philosophy of the Scientists (1966). Here, he argued that – insofar as they act as a critical liaison between scientists and the public – the role of the Marxist materialist philosopher is to intercede in politics on behalf of science and in science on behalf of politics such that ideological positions that inform politics and that retard political change might be overcome.[58]

In regard to Althusser's and Bohman's understanding of when a critical social theory can be judged to be correct, Bohman provides a criterion that seems more adaptable than that of attending a successful transition to communism. As Althusser had given up the dream of full human freedom long before his championing of concrete analysis in the late 1970s, this more modest measure is also consistent with Althusser's mature understanding of history and ideology.[59] In addition, Bohman's criterion that we understand critical social theory to be correct when people use its insights to change their lives is realistic in the Althusserian (and, indeed, Marxian) sense of the term: the real is what is realised in the course of human social relations.[60] By appealing to this manifestly pragmatic criterion, both concrete analysis and pragmatic critical social theory have the advantage of avoiding problems with external verification that plague positivist and constructivist understandings of scientific truth.

---

55   Bohman 1999b, p. 460.
56   Bohman 2008, p. 102.
57   Bohman 2008, p. 96.
58   W.S. Lewis 2005a, p. 464. See Chapter 6, section 1 for more details.
59   Althusser 2006a, pp. 53–4. It is also consistent with the rethinking of ideology as immanent critique developed in Jaeggi 2008, p. 24.
60   Althusser 2003b.

5   Historical Materialism and Critical Theory

If Bohman's work on pragmatic critical social theory pretty much gets it right and corrects for the more obvious holes and contradictions in Althusser's method of concrete analysis and if, in the process, it delivers a tenable critical social theory, then why take the long detour this chapter has made through the theory of concrete analysis, a theory and practice that Althusser himself never fully developed? Well, in addition, to the historical value of such a study, there is reason to emphasise and support certain of Althusser's claims that differ from Bohman's. These differences remain even after – with Bohman's help – concrete analysis and historical materialism have been reconstructed so as to be more in line with contemporary philosophy of social science and with Althusser's mature understanding of the relationship between philosophy, science, ideology, and politics. This understanding is provided in Chapter 3, Section 2.3 and is given more detail in this chapter. Nonetheless, it will be useful here to rehearse Althusser's post-1965 understanding of historical materialism after first detailing Bohman's general criticism of historical materialism. This accomplished, we can then examine whether and to what extent the historical materialist aspect of concrete analysis needs further reconstruction. At that point, we can also take inventory of that which is distinctive and valuable about Althusser's understanding of historical materialism and answer the question of whether a critical social theory ought to preserve it.

In the lead up to his dismissal of historical materialism, Bohman distinguishes two ways in which critical social theories are critical. In the first sense, social theories are critical inasmuch as 'they employ a distinctive theory that unifies such diverse approaches and explanations'. In order to affect this unification, 'a comprehensive theory' is needed 'that will unify the social sciences and underwrite the superiority of the critic'.[61] Bohman gives the philosophical anthropology of Hegel and the social theory of historical materialism as examples of such unifying schemas and, on pragmatist epistemological and empirical historical grounds, he rejects this general form of criticism.[62] Rather than being comprehensive and universal, being for practice is the second way in which theories can be critical. 'Such theories' Bohman notes, 'are distinguished by the form of politics in which they are embedded and the method of verification that this politics entails'.[63] In addition to being embedded in a spe-

---

61   Bohman 2008, p. 92.
62   Bohman 1999b, pp. 460, 470.
63   Bohman 1999b, p. 460.

cific historical conjuncture and reflecting its ideals, these theories are practical inasmuch as they facilitate collective inquiry into, and the collective realisation of, those ideals.[64]

The distinctive, unificatory theory historical materialism offers, Bohman argues, is riddled with metaphysical and epistemological problems. In terms of its theory of knowledge, historical materialism is guilty of reductivism and objectivism. Specifically, Bohman claims that Marxist science endows the 'critic with an epistemically superior status over and above the limits of the participants' perspectives' and that its general theory 'provides the basis for going beyond a "mere" pluralism and for adjudicating among the often contradictory claims of theories and explanations in the social sciences'.[65] The problem with this universal point of view is that the critic is always already embedded in the very processes she wishes to critique; there is no view from nowhere, no objective 'facts of the matter'.[66] In terms of methodology, Bohman contends that the reduction of all social behaviour to 'large-scale macrosociological and historical theories' ends up reducing a theory's usefulness and explanatory power.[67] In addition, relying on such theories leads to a rejection of 'those explanations that cannot be organised into the unity of the comprehensive social theory'.[68] Finally, when historical materialist critics actually offer analyses, they do explain every social phenomena by economic relations but, 'typically appeal to many different social theories at many different levels'.[69]

On the metaphysical side, Bohman criticises historical materialism for its determinism and for its normative eschatology. As he writes, 'historical materialism has long been tied to the project of a politically and scientifically determinate critical theory'.[70] 'This theoretical conception', Bohman adds, 'is not devoid of politics'. Instead, there exists an all-too-happy synchrony between 'this single comprehensive theoretical framework [and] the comprehensive political goal of human emancipation'.[71] It is this goal, he argues, that motivates the objectivist and reductivist philosophy of social science championed by historical materialism and which prematurely prejudices an investigation as well as its results.[72] Indeed, according to Bohman, its advocates champion

---

64   Bohman 2002, p. 518.
65   Bohman 1999b, p. 460.
66   Bohman 1999b, pp. 460, 476.
67   Bohman 1999b, p. 470.
68   Bohman 1999b, p. 460.
69   Bohman 1999b, p. 471.
70   Bohman 1999b, p. 473.
71   Bohman 1999b, p. 460.
72   Bohman 1999b, p. 468.

this normative-ontological pairing so strongly that the views of those who may reject historical materialist explanations 'for good reasons does not matter for the correctness or incorrectness of criticism'.[73] Instead, as with psychoanalysis, the theory is self-reinforcing: the historical materialist critics always have an explanation for why one is rejecting their insights.[74] To summarise, Bohman claims that historical materialism is designed to give comprehensive explanations of social relations by reducing them to economic relations. However, this method is unable to make sense of many social phenomena and historical materialists habitually resort to plural explanations when they actually engage in their analyses. Further, its objectivist and universal pretensions endow the critic who 'understands' these causal economic mechanisms with explanatory superiority such that the normative project of the critic be underwritten and such that other normative projects and other explanations of social phenomena be dismissed.

Undoubtedly, Bohman's description of Historical Materialism captures much of the tradition which this book in Chapter 5 labels 'Classical Marxist Theory'. But does it describe Althusser's historical materialism? As discussed above, Althusser repeatedly rejects the claim that the historical materialist critic has an 'epistemically superior status over and above the limits of the participants' perspectives'. In fact, the thesis of his most well-known texts is that, despite founding the science of historical materialism, Marx himself could not see beyond the limits of his times and circumstances.[75] The charge of reducing historical and casual complexity to a large-scale macrosocial theory also does not fit Althusser, who is, again, well-known for rejecting all teleology, for resisting mechanistic theories of history, and for proposing, alternatively, a historiography in which particular historical forces overdetermine multiple productive practices, and of which the structure in dominance may or not be the economy.[76]

In terms of the practice of concrete analysis detailed above, it is also clear that Althusser welcomes investigations from methodologically and disciplinarily diverse social sciences and that he does not demand that each employs a historical materialist template. Further, the normative and eschatological framework which Bohman (and more recently Allen and Jaeggi) rightly censures and which Bohman identifies with the Frankfurt school of critical theory is

73   Bohman 1999b, p. 472.
74   Bohman 2008, p. 93.
75   Althusser and Balibar 1970, pp. 29–30.
76   Althusser 1969b, pp. 100–2; Goshgarian 2019.

nowhere evident in Althusser.[77] Yes, Althusser desires a future free from oppression and exploitation. However, he consistently argues against the whole tradition of Marxist philosophical anthropology which holds that human beings are engaged in a historical process of overcoming their alienation and coming to be who they are, in their full freedom.[78] In Althusser, there is therefore no overarching narrative about human beings or about history. What exists are particular socio-economic circumstances that are productive of and rely upon the production of particular classes of human beings for their continued existence. These conjunctures and their tendencies can be studied, understood and, from our collectively arrived at understandings of how they function, possibly changed. If altered, there will not then be full emancipations and full human flourishing but different human beings, engaged in new productive practices, which are characterised by novel productive relations and who embody new ideologies supportive of these practices.

If the last few paragraphs defend Althusser's version of historical materialism by specifying what it does not contain, then the next few will try to delineate that which it does. Historical materialism, Althusser maintains, is the only theoretical practice that allow us to reliably understand politico-socio-economic structures such that we might intentionally assist in their transformation. As a critical and *overarching* social scientific discipline, historical materialism makes use of the results from specific sciences while also engaging in their critique and in their synthesis.[79] This process of inquiry, Althusser argues, allows us to critique ideological ideas about why we act and desire in the ways that we do and to replace them with scientific understandings of how present social relations are maintained and may potentially be transformed.

In terms of methodology Althusser contends that historical materialism is, like other sciences, social or otherwise, experimental. It makes abstractions from experience and then relies on demonstration for its proof.[80] Althusser does not assert explicitly whether historical materialism relies on evolutionary, functionalist, structuralist, holistic, normative, collectivist, or individualist assumptions. Nonetheless, as he rails against evolutionism and functionalism from 1960 onwards, abandons structuralism after 1966, and inasmuch as he makes the point over and over again that 'history is a process without a sub-

77   Allen 2016; Bohman 2008, p. 93; Jaeggi 2017.
78   Goshgarian 2003; W.S. Lewis 2007a.
79   Althusser 2003b, p. 161.
80   Althusser 1966a; Goshgarian 2013, p. 105.

ject', it can be safely assumed that the starting point for historical materialism is neither the choices of individuals nor a pre-ordained dialectic of history, but the process of class struggle itself.[81]

The object of historical materialism is, according to Althusser, class struggle and, more specifically, the particular conditions and forms of class struggle. Just as canyons are the results of erosion and do not pre-exist it, classes themselves do not precede the class struggle but are the effects of the exploitation, domination, and oppression of one class by another.[82] As discussed above, historical materialism investigates the relatively stable structures or tendencies by which societies materially reproduce themselves as well as the incongruities endemic to these structures, strains which drive the change of these relatively stable formations into different formations marked by different struggles. Typifying capitalist formations, such tendencies may include a generalised belief in a kind of property known as private or 'a functional relation between changes in two variables, the rate of profit and time, such that the former decreases and the latter increases'.[83] In addition to other pervasive norms, technologies, modes of exchange, laws, ideologies, etc., it may also be found that, 'under conditions of austerity (i.e.: reducing social spending and increasing taxation), childhood morbidity rates increase' among impoverished populations.[84]

As for the proofs furnished by historical materialism, Althusser maintains that these are not of the sort produced by mathematical science or (sometimes) thought to be furnished by natural science. As a practical science, historical materialist knowledge is only validated as *juste* or correct when it is successfully applied, that is, when it transforms the forms and conditions of the class struggle. This practical science achieves these mutations by two means: first by replacing ideological knowledge of how and why we behave the way we do with scientific knowledge of our comportment; second, knowledge of the specific social tendencies and tensions which maintain a social formation, permitting the social agent to proceed from an understanding of the forces that produce a situation to hypothesising definite actions which may transform it.[85] By dispelling folk beliefs about who we are and why we act as we do and in producing a scientific understanding of the institutions, practices, and beliefs which govern our social relations, historical materialism

81 Althusser 2003a; 2015, pp. 179–84; 2018c, p. 112.
82 Althusser 1976b, pp. 49–50.
83 Suchting 2004, p. 42.
84 Rasella 2018.
85 W.S. Lewis 2013, pp. 46–7.

provides the political agent 'effective knowledge of the conditions, mechanisms, and forms of the class struggle'.[86]

Given these specifications, it can be seen that, unlike, Althusser's understanding of historical materialism and of the role it plays in concrete analysis does not fall prey to the criticisms made by Bohman of historical materialism as a universal, infallible, macrosocial theory. Althusser's Marxist science is neither reductivist nor objectivist. Nor is it determinist, telic, or universalist. Further, concrete analysis is critical and practical in the second sense identified and endorsed by Bohman. Inasmuch as its success is to be judged by its effectiveness in encouraging and enabling the transformation of particular, existing exploitative, unsustainable, and oppressive socio-economic relationships into more egalitarian, durable, and rich associations, historical materialism is 'embedded in some practical context that in large part determines its relevant standards of justification and conditions of success'.[87] If there are remaining tensions between the two critical social theories, then this friction is to be found in three places: first, with Althusser's claim that historical materialism is a 'critical and *overarching* social scientific discipline'; second, with his insistence that the class struggle is the object of historical materialism and third, with Althusser's endorsement of a non-democratic mode of transition to communism.

The third source of friction is perhaps the easiest to address. As should be clear from the account of the historical and political context for concrete analysis provided above, Althusser intended these inquiries and the historical materialist research which informed them to be used democratically: social scientific data on the present conjuncture were to be directed and assembled in a historical materialist fashion such that the current contours of the class struggle be understood and so that this knowledge might be used to inform debates regarding policy. Though Althusser might challenge the fact-value dichotomy, he did not think that scientific research alone revealed 'what is to be done'. Rather, he argued that, without this research, political decision-making would consist exclusively of spontaneous (and therefore ideological) choices by party leadership and that these initiatives were less likely to succeed than those informed by data and deliberation.

Given this call for democracy, why then did Althusser argue for much of the 1970s for the Dictatorship of the Proletariat and often against parliamentary participation for the PCF? Thought the story is a longer one and Althusser tells

---

86   Suchting 2004, p. 59.
87   Bohman 2002, p. 499.

it well himself in *On the Reproduction of Capitalism* (1969/2014), it is because, based on his philosophical analysis of the capitalist state, he judged it incapable of categorical economic and normative reconstruction by democratic means.[88] That he judged the PCF capable of such discussion might bespeak a certain wilful naiveté on Althusser's part, but it also demonstrates his belief that, given sufficiently supportive background conditions, social-scientifically informed public deliberation is epistemically and politically advantageous for deciding upon and for realising a group's political goals.

That Althusser endorses democratic deliberation as part of an effective Marxist-Leninist political practice and that his idea of concrete analysis is otherwise compatible with pragmatic critical social theory leaves two remaining tensions. Both of these have to do with historical materialism: one, with its object and, two, with its purview. The object of historical materialism is, according to Althusser, class struggle and, more specifically, the conditions and forms of class struggle. Further, as Marxist science is introduced in relation to the other social sciences in the context of how to produce concrete analyses, it is said to be 'critical and overarching'. Granted Bohman's criticisms of universalist critical theories, one presumed fear is that there is something about class struggle as theoretical object which makes it significantly different from the social relations studied by other social sciences. Another worry is that, though the study of class struggle may be a scientifically legitimate and politically useful endeavour, historical materialism has no claim to be critical or overarching.

Bohman's chief worry about universal theories is that their 'single comprehensive theoretical framework' unnecessarily restricts scientific investigation as well as public debate and initiative. Every social problem, he worries but does not say, will be reduced to and understood only in terms of class-based exploitation. Similarly, given the 'comprehensive political goal of human emancipation', the solution to every social problem is pre-ordained as economic class struggle or as economic transformation. In this scenario, many legitimate claims of domination will fail to be recognised and many potential solutions to public problems will fail to have a hearing. However, as we have seen, this is not Althusser's historical materialism. Famously, for Althusser, 'the lonely hour of the last instance' when all human relations will be reduced to economic causes 'never comes'.[89] Like the other social sciences, historical materialism is a human practice, it helps us to understand how social relations that are char-

---

88   W.S. Lewis 2013, pp. 34–5; Anonymous and Althusser 2010, pp. 11–13; Althusser 2014a, pp. 151–2.

89   Althusser 1969b, p. 113.

acterised by class relations are produced and sustained; it is effective insofar as the knowledge it produces allows us to transform these relations.

But is historical materialism still different from other social sciences in terms of being a 'critical and overarching' form of knowledge? Despite Althusser's consistent rhetoric to the contrary, his more considered thoughts on the connection between politics and scientific knowledge as well as Bohman's criticism of universalist theories suggests that we should not treat it as such. All history is not the history of class struggle and neither is historical materialism an over-arching science in the sense that the results of other social sciences serve only to flesh out a long story of wars between classes. The rare times when Althusser repeats the shibboleth of classical Marxist theory that 'all history is the history of class struggle', it is only to complicate and to challenge it.[90] Given this diminution, historical materialism is in one respect a social science like any other, one which tries to understand patterned human behaviour. What distinguishes it from, say, descriptive linguistics or ethnomusicology, is its focus on class and class struggle. In another respect, and this is perhaps a third meaning of a practical theory different from the other two Bohman specified (or at least a particularist modification of the first meaning), it is a practical as well as critical social science. It is so not because it has found in class struggle the key to understanding the full sweep of human social relations and history. It is also not so only because it produces practical knowledge of a specific conjuncture. What makes it practical is that it is social science undertaken and advanced from a specific class position: that of the dominated, oppressed, and exploited, and with the intent of transforming this relation.

If historical materialism is critical and overarching, it is overarching in the way that feminist or anti-racist social science also 'commands' other social sciences. That is, from a particular and engaged ideological position, each variety of critical theory integrates the results of diverse social studies to understand, and with the goal of transforming, one aspect of our social situation.[91] To understand the past and present oppression of women, feminist social science may organise and employ demographic, economic, and linguistic evidence. Anti-racist social science for its part may employ these sciences, as well as others, to comprehend white supremacy. Similar to both, historical materialism critically engages the other social sciences with the goal of understanding and transforming class relations. If, therefore, as partisans in the struggle against class domination, we want to understand and to transform the 'terms and conditions

---

90   Althusser and Balibar 1970, pp. 203–4; Althusser 2018a.
91   Ideological positions as the starting point for deliberation are discussed in Chapter 7, section 3.3.

of the class struggle', then we have every reason to pursue Concrete Analyses of the sort championed by Althusser. We should make them a part of our collective inquiry about what is to be done in order to encourage and enable the transformation of exploitative, unsustainable, and oppressive socio-economic relationships into more egalitarian, durable, and rich associations.

CHAPTER 5

Class as Concrete and Normative

Introduction[1]

Louis Althusser famously asserted the thesis 'philosophy represents class struggle in theory'.[2] If this claim holds some truth, then it must also be correct that theorising class is a part of this struggle. We can know this analytically, but there is also empirical support for the claim that theorising class is a part of class struggle. Since the eighteenth century, thinkers have debated whether or not regimes need to add the category of social class to their constitutions and they have done so from explicit class positions. In addition, since the late nineteenth century, there has been a long line of political philosophers and social scientists declaring the Marxian concept of class dead, false, unscientific, and unphilosophical. There has also been a similarly extended counter-tradition of philosophers and social scientists working to theorise class and to show how it is a concept necessary to the comprehension of social and political relationships.[3] Historically, therefore, we can say that philosophy is – to some extent – class struggle in theory and that the theoretical struggle over the meaning and ontological and political status of the concept 'class' has been a primary terrain of class conflict.

Right now, if part of the class struggle remains the theorisation of class, philosophers who recognise the usefulness or necessity of the concept of class for understanding contemporary, historical, or universal social and political relationships seem to be losing the battle. A search of *The Philosopher's Index* from 1995–2019 reveals only 104 articles or books with 'class' in the title where this word denotes a political concept having to do with social identity rather than synonymous but semantically distinct uses of the term in logic, law, or pedagogy (e.g.: 'class logic', 'class-action', 'class room'). Further, the overwhelming majority of these articles are found in Marxian journals like *Nature, Society and Thought, Telos, Constellations*, or *Radical Philosophy*. Finally, many of these essays do not take the trouble to define class but use the term as if it were transparent, as in the phrase 'middle class'. We can profitably contrast this lack of

---

1   The author wishes to thank Mari Mikkola for her helpful clarifications as well as Jennifer Hansen, Paul Reynolds and Taylor Rogers for their perspicacious criticisms and questions.
2   Althusser 1972d, p. 18.
3   Kwame Anthony Appiah 2018.

theorisation with the concept of 'justice' where 4,585 separate books and articles employ this term in their titles. Interestingly, when we search within those articles for the subject category of 'class' we obtain only 5 articles combining it with justice. Even searching the full text of the 4,585 articles yields an extremely modest 48 hits. In general, it is abundantly clear, contemporary philosophers do not link justice and class. This is a connection that must be theoretically and politically forged anew.

Those who think of themselves as engaged in the tradition of theoretical class struggle are in need of new arguments and need to take up new strategic positions. However, if they are to be part of a Marxist political project, these positions should not only be helpful in the intra-philosophical struggle but must also have pragmatic justifications. That is, once applied to the analysis of our socio-economic conjuncture, the resulting research must help us *to understand and to transform unjust socio-economic situations more effectively than do other theories*. Though clearly on the side of Marxist philosophers and social scientists, this chapter presents and scrutinises ideas and arguments about what social class is from sources both bourgeois and Marxian, historical and contemporary. The aim of this exercise is to develop one part of a holistic theory of class that is flexible enough to conceptualize the multiplicity of class positions occupied today, that avoids some of the theoretical and practical problems that previous definitions of class have met, and which provides us with an explicit understanding of what is *wrong* or *bad* with occupying some concrete, particular and existing class position. This new theorisation should also have the advantage over the traditional Marxist understanding of the goal of class struggle where the wholesale solution of abolishing class has been offered without specifying clear means to this eradication. Further, the new conception of class should help us to identify particular class-based wrongs that need redress (and which can therefore be struggled toward), rather than waiting for the development of a universal class subject or aleatory political event to transform class relations. Ideally, this new model of class should enrich other social scientific and humanistic analyses of oppression, including those that focus on race, ethnicity, gender, or any intersectional combinations thereof.

Lofty aspirations aside, this tool is not intended to be comprehensive, nor is it designed to provide satisfactory causal explanations at the micro (individual) or macro (group) level of class formation and transformation. Rather, it is conceived as a contribution to the type of methodologically pluralist integrative analysis championed by Erik Olin Wright and, less famously though presciently, by Mary Davis.[4] In this pragmatic realist model, capitalist relations of exploit-

---

4   Davis 1995.

ation and domination are understood to work alongside other forms of social and economic resource hoarding to structure the identities and life choices of individuals along class lines.[5] For the most part, this exercise makes a contribution to the third part of such analyses: 'stratification' or the study of individual attributes and material life conditions.[6] Stratification studies like these do not usually explain why some social positions are better than others but the model adapted here includes the value judgments associated with class markers. The crucial innovation here is that the *normative dimension* of class-structuring interpersonal relationships is privileged.[7] While attention to this dimension will not give the reasons for the existence of these value judgments (these may be found at lower levels of the integrative analysis), it strengthens the explanatory power of the model by clarifying how individual traits are differentially valued, thereby sorting people into classes, and furthering exploitation and domination. Significantly, inasmuch as the possessors of certain traits are negatively valued and sorted into subaltern classes, it gives reasons for those so valued to resist those evaluations as well as the practical effects that stem from the normative judgments.

As mentioned above, this is an adapted model. Where it is adapted from is analytic feminist philosophy. Unlike Marxist philosophy, which sometimes seems to be caught in endless debates that had their origins in the 1960s (or even 1860s), feminist philosophy has made great advances over the past 40 years. Its practitioners organised, attuned themselves to lived experience and to the social sciences and they made impressive contributions to epistemology, value theory, aesthetics, and social ontology. One recent conceptual advance in feminist social ontology can help us to reconstruct the moribund Marxist concepts of 'class' and 'class struggle'. The apparatus is one developed by Mari Mikkola in her 2011 paper 'Ontological Commitments, Sex and Gender' and elaborated in her 2016 book: *The wrong of injustice: dehumanisation and its role in feminist philosophy*.[8]

Due to the political effects of its conventionalist conclusions, Mikkola targets the conventionalist sex/gender model of identity, which is currently dominant in the academy. Because a gender-free world is one most existing humans would neither want to live in nor struggle towards, this conventionalist model, she argues, makes it difficult to achieve the liberation from gendered oppres-

5   E.O. Wright 2015, pp. 109–10.
6   E.O. Wright 2015, p. 102.
7   E.O. Wright 2015, p. 104.
8   Mikkola 2011, p. 2016.

sion which is that analysis' ostensible goal.[9] In place of the sex/gender dichotomy, Mikkola offers a 'trait-norm covariance model' in which certain traits of
femininity (or masculinity) mark persons as subject to differential and unjust
treatment within a patriarchal system.[10] She contends that we must examine
the actual relationships of privilege and oppression that accrue with the material possession or dispossession of certain gendered traits in a definite historical
culture. This attunement will allow us to discern which traits are associated
with oppressive values and then to politically and socially target these associations rather than gender as a whole, as conventionalist analyses demand.[11]

Like gender, class identity has progressively become unmoored from essentialist analyses. The Marxist idea that capitalism will produce a transformative battle between proletariat and bourgeoisie has been decisively challenged.
Just what class 'is' has also been subject to debate. This chapter defends the
thesis that, following Mikkola's example, we can – in part – define 'class' as
the possession of certain differentially valued ascriptive traits in a particular
historic and socio-economic conjuncture. This social valuing, in turn, explains
and motivates differential interpersonal relationships of oppression as well as
the resistance to these relationships. Such ascriptions and associations cannot
be known in the abstract, universally. Rather, they must be studied and understood in their particularity (and in their particular interrelations). In other
words, understanding class in this way demands the concrete analysis of concrete situations. As with the analysis of gendered oppression, the result of these
concrete analyses of concrete class situations is the ability to better grasp and
to more successfully target and challenge oppressive class relationships.

The first section of this chapter explains Mikkola's trait/norm covariance
model of gender and gendered oppression. It then contrasts trait/norm covariance with the theoretically dominant conventionalist understanding of gender
as well as with the classical theory of gender in which gender identity is
understood to relate essentially to biological sex as the latter's expression. This
section also details Mikkola's arguments for why the latter two models are
theoretically and politically problematic and for why trait/norm covariance
offers advantages in both domains for understanding and overcoming women's
oppression. The second section draws out the analogies between past theorisa-
tions of gender and those of class, while also noting their specific differences.
To this end, classical Marxist theory and more recent post-Marxist models of
class and class struggle are examined. Necessarily, given the scope and variety

9   Mikkola 2016, pp. 87–8.
10   Mikkola 2016, pp. 128–37.
11   Mikkola 2011, pp. 80–1.

of Marxist theory, this assessment will be sketchy. The aim is that the account be accurate enough to help us recognise the generic flaws of each schema and to motivate the move to a trait/norm covariance model of class. It is with this model and third section that the chapter concludes.

1   Gender Theories

1.1   *The Classical Theory of Gender*
The classical theory of the relationship between gender and sex is essentialist and universalist: it holds that biological sex necessarily and significantly determines an individual's gender. It has roots going back to Aristotle but its modern form was set by Rousseau in the eighteenth century when he described women as naturally and 'specially made for man's delight' and 'to be in subjection' to him.[12] The exact mechanisms of femininity's fabrication Rousseau could not divine but he reasoned that 'where man and woman are alike, we have to do with the characteristics of the species; where they are unlike, we have to do with the characteristics of sex'. The theory holding that biology is the essence of gender was updated at the end of the nineteenth century by Freud who, in his 'Lectures on Femininity', provided a subtle family-dynamics based account of how a person born with female genitalia becomes a woman (with characteristics more or less feminine) and how a person with male genitals becomes a man (with characteristics more or less masculine).[13]

The classical theory of gender is an *essentialist* theory inasmuch as the sexed body is the essence of which feminine characteristics such as passivity, pleasantness, delicacy, sentimentality, and heightened moral sense are the appearance. It is a *universalist* theory inasmuch as every individual is sexed (and therefore gendered) by her or his pheno- or genotype and because historical and cultural differences in gender identity are explained as merely particular variations of a universal type. Finally, inasmuch as these are seen to follow from the characteristics that women naturally manifest in relation to those manifested by men, the classical theory explains and often justifies oppressive and inegalitarian familial, social, economic, and political treatment of women.

---

12   Rousseau, Kelly, and Bloom 2010, pp. 531–4.
13   Freud et al. 1964, p. 116.

1.2 *The Conventionalist Understanding of Gender*

The conventionalist understanding of gender is similarly universalist, but it is not essentialist. Theorised in the 1950s by de Beauvoir in *The Second Sex*, it also has antecedents in certain nineteenth- and early twentieth-century feminisms.[14] More recently, this model has been reworked using tools from analytical philosophy of language and conceptual analysis, most characteristically by Haslanger. Believing that the classical model has been thoroughly unseated within contemporary feminist philosophy, it is the conventionalist model Mikkola judges hegemonic and that she aims to challenge with the trait/norm covariance model. Concerned chiefly with the question of ontology, of what kind of objects we mark out when we refer to men and women, the conventionalist model begins with the contention that biological sex is a natural kind and that it has no relation to gender identity. 'Sex', in this sense, is understood to be merely the expression of genotypes in a particular natural environment, a combination which gives rise to certain phenotypical sexual characteristics. As natural kinds, these characteristics are what they are no matter what anyone thinks about them.[15] In contrast, neither a person's gender characteristics nor their gender identity is said to stem from natural causes. Instead, gender identity is the product of purely social causes. As Mikkola quotes Haslanger, rather than 'tracking a group of individuals defined by a set of physical ... conditions [the term "woman"] is better understood as capturing a group that occupies a certain ... social position'.[16]

What social position do women occupy? According to the conventionalist model, it is one of oppression and exclusion: those who are identified as belonging to the group 'woman' are limited in their freedoms, are prescribed different life possibilities, and have different social expectations placed upon them than those humans identified as 'men'. In short, a person belongs to the social kind 'woman' iff she is part of a socially defined group distinguished from other social groupings by a specific set of oppressive social forces, whose net effect is to gender someone as a woman.[17] Because woman is exclusively a social kind, one implication of this theory is that, if these oppressive forces ceased to exist, the social category 'woman' would disappear as well.[18] Another implication is that biological females not subject to the specific set of social forces that causes women to be are not women.[19]

---

14   Chetcuti 2009.
15   Mikkola 2016, pp. 136–7.
16   Mikkola 2011, pp. 70–1.
17   Mikkola 2016, pp. 80–1.
18   Mikkola 2016, pp. 118–19.
19   Mikkola 2016, p. 81.

In addition to doing away with the empirically untenable claim that biological sex determines gender, this theory has other advantages over the classical model. First, this model includes in the category 'woman' those who believe themselves to be women and who express themselves as such despite lacking some of the genotypical or phenotypical characteristics of biological females.[20] Because such persons face comparable oppression, they are equally members of a social group distinguished precisely by its being the target and result of these oppressive forces.[21] Second, with the essentialist connection to biology severed, this model helps to reveal the historical and social construction of women as an oppressed group.[22]

Politically, if we are concerned with justice and wish to overcome oppression, the constructivist theory means that we now know where to focus our efforts: on social norms, on the practices and institutions productive of these oppressive relationships and thereby of women in general. If being a woman is to be oppressed and if women do not have to exist, then we also now discern our political goal: the *abolition* of woman as a social and identity category. Given these advantages over the classic theory, the conventionalist model can therefore be said to have both pragmatic and strategic justifications.

Despite manifest theoretic and strategic advantages over the classical theory, Mikkola argues that the conventionalist model of gender identity is likewise problematic. Why? First, because the conventionalist model is counter-intuitive. Many or most people who think of themselves as women perceive some kind of relation between their possession of female biological characteristics and their feminine gender. While one can imagine altering society and thereby eliminating such social kinds as lamplighters or senators, most people do not believe that 'woman' is the kind of thing that disappears under a new constitution or with a new economy.[23] Being counter-intuitive, the theory also presents a huge hurdle in terms of its acceptance and adoption. Many who think of themselves as women and who may also recognise this identity as complicit in their oppression would simply not sign-up for a political project that promised the *abolition* of this aspect of their identities. Neither would they accept that their identity as a woman is entirely constituted by oppressive forces.[24]

---

20   Mikkola 2011, p. 76.
21   Mikkola 2011, p. 76; 2016, pp. 112–14.
22   Mikkola 2011, p. 71.
23   Mikkola 2016, p. 119.
24   Mikkola 2016, p. 121.

It is here that the universalism of the conventionalist theory becomes a problem. Simply put, for many potentially feminist women and for their allies, the abolition of woman as a social kind may be as undesirable as it is unthinkable. Therefore, along with its promise for a politics of anti-oppression, the conventionalist model presents *epistemic* and *pragmatic* obstacles.

1.3   *The Trait/Norm Covariance Model*

If the classical theory of gender is empirically wrong and justifies political oppression and if the conventionalist model has theoretical and practical problems, then what is an alternative? Mikkola argues that concepts borrowed from biology and from value theory might be helpful in theorising what it is to be a woman. Further, this borrowing can be done such that the anti-essentialist strengths of the conventionalist theory and its emphasis on women's oppression be preserved, but without this theory's pernicious political and theoretical consequences. In her model, Mikkola emphasises the *particularity* of what it is to be a woman, rather than this identity's universality. As indicated in the introduction to this chapter, this emphasis on particularity as well as the concepts and the relationships Mikkola describes in her trait/norm covariance model may also be useful to theorising class and to the class struggle. Therefore, this chapter briefly summarises her theory before showing how it can be ported to Marxist political theory in order to give a model of class that is more accurate and politically useful than classical Marxist and post-Marxist analyses.

Both the classical and the conventionalist models of gender described above make a distinction between natural and artificial traits. The former does so to emphasise the causal primacy of the natural in producing feminine characteristics while the latter does so in order to ontologically separate the two and thereby deny any causal relation between them. Unlike classical and conventionalist theories of gender, Mikkola makes no such distinction or, at least, makes very little of it. Rather, what she notices (and this becomes the basis of the trait/norm covariance model) is that those who are recognised and classified as women share certain physical, moral, and social traits.[25] Mikkola agrees with Haslanger that the possession of certain biological traits do not 'make one a woman' However, she also does not think that social forces are exclusively what make one a woman. For Mikkola, a woman is 'made' when she herself or others in a society ordinarily attribute to her the possession of a sufficient number of associated traits that are recognised in a specific society as female

---

25   Mikkola 2011, pp. 127–8.

or feminine.[26] Despite traits such as wearing makeup and possessing a uterus being paradigmatic, there is not one trait or set of traits that marks one definitively as being a woman universally and for all time.[27] In addition, any individual trait can be more or less associated with being a woman in a certain society, or with being a man, or it can be a gender-neutral trait.[28]

So, what does a woman look like or what does it feel like to be a woman for Mikkola? Well, this depends on the society she lives in. Today, in the United States, there are certain descriptive traits that are normatively associated with being a woman. These may include but are by no means exhausted by: thinking oneself a woman, lactating, brow waxing, disproportionately performing care-work, persistent apologies in work emails, and feeling vulnerable when walking home alone after an evening out. What all of these traits share is that they are 'facts of the matter'. That someone feels vulnerable as a woman or that they are lactating does not depend on any value judgments.[29] What does depend on value judgments, however, are the *norms* associated with gendered traits. For example, that waxing one's brows appears feminine is an evaluation made by others about a certain trait. So too is the judgment that women as lactating or as potentially lactating mothers make poor employees. Unlike 'facts of the matter', these values are social constructions.[30] Some judgments, like associating social reproduction with femininity, are relatively constant and widespread. Others, like associating masculinity with short hair, are extremely localised and variable.[31]

As indicated by the examples having to do with care work and walking home alone, many gendered traits co-vary with particular judgments about an individual's emotional states, physical capacities, character, intelligence, sociability, political agency, status, and dessert. Depending on the society that one lives in, the specific judgments that co-vary with gendered traits mean that those who manifest certain traits and are ordinarily categorised as male or female are likely to find some social situations open and to find others unavailable. The same goes for privileges, employments, communications, alliances, gifts, specific recognitions, and many other social and economic relationships.[32] For example, in the USA in 2021, guarding one's emotions is male ascribed (rather

26   Mikkola 2016, pp. 127–8.
27   Mikkola 2011, p. 69.
28   Mikkola 2016, pp. 133–4.
29   Mikkola 2016, p. 129.
30   Mikkola 2016, p. 130.
31   Mikkola 2016, pp. 133–4.
32   Mikkola 2016, p. 139.

than female or gender neutral) and, also in the USA in 2021, those identified as men by their possession of traits sufficient to gender them male are negatively valued for some relationships and tasks and positively valued for others. This valuation, in turn, leads to certain opportunities and relationships generally being granted or encouraged and others seldom offered or foreclosed. Continuing with the above example, if stoicism is generally valued among leaders, then, in the USA in 2019, those taken to be men will be able to access positions of leadership more readily than women. Because this norm-based sorting is based on generalisations made at the level of gender and not necessary at the level of judging whether an individual possesses a trait, access to leadership positions are more likely to be granted a man even if the selected individual imperfectly manifests the gendered trait.

To summarise, what Mikkola argues is problematic about being a woman is not the possession of certain traits that covary with femininity. After all, these traits are merely facts of the matter and, at different times and in different places, the same traits may have had different or neutral gender associations. What matters to Mikkola is that – right here and now – the negative patriarchal value judgments about the category of women and the negative actions towards those who fit into this category result in women's oppression.[33] While Mikkola leaves the concept of 'oppression' undefined, it is clear that she means by it something akin to how both Marxists and feminists have understood the term. That is, the 'imposition of systematic disadvantage on members of a social group ... such as a gender, race, class, etc., generating a pattern of unfavorable ratios of benefits to burdens, and impaired opportunities to establish and maintain positive relations-to-self'.[34] Given this definition, the systematic disadvantaging of persons identified as women due to their manifesting certain traits would be a form of group oppression by (a) those persons who share these negative value judgments; and (b) those that have the personal or institutional power to structure the social and economic world in accordance with these normative evaluations.

This does not mean that women cannot oppress other women or hold values that contribute to their own oppression. Quite the contrary, inasmuch as the evaluations that co-vary with the possession of certain traits in a specific society are more or less generalised, women can be expected to make these judgments about other women as well as about themselves. The latter phenomenon is referred to as the 'psychology of the oppressed' and contributes

---

33   Mikkola 2016, pp. 236–7.
34   D'Arcy 2014; Frye 1983, p. 4.

to an 'impaired opportunity to establish positive self-relations'.[35] That said, if some of the facts marking one as a woman is a relative lack of social, political, institutional, and economic power and if men are marked by a relative surplus, then, in the absence of other matrices of oppression, domination, and exploitation (such as race, caste, or capital), women would be less likely to successfully oppress other women than would men and they would also be less able to forcibly constrain other women and thereby enforce other forms of class inequality by their choices.

1.3.1   Advantages of Trait/Norm Covariance Model

Now that the trait/norm covariance model is explained, its advantages over classical and conventionalist models of gender identity can be enumerated. The classical theory of gender holds that biological sex necessarily and significantly determines an individual's gender or gendered characteristics. Though plastic enough in its Freudian form to admit of variation in these characteristics' ontogenetic expression, this model is still universalist in that the spectrum and variety of gendered traits associated with women are relatively fixed. And, though useful for demographic purposes (one can survey who manifests these characteristics in a given society), it is woefully inadequate for explanatory purposes, especially when the model is confronted with individuals who manifest feminine characteristics but are not biologically women. In contrast, the trait/norm covariance theory demands an *empirically accurate description of the particularity of women's oppression in a given society and at a given time*. It thereby avoids the universal claims of the classical model in which all women are said to share, for all time, certain characteristics. In addition, this model does not anchor, let alone metaphysically justify, women's oppression in their biological bodies or by dint of the gendered characteristics that are 'essentially' these bodies' expression.

In relation to the conventionalist model, where gender is said to result from social causes rather than from biology, the trait/norm covariance model preserves Conventional Gender Theory's anti-essentialism and thereby its superior explanatory and ameliorative powers. Like conventionalism, it severs the essential ties between biological sex and gender. With both theories, one can explain, for instance, why and how a transwoman is a woman insofar and inasmuch as she is distinguished from other social identities by a specific set of oppressive social forces.[36]

---

35   Ratner 2014.
36   Bettcher 2012, p. 243.

However, conventionalism, as we have noted, presents some problems. Chief among them is the *universal* claim that gender is exclusively a social kind and that the gender 'woman' can be abolished if the social conditions productive of this kind are overcome. For many, this claim is counter-intuitive and, as Appiah has argued in regard to analogous abolitionist claims about race, it is an assertion unlikely to be accepted by the general population even after much re-education.[37] In contrast, the trait/norm covariance schema coincides with folk conceptions of what is to be a woman. Specifically, that being a woman involves the possession of many of the primary and secondary sexual characteristics associated with women as well as the expression of some of the gendered traits that are also so-linked.[38] Because it fits with our ordinary language understanding of what it is to be a woman, the trait/norm covariance model has none of the epistemic hurdles associated with Conventional Gender Theory's redefinition of a commonly accepted term. Further, like the conventionalist model, it preserves the idea that part of what it is to be a woman is to be oppressed, an idea that can motivate feminist political struggle. However, it does not face the pragmatic problem of how to motivate women and others to the feminist cause when the end goal of feminist action is seen as the abolition of women as they are commonly understood to be.[39]

2   Marxian Class Theories

This chapter argues that, drawing inspiration from the trait/norm covariance theory of gender, we can usefully enhance social scientific stratification analyses of class and, using this information, better strategise about how to end class-based oppression. This is accomplished by defining 'class' as, in part, the possession of certain differentially valued ascriptive traits in a particular historical and socio-economic conjuncture, traits which are commonly understood to mark one as belonging to one class or another and therefore as valued for certain social positions and relationships and as not valued for others. Wright refers to these traits as 'material conditions'.[40] Davis calls them 'material and ideological facts'.[41] Following Mikkola, we can usefully include among these

37   Mikkola 2011, p. 69; Kwame Anthony Appiah 2001, pp. 286–8.
38   Mikkola 2016, pp. 88–9.
39   Mikkola 2011, p. 75.
40   E.O. Wright 2009, pp. 102–3.
41   Davis 1995, p. 109.

conditions all 'facts of the matter' about one's identity, including those often thought of as psychological such as self-identification and affective responses to social stimuli.

Despite the ease of this transcription, the analogy between gender and class is not exact and the differences matter theoretically and practically. Rather than being a biosocial phenomenon, class has been understood since the advent of modern political economy as socioeconomic. Given its ontological status, those on the egalitarian left have, like gender conventionalists, taken the possibility of its abolition as both a given and as political goal. This assumption is true of Marxist theory in its classical form, which stipulates that classes are economically determined and that economies (and therefore classes) are subject to transformation. The prospect of abolition is also true of Marxist theory in its Post-Marxist form. However, Post-Marxism downplays economic transformation and, instead, emphasises the social construction and transformation of class identity, consciousness, and agency.

2.1   *Classical Marxist Theory*

In the Marxian tradition, the classical mode of theorising explains class formation and reproduction through the economic, political, and social mechanisms of exploitation, domination, and oppression. Characteristically, it privileges the economic relation as ultimately determinant of class identity and of conflictual class relations. As mentioned above, this model is useful but not sufficient for identifying who belongs to a social class and why. However, oppression, which consists of different as well as more multifarious phenomena than the harmful appropriation by one class of another class's labour, i.e., exploitation, or of the political subjection of one class to another, i.e., domination, is not explained well by classical Marxist theory, nor are the relations between oppression and exploitation well-theorised.[42] In addition to its emphasis on economic determination and, therefore, on explanations of class linked to one's role in the economy, Classical Marxist theory is burdened by its relation to an ill-proven, telic theory of history that, if embraced, gives too strong an explanation for class struggle related political activity. Further, if this purposiveness be rejected, the theory becomes merely descriptive and provides insufficient explanation for such action. As such, like the classical and conventionalist understandings of gender, it faces both theoretic and pragmatic obstacles.

Though dealing with social rather than natural kinds, classical Marxist theory is no less essentialist than those theories that find in sex the truth of gender.

---

42   Davis 1995, pp. 102–3.

Indeed, it can be argued that this variety of class explanation is both more essentialist and more reductionist than the models of gender developed by Rousseau and Freud, both of whom provided explanations for normative and counter-normative gendered behaviour on the basis of interactions between sexed body and gendered environment. Similar explanatory subtlety only came to classical Marxist theory in the 1960s, when its predictions about class development and class struggle failed to come to pass.[43]

Classical Marxist theory was famously and pithily formulated in 1847 by Marx in *The Poverty of Philosophy* when he wrote 'the hand-mill gives you society with the feudal lord; the steam-mill society with the industrial capitalist'.[44] Its principle was more clearly iterated a decade later in the 'Preface to *A Contribution to the Critique of Political* Economy', when Marx informed his reader about the general conclusion to his extensive study of political economy, namely that,

> In the social production of their existence, men inevitably enter into definite relations, which are independent of their will, namely relations of production appropriate to a given stage in the development of their material forces of production. The totality of these relations of production constitutes the economic structure of society, the real foundation, on which arises a legal and political superstructure and to which correspond definite forms of social consciousness.[45]

Despite such clear assertions, Marx and Engels inconsistently reduced all social phenomena to economic foundation. Sometimes, they privileged social relations of oppression and domination or even individual human agency as determinative of class relations and, reciprocally, of the economic structure of society.[46] Nonetheless, in influential texts like *Anti-Dühring* (1878), Engels' theory reads as determinist and unidirectional with all history driven by contradictions within a mode of production.[47] Indeed, it was Engels' necessitarianism that the Russian philosophers Bukharin and Plekhanov set into 'orthodox' form at the beginning of the twentieth century.[48] There, it took the guise of a telic naturalism and technological determinism, a philosophy of 'dialect-

---

43   Gorz 1964; E. Mandel 1964.
44   Marx and Engels 1976, p. 166.
45   Marx and Engels 1987, p. 263.
46   Marx and Engels 1976, p. 166; 1987, p. 263; Stillman 2005.
47   Hunley 1991, pp. 113–26.
48   Mendelson 1979.

ical materialism', which explicitly underwrote the Marxist science of 'historical materialism'.[49] In 1938, Stalin's vulgarisation of this philosophy rapidly achieved theoretical hegemony within the international communist movement before declining in authority during the Khrushchev era.[50] Though challenged by Neocapitalist theory and by nascent Post-Marxisms, classical Marxist theory enjoyed a brief revival in the 1970s when it was stripped of its dialectical materialist metaphysics and reconstructed as a methodologically individualist social science by G.A. Cohen and other Analytic Marxists.[51]

That classical Marxist theory is determinist and essentialist does not mean that it is simple. Each of the aforementioned Marxist thinkers developed more or less sophisticated accounts of how economic modes of production give rise to diverse social relationships and inequalities and of how the economy interacts with non-economic social relations and institutions such as family, law, morality, art, religion, and gender to produce class and class struggle. Fundamentally, advocates of this monocausal model held that all class differentiation and, therefore, all class struggle is ultimately determined by the economic mode of production. To connect it to the classical theory of gender, the economic is the 'real' or 'essence' of which all history and all historical identities and interactions are merely the appearance. Simply put, each characteristic of an individual's class identity can be traced back to the role that that person plays in a particular socio-economic structure. These include obvious economic identifiers or 'traits' like income level, job precarity, and skill. Less evidently, this mode of explanation may account for an individual's social status, gender, race, ethnicity, political agency, morality, language, philosophy, as well as their subjective identification with other individuals recognised to be members of the same class.

According to classical Marxist theory, each of these facets of class identity serves to situate one in a set of productive relations, interactions that are, ultimately, determined by a particular mode of economic production. Further, under the capitalist mode of production, it was argued that a multiplicity of class identities (bourgeois, proletariat, peasant, rentier, petit-bourgeois, pauper) would be reduced by economic necessity to just two classes: a proletariat whose members have to sell their labour to survive and a bourgeoisie who lives off the labour of others.

Given the similarities between classical Marxist theory and the classical theory of gender, it is not surprising that both run into comparable theoretical and

---

49   Bukharin 2012, p. 148; Plekhanov 1964, p. 13.
50   Meikle 1999; I. Stalin 1949.
51   Bimber 1990; G.A. Cohen 2000; Hodges and Gandy 1980.

practical problems. If exploitation is understood at the microeconomic level as one party harming another person 'materially, intellectually and morally' in order to derive some benefit which the other is wholly or partially denied and, at the macroeconomic level, as the members of one class harming the members of another class in order to derive some benefit, then classical Marxist theory explains such relationships well.[52] Analytically and in terms of exploitation, one can use this concept of exploitation to differentiate husband from wife, master from slave, feudal lord from peasant, and proletarian from bourgeoisie. Depending on one's reading of Kant, one may even use this definition to explain just what is wrong about these relationships.[53]

However useful this description may be in the abstract, it has difficulty explaining the varieties of exploitation, domination, and oppression which combine to result in class formation and that may result in class struggle. As with employee participation in joint-stock companies, union pension plans, or with the middle class in general, when members of a certain class both benefit from and participate in their own exploitation, the concept loses some of its explanatory and predictive power.[54] In addition, when it comes to elucidating the complicated psychological attitudes that accompany and allow exploitation, this model again meets problems.

At first, solidarity or ideological cohesion among the members of an oppressed class seem easily explained using folk psychology and classical Marxist theory. If members of a class are forced together, collectively targeted, and repeatedly and progressively harmed by another class, then feelings and beliefs about the need for collective relief are likely to be engendered and shared among the affected group. But can exploitation illuminate a complicated phenomenon like negative solidarity, where members of the same class – each similarly employed and exploited – are driven not to empathy and mutual identification but instead evidence indifference to, or even contempt for, one another's suffering?[55] Think here of the senior co-worker who resents a junior colleague's 'taking advantage' of maternal leave policies that were unavailable to her. To preserve classical Marxist theory's explanatory power in such cases, one has to introduce a very complicated story where exploitation is shown to result in diverse and contradictory instances of class-consciousness among members of the same class. Alternately, one may grant explanatory power to other social sorting mechanisms such as oppression and domination (detailed

---

52   Furner 2015.
53   Furner 2015, pp. 40–1.
54   E.O. Wright 1979, pp. 42–55.
55   Durkheim and Simpson 1933, p. 119.

in section 1) or to universal psychological tendencies.[56] Both options, however, undermine the essentialist and universalising story that classical Marxist theory tells about history and class struggle: namely, that 'all history is the history of class struggle' and that the capitalist chapter of this history can be reduced to a simple account. This simple tale is that the necessity to employ and re-employ capital leads to the rapid expansion of a class of exploited workers who, once sufficiently numerous, immiserated, and engaged in collective production, will be motivated to revolt against their exploiters, to overthrow them, to reorganise productive relations and, triumphing as the universal class, to abolish all social classes and class relations. This historical schema brings us to the main empirical problem with classical Marxist theory. Simply put: this model has not predicted the future well and it has not, like other successful sciences, yielded explanations of a social phenomenon, in this case class-based socio-economic behavior, such that this behaviour can be predicted, and intentionally transformed by human activity.[57]

In terms of intentional transformation, Chapter 7 of this book shows how, why, and to what extent social scientific knowledge can be useful to political decision-making and to political strategy in a democratic context. Chapter 4 argues that historical materialism is a social scientific metatheory that bears structuring and orienting relations to the other social sciences and it suggests how an historical materialist orientation may usefully inform social scientific analyses in a way productive of social transformation. This chapter, along with Chapters 4 and 7, argue that there are fatal problems with the classical Marxist version of historical materialism. Specifically, and to the aim of this section, when historical materialism is wedded to dialectical materialism and to a telic philosophy of history, it suffers from multiple problems, rendering its employment theoretically and strategically detrimental. For one, it suffers from the oft-discussed 'transition problem' or the enigma of how capitalism becomes communism.[58] This problem comes in various forms but most who attempt to solve it focus upon the agency of the working class. Under classical Marxist theory, the activity of this class is understood as produced and reproduced by the productive forces of capitalism. Productive forces come first or are, in the last instance, said to determine the working class's collective self-consciousness and political will. Consequently, the most rigid and mechanistic answer to the transition problem is that, when the productive forces are sufficiently advanced and the proletariat sufficiently numerous, immiserated, and organised into

---

56   Schriber et al. 2017, p. 281.
57   Sesardic 1985, pp. 34–8.
58   Rockmore 2014.

economically fecund productive social relations of production, then this universal class will seize the means of production and will transform capitalist relations into communistic ones.[59]

2.1.1   Criticism of Classical Marxist Theory

This mechanistic solution to the transition problem leaves little room for individual or collective free agency. Just as women and men are merely the expression of biological sex under classical theory of gender, proletarian class-consciousness, agency, and politics under classical Marxist theory are merely the expression of the necessary dialectical unfolding of the economy. However, because individual and collective agency is assumed to be determined rather than free or partially free, classical Marxist theory gives no one reason to engage in revolutionary politics and every excuse not to do so. According to this model, if someone does not agree about the need for socialising private property, then it is because their role in the economic mode of production has not yet produced this awareness. What to do? The answer that classical Marxist theory gives is to wait until the productive relations have changed and until enough people are sufficiently immiserated such that a critical mass shares this ideology. At this point, revolutionary action becomes possible.

This strict, deterministic version of classical Marxist theory was, perhaps, never fully embraced by anyone, least of all Marx himself, who inveighed against 'Iron Laws' in economics.[60] Lenin, for his part, designated the communist party as the avant-garde agent capable of leading the people and of changing economies and ideologies along with them, hardly a necessitarian position.[61] Even Stalin made exceptions to this essentialism, singling out language as a cultural product not subject to determination by the economic infrastructure.[62] As such, tagging this theory 'classical' may be to pin a label on a strawman.

From the standpoint of first-person experience, classical Marxist theory also seems quite dubious. Though our agency may be limited by what we have to work with in terms of ideas, existing social relations, traditions, laws, language, raw materials, manufactured goods, and other tools – that is, by the material conditions in which we find ourselves – most of us sense ourselves as somewhat capable of changing our economic and social circumstances through action both individual and collective. This phenomenal awareness, combined with the actual, historical experience of people organising for and achieving social,

59   Engels 1973, pp. 145–50.
60   Addis 1966, pp. 112–13; Baumol 1983; Marx and Engels 1989, p. 91.
61   Le Blanc 1990, pp. 64–5.
62   J. Stalin 1951.

environmental, and economic change present empirical challenges to classical Marxist theory and demands a theoretical modification of some sort.

2.2   *Post-Marxism*

To perhaps oversimplify and for one of the purposes of this chapter, which is to develop a helpful analogy between feminist and Marxist social ontology, classical Marxist theory has been modified to account for the role of self-directed human agency in historical change in two basic ways. The first modification follows classical Marxist theory closely and acknowledges that our ideas and our agency are produced and limited by the mode of production in which we find ourselves. It also accords with classical Marxist theory in holding that our volitions as well as our 'takes on the world', or 'spontaneous philosophies', mostly serve to reproduce these economic and political relations. Nonetheless, it admits some agency on the part of individuals, groups, classes, and parties to inquire about the material conditions in which they find themselves and, from this understanding, to actively and self-consciously direct these structures' modification towards liberatory and egalitarian forms of association and production. For the most part, and with better and worse applications, those adopting this modification have associated themselves with the tradition of Marxism-Leninism. This chapter, which seeks to develop a modest methodological tool towards this understanding and modification, positions itself – as does the rest of the book – as self-consciously a part of this tradition.

The alternative methodological adjustment from classical Marxist theory emphasises cultural forces, human agency, ideas, art, emotions, and volition as determinative or as co-determinative of our economic and social conditions. Often, this tradition has been called 'Western Marxism'. However, as many of the theoretical figures associated with it were not from Western Europe and because many wholly identified with the Marxist-Leninist project, this appellation is confusing.[63] Because this method emphasises the power of ideas to drive or to change history, Hegelian or Lukácsian Marxism may be a better name for this tendency.[64] As with Marxism-Leninism, whole books have been written considering its development.[65]

Rather than being constituted by a divide between Hegelian Marxism and Marxism-Leninism, it is more useful and accurate to locate the various Marxist philosophies from the last century or so along a spectrum. One side is marked by a strict, technocratic historical determinism and the other end by an

---

63   Therborn 2008, pp. 84–5.
64   Therborn 2008, pp. 90–1.
65   P. Anderson 2016; Jacoby 2010; Jay 1984; Merleau-Ponty 1993; McInnes 1972.

emphasis on the power of human agency and ideas to produce historical transformation. Most Marxist philosophy falls somewhere in the middle. However, classical Marxist theory – as it is sketched above, and post-Marxism – as it is represented by volontarist, eventalist, aleatory, and hegemonic variants, can be considered to occupy the two poles. For the purposes of this chapter, what is interesting about the two extremes is that they are analogous to the two models of gender theory discussed above: classical Marxist theory, at its pole, is essentialist, universalist, and reduces all history, culture, and politics to the economy. Similarly, the classical theory of gender holds that gender is determined by biological sex and that this determination is universal. Like gender conventionalism, post-Marxist theories locate the endurance of capitalist economic formations as well as the potential for revolutionary change within the realm of ideas, culture, and social sentiment: that is, with convention. With their rejection of economic determinism and embrace of volontarism and social constructivism, they are similarly universalist if not essentialist.

Surveying or composing a typography of post-Marxism is beyond the scope of this chapter. So, as with the account of classical Marxist theory provided above, this section will use established post-Marxist works along with secondary sources to sketch post-Marxism's main positions and to highlight its conceptual similarities with the conventionalist understanding of gender. This accomplished, the chapter will conclude with an account of how a trait/norm covariance theory of class can overcome some of classical Marxist theory's and post-Marxism's theoretical and practical flaws.

Post-Marxist theory has no definite origin. Historically, many accounts link it to disillusionment with the Marxist-Leninist and Soviet project in the post-WWII period. Textually, intellectual historians begin with Luxembourg, Merleau-Ponty, Castoriadis, or Adorno.[66] However, some settle on a diverse and international cadre of theorists inspired by Althusser (and his students') theoretical severing of the economic mode of production from its determinative role in regard to other productive social practices in 1965 with the books *For Marx* and *Reading Capital*.[67] This splitting, it is claimed, challenged and removed the essentialism from Marxist historiography and philosophy of nature. While leaving the dialectical method intact, Marxist concepts such as class and contradiction were exclusively to be applied to social or discursive structures, rather than to economic ones. Similarly, subjectivity, agency, ideology, history, politics, religion, science, and revolution were now understood to be autonomous

---

66 Baldacchino 2018; Breckman 2013; Sim 2013, pp. 70–91.
67 Althusser 1969b, p. 229.

or 'relatively autonomous'. Following this reading of Althusser, thinkers such as Butler, Hindess and Hirst, Laclau and Mouffe, Hardt and Negri, and Resnick and Wolff competed with other post-Marxisms to give explanations of these phenomena without recourse to the economic.[68]

If there is no definite origin for post-Marxism, then there may at least be a quintessential post-Marxist text: Laclau and Mouffe's 1985 *Hegemony and Socialist Strategy*. Indeed, Therborn refers to it as 'seminal' and as Post-Marxism's 'most intellectually powerful contribution'.[69] What is this contribution and how does it typify post-Marxism's innovations? Wood argues that its novelty lies in denying essentialism in all its forms and, instead, positing a world where 'there is no [economic] determinacy, no relationship, no causality at all ... no historical conditions, connections, limits, possibilities'. At the level of the individual and of social class, this means that there are no '"fixed" social interests or identities'. Instead, all social identities are understood to be discursively constructed and "politically negotiable"'.[70]

How is this contiguous with Marxism? Well, along with other Post-Marxists, Laclau and Mouffe still believe in the existence of classes, class struggle, and in the revolutionary, egalitarian, and liberatory project inaugurated by Marx and Engels.[71] Denying economic determinism, however, they locate identity, class formation, as well as class conflict in historically contingent discursive relations. Particular and protean, these classes, however, will never be universal in the sense that Marx and Engels spoke of a 'universal class'.[72] It is also always within discourse, that is, within the systems of meaning available to a subject, that individuals and classes come to struggle with one another and to make competing political claims.[73]

As distinct from classical Marxist theory, there is no essential relation between the assertions that a subject makes and their role in the economic mode of production.[74] As Laclau and Mouffe write, '... there is no logical and necessary relation between socialist objectives and the positions of social agents in the relations of production'.[75] This is to say that, as distinct from clas-

---

68   Goldstein 2005, pp. 67–78; Park 2013; Rekret 2016; Sim 2013, pp. 57–60.

69   Therborn 2008, pp. 141, 155.

70   Wood 1998, p. 62.

71   Laclau and Mouffe 2001, pp. 4, 183.

72   Or, more precisely, they deny that the economic can be known separately from and in terms of its causal effect on the production of the social or discursive. Laclau and Mouffe 2001, pp. 120–1, 128, 191.

73   Laclau and Mouffe 2001, p. xiii.

74   Sim 2013, pp. 20, 42.

75   Laclau and Mouffe 2001, p. 76.

sical Marxist theory, there is no essential relation between the assertions that a subject makes and their role in the economic mode of production.[76] Subjects recognise themselves as being part of certain social groups, as having certain claims on the body politic, and they collectively struggle against others who do not recognise these claims. The struggle for recognition is the terrain of politics and it is crisscrossed by battles for hegemony, for having a certain class's viewpoint dominate such that their perspective on justice, right, and morality becomes constitutionally universal.[77] Dissimilar to classical Marxist theory, the side that one picks has to do with available discourses rather than with an individual's place in the mode of production.[78] In this model, there is no place for epistemic or agential privilege, no true (or truer) understanding of the social whole from the position of the subaltern, nor special powers granted by dint of occupying a certain economic position.[79]

Therefore, to the exemplary post-Marxists Laclau and Mouffe, history still exists and contradiction or 'antagonism' is still its motor. However, class struggle must now be positioned alongside fights against racism, sexism, and environmental devastation as ontologically equivalent skirmishes.[80] Rather than being powered by persons playing the subject roles that the economic structure needs individuals to inhabit and to self-identify with in order to reproduce itself, the motor of history is now said to be fuelled by a public's identification with certain discursively situated universals or 'nodal points' such as equality, freedom, anti-racism, or democracy.[81] As Paul Rekret writes, 'the definitively *post*-Marxist move [Laclau] enacts is to rearticulate the theory of hegemony by pushing the element of political contingency to its limits so as to undermine all notions of historical necessity such that the category of an essential and unified subject is displaced by a "plurality of subjects"'.[82]

With its insistence that all politics takes place in discourse, Laclau and Mouffe abandon historical materialism's essentialism for a type of discursive or cultural universalism.[83] For them, the mode of production no longer explains political subjectivities or political movements. Instead, historically mutable nodal points – more or less unconnected with the economy – are understood to be the universals by which political subjectivities are constituted and for which

---

76   Sim 2013, pp. 20, 42.
77   Sim 2013, p. 23.
78   Sotiris 2019, p. 8.
79   Laclau and Mouffe 2001, pp. 163–4; Sim 2013, p. 44; Turner 2019, p. 31.
80   Laclau and Mouffe 2001, p. xix; Rekret and Choat 2016, p. 282.
81   Laclau and Mouffe 2001, p. 155.
82   Rekret 2016, p. 136.
83   Nash 2001, pp. 78–9.

they struggle. The denial that the economy determines class identity and class struggle and the recourse to what are, at base, cultural explanations of class, subjectivity, agency, ideology, history, politics, and revolution are the hallmarks of post-Marxism.

Post-Marxism's embrace of cultural explanations for change disunited from economic determinism provides distinct advantages over classical Marxist theory. Stripped of classical Marxist theory's necessitarianism, it provides explanations of class, political consciousness, ideology, agency, and revolution in their integrity and without fitting them to a grand metaphysical narrative. A distinct gain, therefore, is that the predictive and explanatory failures of classical Marxist theory are obviated. With post-Marxism, there is no need to link every shift in ideology to a previously occurring change in the mode of production. Similarly, with the Marxist dialectic of history denied, the problem of why capitalism has not yet become communism disappears. Finally, a decided practical advantage is gained: one is obliged to focus on political work in the here and now.

Another achievement, which has both theoretic and pragmatic consequences, is that the role human agency plays or may play in political change is foregrounded. Humans are treated by post-Marxist theory as (somewhat) free agents capable of acting and of influencing one another. Yet another is its flexibility. Whereas classical Marxist theory posited that the economic is the 'real' or 'essence' of which all historical identities and interactions are merely the appearance, post-Marxism argues that history and historical political identities are particular and contingent, that is, that they are subject to change. Post-Marxism does not deny that social classes exist, that they are often united by a shared consciousness, and that, once constituted, members of a class may struggle collectively for political goals. This unity, though, is not demanded by being similarly opposed to other classes in economic terms but by individuals being proximally located in the symbolic or cultural order such that collective identification is achieved. By abolishing class determinism, post-Marxism reveals something of the freedom and potential that subjects have to organise politically and to alter class relations, notwithstanding the mode of production in which they act.

Further, whereas classical Marxist theory resorted in the 1970s to Mandelian epicycles to explain the failure of the world-wide socialist revolution and so as to include middle-managers among the proletariat. Post-Marxism readily explains both phenomena. Inasmuch as middle-managers identify with working-class struggles under the banner of equality or the feeling of shared precarity, they become part of that class. Correspondingly, troubling social phenomena for classical Marxist theory to explain, like negative solidarity, are effortlessly elided by the fact that multiple political projects can compete for any given subject's allegiances: a worker can as easily embrace frontier individualism as cosmopolitan fraternity. Further as to its explanatory powers, the occurrence of worldwide, national, or local revolutions, or their failure to occur, can be explained by the sufficient or insufficient identification of a critical mass of subjects with a revolutionary socialist political project such that they are able to wrest hegemony from those who previously held it.

2.2.1   Criticism of Post-Marxism

In terms of retrospectively explaining and prospectively modifying social behaviour in terms of class dynamics, however, post-Marxism is underpowered. According to post-Marxism, people happen to identify themselves with certain social groups and are inclined to act in solidarity or are not so inclined. Because all claims are equal in the symbolic, any reason for a subject's identification, whether economic, physiological, psychological, normative, or capricious, is taken to be as sufficient an explanation for affiliation as any other. Though it rightly takes such forces into account, post-Marxism overestimates the role of discursive formation in political change. This is because it ignores all of the other material relations influencing political outcomes which can be separated out from discursive systems. These include natural resources, built environments, modes of production, and fundamental human psychology. It also overlooks the non-discursive aspects of educational, economic, religious, scientific, political, and military institutions and their associated powers. In addition to discursive appeals and their reception or non-reception, it is the relation among these concrete environing conditions which permit some political outcomes to be realised and which prohibits or inhibit the realisation of others.

Retrospectively, post-Marxism provides neither an explanation for historical stasis nor for historical change. It can only observe that the politico-discursive field has changed and suggest that it might again be reconfigured. Though classical Marxist theory overreaches by positing that all class consciousness and all historical transformation can be explained by appeal to the economic, post-Marxism cannot justify why subjects in a social formation are wont to embrace a specific political cause or, indeed, why they should. Correspondingly, the political agency based upon such an identification is reduced to a type of volontarism, albeit one that can be explained psychologically by the belief that one is exploited, dominated, or oppressed. These feelings of subjugation do not, however, have an objective basis. Revolutionary formations based on calls for non-domination or to save the environment come to be uttered, heard, and heeded or they do not. According to post-Marxism, such developments are not necessarily the result of changes in the concrete material conditions in which subjects find themselves. In fact, one cannot even make the useful theoretical distinction between material economic conditions and the subject's knowledge of these conditions. If one judges that capitalism has led to material inequality, then for post-Marxism this is as much a political statement as it is a scientific one.

These theoretical problems lead to practical problems. As Rekret and Choat point out, 'post-Marxist political theories tend to locate the sources and conditions of social struggle and emancipation within some axiomatic, irreducible principle ... of contingency, agency or subjectivity'. This, they continue, leads to two problems:

> First, the possibility of meaningful social transformation is sustained but at the cost of divorcing the concept of the political from any critique of political economy and from the quotidian work of political organising, analysis, and even conciliation ... [S]econd ... insofar as the political is analytically distinguished and separated from every determinate order, the historicity of the concept of the political itself is not interrogated. A circularity is introduced in which the political is affirmed in terms of some sui generis principle which is itself never situated politically or related to its own historical conditions.[84]

Like the conventionalist understanding when compared to the classical theory of gender, post-Marxism gains theoretical suppleness in relation to classical Marxist theory but at the cost of its power to explain class consciousness, class struggle, and, ultimately, political change by dint of how each of these phenomena relate to and are produced within a particular economic and historical context. Emphasising discourse, post-Marxism cannot explain why certain schemes are taken up at certain times, nor can it identify the material obstacles to these projects' realisation, acceptance, and endurance. That such transformations may happen is assumed. This is because granting contingency, agency, and subjectivity ontological status allows it to posit revolutionary transformations as always, perchance, just around the bend. Post-Marxism thereby solves the transition problem by dissolving it. Post-Marxism's theoretical suppleness allows it to describe in detail, at the level of rhetoric and identification, how certain political projects arise, are taken up, and struggle for domination. However,

84   Rekret and Choat 2016, p. 281.

adopting its assumptions renders political theory impotent as critique and rud-
derless as a guide for practical direction.

As with the conventionalist understanding of gender, the embrace of post-
Marxism as political theory presents pragmatic obstacles to a political movement which wishes to explain *why* a subject should engage in a particular
political struggle rather than another. Both theories of identity render arbitrary or obscure the relationship between a subject's particular gendered traits
(in the case of conventionalist understanding of gender) or socio-economic
class markers (in the case of post-Marxism) and gender or class identity. In
the case of the conventionalist understanding of gender, the identification
of certain subjects as woman or man is historically particular. As neither are
natural kinds, both categories are subject to abolition. The identification or
self-identification of certain subjects as lower class and deserving of a different social and political status is similarly underdetermined according to post-
Marxism. Neither anti-essentialist model provides objective reasons for why
certain subjects, sharing certain concrete attributes, might organise or be per-
suaded to organise around a certain set of goals, nor does it provide them with
objective reasons to organise around and advocate for certain changes rather
than others.

3   Trait/Norm Covariant Class Model

Class stratification studies seek to partially explain and to define social class
by appealing to the individual attributes and material life conditions shaping a
person's identity. Similarly, the trait/norm covariance model seeks to comprehend gender by cataloguing the 'facts of the matter' or 'gendered traits' which
mark one as being a woman or man in a *particular historical conjuncture* and
place and as subject to certain oppressive forces. Further, the trait/norm covariance model promises to explain gendered oppression and to motivate political
action in a feminist direction by showing how these traits covary with patriarchal valuations and contribute to the systematic disadvantaging of persons
identified as women. Building upon the critical account of classical Marxist
theory and post-Marxism just offered, the argument pursued in the final section is that a trait/norm covariance understanding of the historically-situated
particularities constitutive of class identity and on the normative judgments
which covary with these traits yields theoretical and practical advantages over
the other two models. These gains are especially acute if one is seeking ways to
pragmatically link class analysis to political agency via oppression and, thereby,
to motivate and direct class struggle. The case for these benefits will be made

after explaining how and to what extent trait/norm covariance can be applied to modelling class stratification.

When applied to social class in a Marxian context, the trait/norm covariance model starts with the supposition that members of a social class can be identified by individual attributes and material life conditions that link them socially, economically, or occupationally. Directly related to these shared conditions and attributes are certain objective interests, interests which place the members of one social class in opposition to the members of another class.[85] Further, in a society structured by the demands of capitalism, some classes are advantaged and others disadvantaged in order that persons be slotted into requisite roles within the relations of production. It is this systematic advantaging and disadvantaging of one or more classes over another which gives members of oppressed classes reasons for struggling politically against another in pursuit of their objective interests.[86]

As the last supposition is similar to that of the trait-norm model in regard to gendered traits, there must be some way of specifying what class traits are and how they differ from other identity markers, such as those for gender, race, citizenship, or ethnicity. Analytically, this is easy to do: class traits are those having to do with social, economic, or occupational status that, irrespective of other identity markers, indicate that one is a member of a class whose interests are objectively opposed to that of another. According to this model, therefore, one might be identified and oppressed as an ethnic minority or immigrant in a way having nothing to do with social class. However, in the actual world, class oppression bears a complex relationship with other varieties of identity-based subjugation such that compound effects often result.[87] The extent to which an individual is granted or denied privileges and opportunities due to different and combined aspects of their identity is therefore difficult to quantify but, at macro levels, such disambiguation is possible.[88]

Neocapitalist and post-Marxist theories are correct in arguing that one can no longer easily separate social classes into proletariat and bourgeoisie. What classes there are and what relationships of oppression and advantage exist among them is an empirical rather than a theoretical question. Further, class

---

85   E.O. Wright 1997, p. 384. Cf. Chapter 4, 'objective class interests' are here defined as that set of interests that members of a social class would come to hold after sufficient public inquiry, deliberation, and experiment into which socio-economic situation would best serve their values and desires.

86   Althusser 1978c, p. 35.

87   Jones 1995.

88   H. Mandel and Semyonov 2016.

complexion differs among societies as well as longitudinally within them. Part of the work of concrete analysis, as discussed in Chapter 4, is to identify and understand these particular relations. That said, if we take our examples from the extremes of the upper and lower classes in the United States of 2021, then a few examples illustrating the trait-norm model's efficacy when applied to class may be generated. Clearly, some traits mark one as upper class while others mark one as lower. Yet others may be neutral in value. For instance, tattoos, once a marker of the lower class, no longer retain this general association. Now, one must pay attention to where the ink is placed, style, and image choice in order to connect a tattoo to class identity.[89] Specifically upper class 'facts of the matter' may include the deeply held conviction that one should choose a job which one loves, the fact that one's parent attended an elite university, and an abundance of social connections. Lower class material conditions may comprise having to drink contaminated water, the conviction that government institutions are mostly malignant, and a relative paucity of social connections. As with gendered traits, persons are differentially valued and value themselves differently according to their perceived membership in a class. One of the clearest examples of the valuation according to classed trait is that many universities and colleges in the United States take a parent's attendance at an elite university as a reason to admit to a prospective student. Similarly, a lack of familial and social connections becomes, for the lower-class person, a reason for refusal.

As with gender – where not all persons who wear lipstick are necessarily female, not all members of a class share every material condition associated with that social grouping. Rather, according to trait/norm covariance, class is a cluster concept, one useful for the diagnosis and explanation of oppression and privilege and, as this chapter argues, for motivating class-based political activity. In its capacity to direct and inform inquiry, trait/norm covariance as applied to class does not differ significantly from contemporary social scientific practice.[90] However, as mentioned above, the reasons for clusterings may be found by different modalities of class analysis, specifically those which focus on exploitation and domination rather than oppression. Such multi-modal reckonings would connect trait/norm covariance and contemporary social science even more deeply with the historical materialist tradition.

One objection to porting a model for gender to class is the supposition that one of the necessary conditions for being a woman or man is the belief that

---

89   Irwin 2001.
90   Savage et al. 2013; Appiah 2018.

one is a member of that gender. By way of contrast, one of the most powerful features of class analysis is that social scientific studies of class can reveal one to be a member of a class with which one does not identity. While this is an apt comparison with most models of gender, trait/norm covariance in fact makes no assumption about the relation between self-regard and gender. According to Mikkola, there are no sufficient and necessary conditions for being a woman. What there are, instead, are 'facts of the matter' or material conditions sufficient for one to be ascribed a female identity and treated more-or-less as a woman.[91] Self-ascription is more often than not part of a gender cluster but there are also cases where someone might identify as a woman and not be treated as one or where someone might think themselves to be gender neutral and yet be valued as a man. Therefore, the trait-norm model has, potentially, the same critical power to identify specific persons as feminised, even if they are not aware of it, as it does of identifying persons members of a class of which they were unaware. In short, according to the trait-norm model neither class nor gender has an essence but both have attributes. This is to say that both identity categories are recognised by the trait/norm covariance model as socially determinative and determining.

When we argue that social scientific studies may reveal one to be a member of a class with which one does not identity and when we maintain that this is one of the most pragmatically powerful features of class analysis, this is what we mean by it. One of the curiosities of class self-ascription in the United States is that most people identify as middle or lower-middle class.[92] In the UK, by contrast, people preponderantly identify as working class.[93] In neither country is it clear that this self-ascription accords with how social classes actually break down, and in neither country does this self-identification directly relate to a politics of class solidarity. Considered only in economic terms, this lack of solidarity makes a lot of sense. In the US, those who identify as middle class vary drastically in terms of income level and income source; they range from manual workers to teachers, coders, and rentiers. When one considers access to quality education and healthcare among the members of this class, there are also pronounced differences. In terms of classical Marxist theory, those who think themselves middle class in the US in 2021 may have no subjectively identified common interest. However, if a class is identified in terms of the commonalities it shares which make it subject to disadvantage according to the norms of a class-in-dominance, then genuine reasons exist for shared class identification

---

91   Mikkola 2016, p. 129.
92   'Northwestern Mutual – Planning & Progress Study 2018' 2018.
93   Manstead 2018, p. 268.

and resistance. Because of these commonalities, objective solidarities can be identified, acknowledged, and serve as the basis for collective action.

Again, the questions of what classes exists and of what complex of traits identifies a social class and covaries with normative judgements about it are empirical ones. That said, using the example of one trait and revisiting the question of self-identification can illustrate how trait/norm covariance functions analytically and pragmatically. If the self-judgement that one is middle class is insufficient to make one middle class, then what is required for object-ive identification of a class? Requisite are traits which are: (a) genuinely shared among members of a class and (b) sufficient for roughly differentiating one class from another. One anthropologist has recently proposed that a trait that marks the US middle class is that its members are terrified about being able to afford a college education for their children and, therefore, to socially and eco-nomically reproduce themselves.[94] Members of the middle class, according to this model, are identified by others as too wealthy for tuition remission pro-grammes and know themselves to be too poor to afford a four-year university degree without incurring life-altering levels of debt. Other linked traits which have both objective and subjective sides and which mark the class divide are those clustered around health care and job precarity. Both the worry about fall-ing ill and losing one's job and the class markings which slot one into precarious jobs and financial situations now affiliate a majority of the American popu-lace.[95]

As with gender, the trait-norm covariance model does not differentiate between essence and attribute when it comes to defining class. Although chronic illness, heightened morbidity, short-term employment, susceptibility to predatory lending, feelings of social alienation, and physicians spending less time with one during an office visit may all be associated with being lower class, none of these markers is taken to be causally primal. Again, as with the trait/norm covariance theory of gender, what matters is that those who, by dint of the possession of such traits, are identified as being from a specific class are normally valued and treated differently than those from another class. For lower classes, this differential treatment results in oppression contrary to the individual's and class's objective interests. For upper classes, the differential valuing results in privilege in conformance with that classes' interests.

Based on the covariant relation between trait and norm upon which this mode of class analysis turns, trait-norm covariance presents advantages over

94   Zaloom 2018.
95   Norman 2019.

both the essentialist universalism of classical Marxist theory and the anti-essentialist universalism of post-Marxism. As detailed in Section 2.1.1., with its emphasis on economic determination and an increasingly bifurcated class struggle, classical Marxist theory has difficulty explaining the varieties of exploitation, domination, and oppression which combine to result in class formation and that occasion class struggle. A trait-norm covariance model sidesteps this difficulty by focusing exclusively on a particular socio-economic conjuncture and by detailing how systematic disadvantage is accorded to one or more groups in this conjuncture through a system of actions grounded in normative judgments about class. By focusing on particularity, it avoids the historiographical problems, including that of the transition to communism, which undermine classical Marxist theory. While preserving the ideas of class and class struggle as well as holding out the possibility of revolutionary political change, a historical materialism informed by the trait/norm covariance model of class makes no claims about where history is going. It does, however, insist that there are reasons for existing class stratification and that we must look at particular histories of class-based oppression to understand it. Further, unlike classical Marxist theory at its most deterministic, the trait-norm covariance model includes individual and collective free agency. In fact, by helping to identify the members of a class and by showing that part of what it is to be lower-class is to be valued unequally, it can be said to focus and amplify the agency of oppressed persons and groups, providing them with reasons to act politically in order to end this discrimination.

As it too focuses on the particular and the contingent rather than on the universal and determined, many of these benefits can be said to accrue to the post-Marxist model of class as well. Just like trait-norm covariance, post-Marxism provides explanations of class, political consciousness, ideology, agency, and revolution without recourse to economic determination, thereby avoiding the predictive and analytic failures of classical Marxist theory. Salutary as well is the way in which post-Marxism tilts Marxist philosophy away from grand narratives of history and focuses those discontented with the status quo on political work.

Where post-Marxism fails, however, and where trait-norm covariance offers promise, is in terms of retrospectively explaining and prospectively modifying social behavior in terms of class dynamics. According to post-Marxism, any reason for a subject's identification with a political cause (economic, physiological, psychological, normative, or capricious) is taken as sufficient a reason for affiliation as any other. With its focus on discourse and affinity, post-Marxism disregards all of the other material practices influencing political activity. With post-Marxism, there is no ethical reason given for *why* a subject, as a member of a specific subaltern class, should engage in a particular political struggle rather than another. In contrast, a trait-norm covariance analysis provides reasons for why certain subjects, sharing certain factual attributes, and oppressed because they are identified as equally members of a certain class, should organise around a certain set of goals. Further, it provides them with a detailed schema for identifying both who is a member of, and what it is like to be in an oppressed socio-economic class. Once inquiries of the sort suggested in Chapters 4 and 7 and incorporating trait-norm covariance analyses are made, then a politics of counter-oppression can be initiated, one which targets class-based valuations as well as the oppressive circumstances, practices, and institutions which are their concrete instantiation. If they are contrary to the interests of the class-in-itself, this can be done by eliminating these circumstances and by targeting the value judgment which makes one think that those identified as lower class do not have the same rights, privileges, freedoms, and capacities as those identified with the dominant class.

In Section 2, we suggested that trait-norm covariance is closer to classical Marxist theory than it is to post-Marxism. If it is, it is not because it revives dialectical materialism in its methodological or metaphysical guises. No, what it preserves is the scientific part of Marxian philosophy, its historical materialism. Like post-Marxism, it starts from the premise that every social conjuncture is particular and that the social balance may be changed. Unlike post-Marxism, it does not hold that every conjuncture and every class formation is contingent and up for grabs. Capitalism structures us and our relations in definite ways. Though classes may ultimately be irreducible to proletariat and bourgeoisie, differentiation among individuals eligible to employ and reemploy the spoils of capitalism and those who produce capital is necessary for capital's accrual and expansion. One of the ways in which this sorting is accomplished is by the normative identification of a group or groups valued for producing capital and by the slotting of individuals into these groups by their possession or non-possession of certain classed traits.

Because these traits and the associated oppression are shared and necessarily identifiable, particular avenues for resistance are suggested. However, unlike with gender, where it is clear that patriarchal norms lead directly to the oppression of those identified as women, historical materialists must continually seek to research and define who, at this particular conjuncture of capitalist history, is being oppressed as well the means by which they are so identified. As argued above, social classes do not have an essence. However, they do have particular causes and functions. By examining the actual relationships of privilege and oppression that accrue with the material possession or dispossession of certain classed traits in a definite historical culture, trait-norm covariance offers us a way to understand how classes are propagated and sustained here and now. Unlike classical Marxist theory and post-Marxism, it helps us to better identify oppressed classes and it offers members of those classes reasons and strategies to resist the reproduction and endurance of unjust class relations.

CHAPTER 6

Separating Racist Science from Racial Science

Whereas fifty years ago it was hard to find academic disciplines outside of sociology and anthropology where the study of race was anything but a marginal part of their practice, it is now hard to find a discipline in the humanities, life, or social sciences that does not devote significant resources to its investigation.[1] Biology, medicine, education, environmental studies, anthropology, psychology, sociology, law, political science, economics, and history all now make it part of their activity to define race or to analyse and describe its effects. Though late to the game, academic philosophy has likewise become a player. As might have been expected of this most abstract of disciplines, philosophy has largely concerned itself with trying to define and understand race as an ontological, experiential, or semantic category. As may also have been expected, academic philosophy's attempts to understand race reflect the split in disciplinary approach and orientation that characterises much of Anglophone academic philosophy. Thus, in certain journals and at certain conferences, one finds philosophers making arguments based in the philosophy of language to demonstrate that race is a social kind or using tools from the philosophy of science to try and conceive race as a natural kind.[2] In other journals and at other conferences one finds philosophers busy developing ontologies of race that are based upon the phenomenological description of racialised experience.[3]

These approaches have been fruitful and it does seem like philosophy has resolved some of the conceptual problems regarding race that trouble the foundations of research programmes in the life and human sciences. Thanks to philosophy's efforts in these areas and to the efforts of scientists themselves, one now finds philosophers, natural scientists, and social scientists much more reluctant than they were a generation ago to explain race away as simply a cultural construct or to reify it as a natural kind.[4] Philosophy, however, can do more for the sciences than provide them with definitions. As critical theory, philosophy can also help to point out where the social and life sciences get race

1   The author wishes to thank Sally Haslanger, Edouard Machery, and Ronald Sundstrom for their helpful criticism and to the students in my Philosophy of Race and Gender seminar who thought through many of the issues addressed in this paper with me.
2   Spencer 2015 offers a useful summary of both approaches.
3   Alcoff 1999; Al-Saji 2014; Balfour 1998; E.S. Lee 2014; Mudde 2014.
4   Nanay 2010, p. 272.

wrong. That is, it can suggest to scientists and to the public where, why, and how the understanding of race that scientific research uses or produces may be ideological in the sense that it contributes to racism or is racist.

Although there is a good argument that racialism, or the view that human races exist, cannot be practically separated from racism, this chapter makes no such assumption.[5] Instead, it treats as open the scientific question of whether or not 'races are real entities'. It also treats as unresolved the ethical question of whether or not 'racial identities are real and valuable properties ... which may help realize such human goods as equality and self-actualisation'.[6] Instead of tackling the ontological question directly, this chapter targets racism as it has developed in the modern era and it seeks to answer the question of whether or not and how modern racist ideology can be separated from racial science.[7]

Following Jackson and Guillaumin, and for the purposes of this chapter, 'racism' will be defined as the ideology which holds that people may be separated and grouped by distinct phenotypic features, that these features correlate with characterological and psychological traits, and that these types are heritable. Necessarily, this modern sense of racism also contains the notions that each racial group 'can be ranked on a hierarchy of value' and that members of a racial group may be treated unequally due to their place in this hierarchy. Inasmuch as these 'ideas are unconscious, experienced as natural, spontaneous and self-evident' rather than conscious, investigated, and explicitly understood, racism functions as a kind of widely-shared background knowledge, an ideology or 'pre-judgment' structuring our interactions.[8]

Over the last half century, historical research has clearly demonstrated that past understandings of race developed by the life and human sciences have been rife with racist notions masquerading as empirically verified truth claims.[9] It is therefore not a bad supposition that contemporary scientific research into areas such as incarceration, facial recognition, immigration, and heart medications may likewise be compromised by racist ideology. Conversely, some have argued that to abandon the idea of race because it is often admixed with racism may lead to bad science, unfortunate political outcomes, and less

---

5   Hochman 2013.

6   Taylor 2000, p. 103.

7   É. Balibar and Wallerstein 1991, pp. 37–68; Hochman 2013, p. 1002; West 1982, pp. 47–65; Taylor 2014, pp. 18–26 and others argue that the 'modern racism' associated with the enlightenment, nationalist, and colonial projects of Europe differs substantively from other forms of group-based discrimination.

8   Guillaumin 1995, p. 36.

9   Barder 2019; Dennis 1995; Finkelstein 2001; Haller 1997; McWhorter 2004; Stepan 1987.

effective health care.[10] Ethically and epistemically, therefore, it matters what race is and that we understand it as best we can, apart from racism. To those who want to know what race is and how it functions, the relevant question, then, is: 'How do we separate scientific knowledge about race from ideological knowledge so that we may obtain a clearer understanding of race and its effects?' This is a vexing problem and, in its general form, it is a conundrum that has been troubling philosophers of science since Hegel noticed that a culture's scientific conceptions mirror and reinforce its metaphysical and normative assumptions. It is not, however, a puzzle without solutions.

For its part, this chapter will focus on Louis Althusser's general solution to the dilemma of how to separate ideological from scientific knowledge. Though developed as a solution to a different problem in a different era, the answer Althusser offered in the 1960s and early 1970s to the dilemma of how to distinguish scientific concepts obscured by class prejudice is applicable to the central problem of this chapter: that of how to separate racist ideology from racial science. This technique is not here presented as the only means for extricating ideological from scientific knowledge. As Chapter 7 suggests in regard to knowledge of public goods and as feminist, underrepresented, and indigenous philosophers of science, indigenous citizen scientists, and collaborative researchers themselves have shown over the last few decades, there are many other ways to aid in this separation and it can be accomplished at multiple points during a scientific inquiry.[11] Philosophers are not objective and they are not above the fray of class struggle and immune from class-based ideologies. However, given the specific philosophical skills of interpreting and assessing arguments and assumptions and given an orientation sensitive to the histories and varieties of oppression, domination, and exploitation, philosophers and, in particular, Marxist philosophers can play a role in this separation.[12] The first section lays out the critical theoretic solution Althusser developed for separating ideological from scientific knowledge. The next section applies this critical method to a definition of race promulgated within sociobiology and suggests that this method of critique may be generalised. In so doing, it makes the case that critical theory can work to separate ideological notions from scientific concepts in every discipline that concerns itself with understanding race or its effects.

---

10   Anomaly 2017; Ferdinand 2008; Shelby 2007, pp. 207–42.
11   Bailey et al. 2017; Basset and Krieger 1986; Fernandez and Tick 1994; Harding 1991a; 1991b; Lennon 1997; L.T. Smith 2012; M. Solomon 1992; Wylie 2015; 2012; Zuberi and Bonilla-Silva 2008.
12   Willett 2008, pp. 298–9.

1   Separating Science from Ideology[13]

Althusser was motivated to think about how to separate science from ideology
in the context of a larger search for alternatives to the understanding of philosophy, politics, and science promulgated by the French Communist Party in
the post-World War II era.[14] In the 1950s and early 1960s, the PCF had a pronounced tendency to second the Stalinist claim that 'bourgeois science' was
ideological and that only the science done by Party members and scientists
was true.[15] When it reconsidered these positions in the late 1960s, it corrected by downplaying the importance of scientific research for the communist
movement and emphasised, instead, the significance of culture and art.[16] For
his part, as an alternative to Stalin's rudimentary standpoint theory and to the
French Communist Party's cultural idealism, Althusser busied himself in the
1960s and 1970s with developing a philosophy of science that neither linked
veracity to class status nor modulated the importance of scientific research for
political direction.

   Trained by Bachelard in the tradition of French epistemology and influenced
by Canguilhem and Cavaillès, Althusser knew that there were theoretical and
practical problems with the Party's official metaphysics of dialectical materialism and with its reduction of Marx's historiography to a few triadic formulas.[17]
In addition, he was convinced that these misrepresentations occluded what
was truly original in Marx: his founding of the science of historical materialism.[18] It was then in an attempt to uncover the philosophical aspects of
Marxism and to demonstrate the scientificity and non-reductivist nature of
historical materialism that Althusser began his re-reading of Marx's texts. This
re-reading began in 1960 with the essay 'On the Young Marx' and culminated
in 1965 with the publication of the collective work *Reading Capital*.

   Chapter 3 engages in a close reading of these texts and shows how Althusser
originally defended the autonomy of scientific knowledge from those who
would reduce it to class interest or ideology. However, it is the contention of this
chapter, of Chapter 4 and of the book as a whole that it is actually Althusser's
later and less well-known work on the philosophy of science and his defence of
historical materialism as a methodological orientation for the social sciences

---

13   This section is adapted from W.S. Lewis 2005a; 2005b, pp. 191–8.
14   Althusser 1969b, p. 22.
15   Langevin 1966, p. 4.
16   W.S. Lewis 2007a.
17   Maruzzella 2019, p. 176.
18   Althusser 1969b, pp. 13–14.

that is more tenable than his earlier work. This work is also more applicable to the problem of how to separate racist concepts from scientific understandings of race. For these reasons, this chapter primarily concerns itself with the period between 1966 and 1978 when Althusser moved away from the conventionalism associated with his 'classic' texts and when he began to suggest that philosophy might play a role in the critique of scientific concepts.

While in the process of re-thinking the conclusions advanced by Althusser and his students during the first half of the sixties, Althusser contended that Marxist philosophers should be in the business of assessing current scientific knowledge.[19] Criticising his former work as 'theoreticist' for its insistence on the autonomy of economic, political, ideological and scientific practices, Althusser modified his contention that science exclusively relies upon its own internal process of verification for truth claims.[20] Though he still endorsed a constructivist position, by the second half of the 1960s, he contended that reality plays some role in the falsification and verification of scientific knowledge. At this point, and for the rest of his career, ideology, philosophy and science were still considered material practices. However, Althusser now maintained that this trio of intellectually productive practices are much more integrated than they were in the descriptions of each he had provided in *For Marx* and *Reading Capital*. By 1967 and in his seminar on *Philosophy and the Spontaneous Philosophy of the Scientists*, ideology was taken to inform every way of knowing and social practice.

As strong a claim as this would seem to preclude the ability to differentiate between scientific and ideological knowledge. However, that every scientific belief includes ideological content does not mean ideology is inescapable. Inherent in the concept of ideology that Althusser developed between 1966 and 1968 is the Spinozo-Freudian presupposition that we enjoy both a 'real' and an 'imaginary' or 'lived' relation between ourselves and the world and that, further, there is a discernible difference between these two relations.[21] It is this difference that Althusser argues scientific inquiry is able to uncover. Science is able to do so by the formulation of rules about the world that, unlike ideological concepts, are testable and subject to revision.[22] Science does not produce 'Truth'. No epistemic certainty is reached. However, its practice permits us to begin to know and to direct the world better than it was known before, by ideology.

19   Althusser 1969b, p. 22.
20   Althusser and Balibar 1970, pp. 188–9.
21   Althusser 1990c, p. 161; 1997b, pp. 5–8.
22   Resch 1992, p. 183.

Given science's role in the progressive disclosure of non-ideological knowledge, philosophy's traditional tasks of truth discovery have, in this account, been superseded. This seems like a strange position for an academic philosopher like Althusser to take. However, because philosophy is likewise contaminated with ideology, it can no longer be understood as the guarantor of truth or as the Theory of theoretical sciences. As it has always been idealist philosophy's goal to provide just such guarantees and overarching theories, it must be abandoned. Claiming no such prerogative, materialist philosophy does have a role to play in the production of knowledge. This role is a critical one: materialist philosophy may help to distinguish for science what part of its concepts are ideological and to make sure that a science's results are not perverted in their reception. In this role, philosophy still works on the elaboration of concepts or categories but it no longer guarantees their veracity. Instead, philosophy is distinguished as that theory which intervenes in theory critically. What this intervention does is 'to draw ... a line of demarcation that separates, in each case, the scientific from the ideological'.[23]

But how does it perform this operation? As Althusser describes the epistemological problem whose partial solution is the intervention of materialist philosophy, science would do quite well if it were not for the scientists who practice it. Because of the nature of their work (and with the exception of some mathematicians), scientists are, in the main, 'spontaneous materialists'.[24] This is to say that they seek answers to questions about what exists and the relations among existences by testing their hypotheses in experience, rather than by appeals to common sense, authority, or revelation. The problem with individual scientists, however, is that, like all of us, they cannot help but be products of a specific socio-economic and historical conjuncture, inhabiting and instantiating the ideology that typifies it and which allows it to be sustained. With the hypotheses scientists pose, the tests they design, and in the interpretations of results they offer, they bring into their research and conclusions the ideology of the wider culture. In fact, it is this ideology which permits certain questions to be posed and findings to be understood. Because they are working on the real, some imaginary relations will begin to be dispersed. This is why science can be said to progress. However, ideology or error will never be totally excised from the body of concepts that allow the science to be established and developed.

---

23   Althusser 1990c, p. 106.
24   Althusser 1990c, pp. 134–5.

Marxist philosophers are subject to the same constraints as everyone else; they likewise live the world in and through ideology. However, a new practice of philosophy, which takes the results of historical materialist inquiry seriously and which inaugurates a 'critical and revolutionary relation between philosophy and the social practices' aids them with this excision.[25] An example of this critical process in regards to the results of a physical science is provided by Louis Althusser in his analysis of a lecture given by Jacques Monod at the *Collège de France* in 1967.[26] In this analysis, Althusser argues that the Nobel Laureate is essentially correct in his contention that the discovery of DNA must cause us to rethink telic assumptions in evolutionary science and to think of the emergent complexity of biological organisms as aleatory. These assertions are correct, Althusser argues, because there is abundant material evidence for this claim and because it makes sense within the conceptual framework of evolutionary biology. The problem with Monod's conclusion though is that he does not stop with this conclusion but goes on to assert that 'humanity is born' when the:

> latest of these [biological] accidents could lead to the emergence in the heart of the biosphere of a new realm, the *noosphere*, the realm of ideas and knowledge which was born on the day when the new associations, the creative combinations in an individual could be transmitted to others through language, rather than dying with him.[27]

In this move, the transposition of the logic of biology onto human social formations, Althusser identifies the effect of ideology on what was theretofore a correct scientific analysis. What Monod did was to 'arbitrarily impose upon another science – which possesses a real object, different from that of the first – the materialist content of the first science'.[28] As Althusser points out, from the standpoint of a materialist philosopher, this is a classic idealist and therefore ideological move to make. Like Hegel or Plato, Monod assumes that there is a universal logic or content (in this case biological) that defines each and every process no matter how materially and functionally disparate each may be. When such a move is recognised, it is the job of philosophy to step in. Its job is to mark-out that which in Jacques Monod's conclusions are ideological and that which are scientific and to suggest what ideological belief(s) inform

---

25   Althusser 1990c, p. 265.
26   Althusser 1990c, pp. 145–65.
27   Althusser 1990c, p. 150.
28   Althusser 1990c, p. 151.

the science. In the case of Monod, Althusser suggests that the ideology distort-ing the scientific theory is Catholic cosmology.[29]

According to Althusser, the intervention by philosophy in science is always political. Through critique, philosophy attempts to vet and thereby to control the way in which scientific knowledge is received by the wider social sphere. Deployed in this way, it has the chance of changing the total conceptual ter-rain. With Monod for instance, Althusser's intervention is intended to defend against 'idealist' assumptions regarding the origins of human culture and to argue on behalf of inquiry focusing on the particularities and 'materiality of [humans'] social conditions of existence'.[30] Anthropology, he argued, should not be reduced to or explained by concepts developed for biology or, for that matter, by idealist philosophical anthropology. Doing its job, Marxist philo-sophy makes both science and bourgeois philosophy reconsider its assumption and its practices. What's more, by identifying where and in what way a science's contents are ideological, Marxist philosophy modifies how scientific know-ledge is received by the wider social sphere. Because the biological and social sciences often influence policy, done well, Marxist philosophy has the possib-ility of limiting the use to which ideological claims made by scientists may be put to justify positions and activities. Because this criticism also removes some of the ideology inherent in a science or encourages a science to rethink its assumptions, it also makes success for policies based on scientific findings more likely.

This does not mean that every philosophical intervention into the sciences will be efficacious. As the positions that philosophy defends are themselves conceptual, philosophy may defend ideological error. In fact, for Althusser, the defence of one dominant historical ideology or the other constitutes most of the history of philosophy. However, and he insists on this point, histor-ical materialism and its emphasis on 'real individuals, their activity and the material conditions of their life' changed all that.[31] With Marx's inauguration of the science of history, it became possible to criticise many philosophical positions and systems as ideological and erroneous. With care and attention, one could now analyse the economic and social relations which caused a spe-cific position to emerge. What's more, this theoretical practice made it possible to continue with this type of analysis in the present and, within science, to separate correct materialist concepts based on the real from ideological con-

29   Dukes 2016, pp. 523–4.
30   Althusser 1990c, p. 151.
31   Marx and Engels 1975, p. 31.

cepts that are erroneous.[32] An example of this technique is given above in terms of an intervention in the physical science of biology but there is no reason that this technique could not be applied to any of the social sciences or to emergent interdisciplinary fields like evolutionary psychology or sociobiology.

2   Critical Technique Defined

In order to furnish a clear exposition of the technique by which philosophy separates ideological from scientific knowledge and to provide an example of the uses to which such a technique may apply, the remainder of this chapter will concern itself with the critique of a recent hypothesis advanced in sociobiology. Before beginning with this assessment, however, a couple of caveats. The first is that Marxist philosophers and scientists have engaged in critiques of sociobiology at least since E.O. Wilson published his seminal text heralding the dawn of this new discipline in 1975.[33] A new voice would not need to be added to the chorus were it not for the detail that a reconstructed version of Althusser's method of differentiating between ideological and non-ideological knowledge has something new to contribute to the debate. For Marxist philosophers, this method's novelty lies chiefly in the facts that it neither reaffirms dialectic as the law of nature, as does clasical Marxist theory, nor does it maintain that sociobiology has no place in historical materialist accounts of human development and association. The place sociobiology should find, however, is one which takes the material practices of language, history, economy, religion, gender, etc., that we use to reproduce our social life as seriously as it does genetics and social statistics. Substantively, then a reconstructed Althusserian critical theory contributes to the debate because it fruitfully criticises not only the biological sciences but also tempers those focusing too exclusively on thought, behaviour, and social relationships.

Before turning to the critique of a specific study in sociobiology, the second caveat to keep in mind is that the great bulk of sociobiological research is done on animals. For the most part, these studies make no supposition about the evolutionary background for behaviours; they only consider the reproductive success rate that specific adaptations bring about as the criterion for suggesting that some expressed traits are evolved or 'selected' for social purposes. In

---

32   Althusser 1968, p. 61.
33   Kitcher 1990; Lewontin 1979; Yudell and Desalle 2000.

that animal studies limit themselves to this type of research and analysis, they are largely immune from the type of criticisms here raised.[34]

That humans represent only a small fraction of what sociobiologists study does not make the impact of these studies negligible. Quite the contrary, the relatively few studies done on humans have been and continue to be enormously influential. One does not need to subscribe to *Nature* or even to *The New Scientist* to read about them. Their analyses have now become part of popular culture and deeply influence the way in which we think about ourselves.[35] Reflect for a second, when was the last time that you heard reference to someone behaving like an 'Alpha Male' or heard a friend explain away relationship problems with the tautology 'Men are from Mars and Women are from Venus?' Both descriptions come from or rely heavily on notions developed by sociobiology. That recourse to both is so reflexive may suggest the extent to which sociobiological conclusions are embedded in popular consciousness.[36] Add to this the distinct possibility that sociobiology and evolutionary psychology will likely have a direct effect on political decisions regarding such matters as public health and the need to keep a critical eye on these fields becomes glaringly obvious. As one example of this potential, studies in evolutionary psychology have suggested that there is a link between step-parenting and child maltreatment.[37] It is but a short move to conclude that children with stepparents need to be monitored by the state in ways that a family consisting solely of biological children do not.[38]

During its infancy, studies in evolutionary psychology and sociobiology were very crudely done and both sociologists and biologists enjoyed pointing out this nascent science's methodological shortcomings. Many times, the relevant sample was too small, the population insufficiently diverse, and the conclusion unwarranted. However, these related fields which started out so crudely a couple of generations ago and that routinely overemphasised the power of genetic expression to account for social behaviour has itself evolved. Both are now much more sophisticated. They have become so because scientists are capable on their own of pointing out when the conclusions of their peers overstep available evidence. Today, any responsible scientist working in the field takes into account not only cultural determination but also the way that envir-

34   Thanks to Cory Freeman-Gallant for his perspective on the field of sociobiology and for his insights into the way that sociobiologists view their own practices.
35   de Waal 1999.
36   Bordo 2015, pp. 229–34.
37   Malkin and Lamb 1994; Tooley et al. 2006.
38   Ardill 2008, pp. 297–347; Heineman 1991; Kuklin 2004.

onments both natural and cultural influence the expression of a particular trait. The effect of sociobiology's acknowledgement of a consort of developmental, cultural, and environmental determinants in addition to innate genetic ones marks the maturation of the field as well as effectively ending the 'nature versus nurture' debate.[39]

So, what is left to critique? Admittedly, not nearly as much as there was a generation ago. However, even recent studies in sociobiology fall prey to pitfalls similar to those for which their predecessors were rightly condemned. Further, then as before, the reasons for these mistakes are sometimes ideological. How can we recognise such mistakes? As detailed above, Althusser's work from the late 1960s suggests a method that may allow us to separate ideological from scientific knowledge. Further, this method presents two distinct advantages in comparison to two other methods of epistemic correction. First, it resists the temptation prevalent in Marxist and some feminist standpoint theory to correlate epistemic ability exclusively with a subject's social position. Second, it corrects for the positivist tendencies of scientists to associate epistemic accuracy with correct procedures and descriptive rigour rather than with collaborative inquiry.

As this method was never stated explicitly by Althusser, any account of it must necessarily be drawn from his examples and from what he writes about the relations between ideological, scientific, and philosophical practices. Departing from these accounts and especially from his critique of Monod, it is apparent that one should only second a scientist's conclusion about human behaviour when there is abundant evidence for the claim, when this evidence accounts for the entirety of the observed phenomenon, when the findings are replicable, and when there is no suspicion that the concepts used to understand the object studied might be ideological. The first three criteria do not differ from the general reasons for why one should accept a social scientific theory and, as was mentioned above, scientists themselves are capable under ideal and even not so ideal conditions of these checks and rectifications.

This kind of work, however, takes a long time and, too often, the faulty knowledge is disseminated and reinforced before a retraction or emendation can take place, the communicative force of which is usually much less than the original study. Further, scientists are not well-trained to ferret out ideology or to confront it.[40] If training in critical theory gives philosophers reason to suspect that material evidence does not account for the phenomenon in a scientific

---

39   De Waal 1999.
40   Marks 2017, p. 23.

study, or if a theory accounts for too many disparate phenomena, or it makes use of theories or concepts developed under heterogeneous circumstances, then it may be the case that ideology is at work and that the science has overstepped its purview. Further, if a claim or set of claims resembles a set of beliefs previously established as ideological, then there is a reason to investigate their role in the study's logic. Therefore, if the conclusions of a specific study can be shown to (a) over-extend its purview, and (b) to second and reinforce a position that has been demonstrated through historical materialist analysis to be ideologically produced, then there is good reason to suspect that part of its content is ideological. The study then is open to philosophical criticism that would seek to differentiate that in it which is correct from that in it which is ideological. Finally, if the background of the scientists and or the funding for the study suggest that its authors are disposed to hold the ideological position in question, then (c) there is additional reason for suspecting that a study is unduly influenced by ideology. However, this last factor is not enough on its own to make the argument that a study has ideological content.

3   Critical Technique Applied

Briefly, let us apply this method to a sociobiological study that seems to have none of the problems historically associated with the interdisciplinary science. The study in question, 'Cross-National variation in violent crime rates: Race, r-K theory and income' appeared in the July 2002 issue of *Population and Environment*. In it, J. Phillippe Rushton and Glayde Whitney argue that race can be a relevant factor in the prediction of crime rates for a population and that it is a factor because specific races have evolved different reproductive strategies, some of which make them more likely to commit crimes like murder and rape. Seeking to place particular races along a spectrum of reproductive strategies, Rushton and Whitney hypothesise that, if it is the case that Negroids tend to 'high fertility, low-investment parenting, fast maturation and low intelligence and learning abilities', then it should be the case that, when these traits are socially expressed, Negroids would commit more murders and rapes than Caucasoids or Mongoloids. This is because, on the spectrum of reproductive strategies, Caucasoids and Mongoloids tend more than Negroids towards 'low fertility, high investment parenting, slow maturation and high intelligence and competitive ability'.[41]

---

41   Rushton and Whitney 2002, p. 501.

At this point in Rushton and Whitney's study, any left liberal worth their 'Celebrate Diversity' bumper sticker will be crying out: 'But what about social determination? Isn't it a fact that the sad history of race in America and ongoing prejudice can account for the higher crime rate among blacks and that there is no need to look for biological explanations?' Well, as noted before, contemporary sociobiology has acknowledged the validity of these types of criticisms and has attempted to take them into account. Thus, in order to explain the relevant causal variables, Rushton and Whitney appeal to international crime registries and look at victims' reports rather than police data. The former appeal promises to cancel out variability in national traditions and the latter accounts for the tendency of police to under- or over-report certain crimes when they are committed by different races. As for the hypothesis that discrimination might totally explain differences in crime rates, the study notes that rates of crime in homogeneous populations where racism is not a problem accord with the trends in mixed populations. 'Aha!' the committed progressive sociologist counters, there is yet another variable for which you have not accounted and that is the 'alternative distributional model in which behavior among populations is explained by overlapping of populations and subtle but deep-rooted cultural affinities such as values and family structure'.[42] Again, though, Rushton and Whitney appeal to international data, pointing out that the percentage of crimes committed by members of specific races has remained relatively constant throughout the whole world and, further, that this sample includes both indigenous peoples with strong cultural traditions, new immigrants who one would expect to be shedding old traditions and embracing new ones, and places like the United States where different races have a long history of shared traditions and associations.[43]

So, is Rushton's and Whitney's conclusion that 'some of the causes of race differences must be sought beyond the local conditions of particular countries or even groups of countries' correct?[44] Has the possibility that ideology influenced this conclusion been expunged? Applying Althusser's critical method, it can be suggested that it has not. Though there is international crime data to suggest that 'Negroids' commit more crimes than 'Caucasoids' and 'Caucasoids' more than 'Mongoloids', this is not sufficient to draw the inference that genetic difference is the relevant variable explaining this phenomenon. In fact, when we appeal to other sciences for help in distinguishing that which in this study is ideological and that which is not, we find that biology and sociology

---

42   Rushton and Whitney 2002, p. 503.
43   Rushton and Whitney 2002, pp. 504–6.
44   Rushton and Whitney 2002, p. 509.

are for the most part in agreement that, at least insofar as it accords with folk notions, race accords with no descriptive category for population at the level of genotype.[45] If race has a meaning, it appears that this is in culture and that it has to do with the way in which racial signifiers are interpreted and used. How then do Rushton and Whitney account for the fact that racial categories are (a) themselves the product of social and historical forces and (b) insufficient to differentiate humans into distinct biological groups? Simply put, they do not and they cannot unless they want to argue the rather absurd position that the proclivity to commit crime is itself the trait that differentiates races. Put succinctly, in the case of Rushton and Whitney, the ideological basis of 'Racial Science', undermines the science of sociobiology.

Appealing to other sciences for clarification, it is apparent that even though lip service is given in the study to the influences of culture, history, and economy on crime rates, none of the particular 'social conditions of existence' faced by those studied is genuinely incorporated. Particular economic situations, for instance, are explained away by the argument that increases in a country's GDP do not necessarily lead to decreases in crime. However, it would seem to most developmental economists that the particulars of a country's development are extremely relevant here. Why, for instance, do crime rates rise with GDP in most African states while they fall in more economically developed nations? More than one economist has noted the relation between oil wealth, government corruption, and impoverishment in African countries such as Somalia and Nigeria.[46] Would it not then be worth investigating whether economic disparity and corruption can account for the crime rates in Africa? Moving from the science of economy to those of history and sociology, we see that neither of these two disciplines and their conclusions have been sufficiently considered by the study. It is the case that murder rates among blacks in the Chicago are higher than those for the city's general population and that murder rates in Johannesburg follow the same pattern. However, no one cognisant of the history and present socioeconomic makeup of each city would cite the same list of factors as being those that contributed to this rate. Isn't it worth considering, then, whether particular material factors in local situations can explain all of the differences between races and yet point to no common 'racial' variable?

All of this is not to dismiss every argument that would seek to link genetic makeup to behavioural traits or to disagree in principle with the conclusion

---

45   Hochman 2016; 2019; Montagu and F 1941; Pigliucci 2013; Pigliucci and Kaplan 2003.
46   Gary and Karl 2003, chapter 2.

that such traits might be shared among distinguishable human populations. Such an argument against genetic determinism has been routinely voiced by sociology and is itself indicative of that discipline's ideological bias. If it is indeed the case that certain breeding populations have certain social and physical tendencies, then this may be socially useful knowledge and it might be established by further inquiry. However, before behaviours are linked with traits and traits with groups, we would do well to investigate whether or not other particular historical and social patterns of activity might account for the phenomena observed. Further, we should be suspicious of those conclusions that seem to echo or reinforce an ideological position. We should be especially suspicious of those, like Rushton and Whitney's, whose research has been funded by racist institutions.[47] Undoubtedly, the supposition that, due to their genetic makeup, blacks 'tend to devote resources to producing greater numbers of children, invest less heavily in them, and provide less parental care' is a little too close to modern racist notions for comfort.[48]

Philosophy, by pointing out both this affinity and reasons why these conclusions should not be readily accepted, might perhaps make science reconsider its assumptions. In addition, by modifying the way in which scientific knowledge is received by the wider social sphere, it may limit the ways in which scientific knowledge is used to justify claims about race that are merely ideological. This should lead to better science. In that scientific knowledge is also useful in the formulation of solutions to human problems, such critique may also lead to better political practices. It is for these reasons that Marxist philosophers should be in the business of making distinctions between ideological and scientific knowledge. Such distinctions, however, should result from the critical analysis and empirical investigation of particular scientific conclusions as these are judged in relation to both the cultural conditions that motivate and frame these hypotheses and in relation to the material evidence justifying a particular set of conclusions.

47   Tucker 2003.
48   Rushton and Whitney 2002, p. 501.

CHAPTER 7

Manipulation of Consent and Deliberative Democracy

For many in the social sciences, the 2004 US presidential and congressional elections became oft-cited examples of the limits of procedural democracy.[1] Pulling on public opinion from before the election as well as other data, political scientists, sociologists, social psychologists, and specialists in communication sought to explain the results of these elections – which guaranteed a continuation of the Iraq War – in terms of elites framing the political discourse; emotional, media, and rhetorical manipulation; appeal to ideology; dissemination of misinformation; group polarisation, and existential triggers.[2] That each of these causal factors bypasses rational and public deliberation, that none results from inquiry into the truthfulness of the political opinions regarding the war and its justifications, and the subsequent public opinion data showing that the public changed its opinion on both the prosecution of the war and on the legitimacy of its rationale, may signal that there are terminal problems with American democracy.[3] If anything, the aftermath of the 2006 congressional elections when Democratic and antiwar majorities were elected to both houses and Iraq policy failed to change may be seen as confirmation of this judgment that democracy conceived and practised as the aggregation of preferences for representative candidates is deeply flawed. That in all subsequent presidential election cycles these same factors have similarly been used to explain elector turn-out and voter choice and that each of these issues is exacerbated by the insatiable growth of social media would indicate ongoing and deep problems with procedural democracy in the United States.[4]

---

1 The author wishes to thank Cynthia Willett and to Peter Breiner for their astute comments.
2 Abramson et al. 2007; Arsenault and Castells 2006; Glazier and Boydstun 2012; Hayes and Guardino 2010; Hillygus and Shields 2005; Holbert 2004; Iyengar 2005; Karol and Miguel 2007; Lanning 2005; Vultee 2010; Zurbriggen 2005.
3 In a Quinnipiac University 2008 poll that asked the question 'Do you think going to war with Iraq was the right thing for the United States to do or the wrong thing?' 62 percent of respondents said that they now think the action was 'wrong.'
4 Depetris-Chauvin 2015; Entman 2010; Gershberg 2017; Giardina 2010; Iyengar 2005; Jost 2017; Major, Blodorn, and Major Blascovich 2018; Persily 2017; Woolley and Guilbeault 2017; Weeks and Garrett 2014; Wingfield and Feagin 2009.

While the social scientists cited above do not usually go so far in their analysis, since the 1980s, political philosophers have consistently argued that it is precisely these types of deficiencies that can be remedied by the adoption of deliberative democratic norms and procedures. Being in agreement with the majority of theorists who argue that the adoption of deliberative norms for political decision making will make for more democratic outcomes, this article will examine the practical obstacles that deliberative democracy may not be able to overcome. Though it does not conclude that deliberative democracy is, because of these obstacles, untenable, impracticable, or unworthy of pursuit, this chapter does claim that one of the *factors* identified by social scientists and philosophers as compromising the legitimacy and practical value of political judgment is ineliminable. This hindrance is ideology. Perhaps unexpectedly, given that this is a book of Marxist political theory, the conclusion is not drawn from this observation that deliberative democracy is fatally compromised and that it reflects bourgeois notions of freedom and politics. Instead, departing from the Althusserian understanding of ideological practices and their relation to politics, it is claimed that ideology is both a hindrance to deliberative democracy as well as its prerequisite. Therefore, this paper concludes, we should not strive for ideologies' elimination from the deliberative space but, rather, we should look for ways to begin with diverse ideologies and to arrive at public knowledge of public goods.

1   Deliberation from Procedural to Feasible

Given the tendency of electoral, representative democracy to produce political outcomes that neither reflect the public's will nor its idea of the good, proponents of deliberative democracy have championed deliberation as that practice by which the public can come to feel responsible for its constitution and laws. Departing from Rousseau's insight that deliberation is the necessary process that facilitates this formation, most theorists of deliberative democracy theory have taken as their project the challenge of ensuring the legitimacy of the decisions reached by deliberation, where 'legitimacy' is understood as the production of a decision that everyone can accept.[5] This emphasis on ensuring the legitimacy of political decisions has led to a focus on the normative and procedural aspects of deliberation. Driven by these concerns and inspired mostly by the work of Rawls and Habermas, political theorists have attempted (a) to

---

5   Bohman 1998, p. 402; Rousseau, Cress, and Gay 1987, pp. 149, 204.

define the pure procedural structure that best allows such consensus formation, (b) to delimit the decisions that can be the subject of political deliberation, and (c) to define the type of individual that can participate in deliberation.
Though there is disagreement among theorists about the specific content of
each criterion for effective and fair deliberation as well as about their respective
necessity, a rough consensus has developed about what deliberation requires.
These provisos include, first, an institutional space or arrangement that guarantees neutrality and protects against the manipulation of the discussion and of
the discussants. Second, effective and fair deliberation needs the participation
of individuals who (a) are aware of the relevant features of the political world,
(b) can reason about political ends, and (c) can look past their own immediate political preferences to rationally and freely choose the general good. Put
succinctly, democratic deliberation requires a noncoercive space and free discussion between autonomous, informed, and rational individuals.

Even as the consensus detailed above was in the process of developing,
political philosophers and theorists began to think about how to apply these
insights so as to reform democratic practice. Comparing existing institutions
and citizens to the deliberative democratic ideal, it was obvious that one or
both were insufficient to guarantee fair and good deliberation. Thus was born
the discussion of deliberative democracy's feasibility, which asked questions
such as whether such reform is possible, how much reform is needed, and
what specific reforms are necessary for deliberative democracy to come into
being.[6] Within the literature that judges deliberative democracy to indeed be
feasible, there is a bit of a split. While some theorists such as Joshua Cohen
and Jürgen Habermas focus on the need to create noncoercive spaces in order
to allow already sufficiently autonomous, informed, and rational individuals
to deliberate on the public good, others suggest not only that our existing forums are insufficient for democratic deliberation but that existing citizens are
insufficiently autonomous, informed, and rational to deliberate about the public good. Though the philosophical literature that makes the latter suggestion
only sometimes pulls on this evidence to make its point, in recent years there
has been a growing body of research in the social sciences that reinforces these
speculative conclusions about the ability of citizens to make informed, free,
and rational decisions.

Drawing on this literature as well as on the insights offered by participants
in the feasibility discussion, this chapter catalogues the practices, institutions,
and psychological proclivities that have been cited as obstacles to the realisa-

---

6   Bohman 1998, p. 401.

tion of a deliberative democratic politics. After this survey, it separates those obstacles that are remediable from those that are not. Because most of the irremediable obstacles are those that compromise the rationality, autonomy, and knowledge of citizens, this separation will have the effect of forcing us to rethink the promise of deliberative democracy as well as the means for its instantiation.

2   Obstacles to Deliberation

The first obstacle has to do with institutions. Because the legitimacy of a democratic decision rests, for deliberativists, on it being the result of a fair procedure, one in which individuals reason and decide without constraints about the public good, an institutional space or arrangement that guarantees neutrality and protects against the manipulation of the discussion and of the discussants is a necessity. This is the case because deliberations are fair only if each of the participants has an equal ability to reason about and then argue for his or her idea of the good. However, as Iris Marion Young and others have pointed out, there are many persons who are ill-equipped to provide reasons in a public forum for their idea of the good. For these people, any institutional structure that sets this type of discourse to be the norm is a nonneutral space in the sense that it privileges those who can argue in rational terms for their idea of the good.[7]

In addition to this institutional bias, there is also the problem of preference change (or decision making) resulting not from reasoned deliberation about the good for oneself and others but from the persuasive effects of fellow deliberators. This result may come about from a fellow deliberator's elite status, from a claim to unique knowledge, or from a claim about expertise in some area of public life. It also may come about simply because some deliberator or deliberators have developed superior rhetorical skills. Contrary to earlier studies, which hypothesised that a subject's perceived social status and expertise have little influence on public opinion, there is a growing body of evidence that suggests that this effect is far from negligible.[8] For instance, studies of the effect of rhetorical tropes used by the Bush administration to encourage support for the Second Gulf War have shown public opinion to be malleable by such devices.[9] Given these effects, a space that protects against the manipulation of the discussion and of the discussants would be one that prohibits claims to authority,

---

7 Sanders 1997; Young 1996.
8 Shapiro 1998.
9 Kellner 2007; Stuckey and Ritter 2007.

expertise, or superior knowledge as well as the display of rhetorical skill. For fair procedures, this may be necessary, and, indeed, some have argued that rhetoric be banned from the deliberative space.[10] It is easy to see why we might also wish to decrease the influence of elites in any deliberative process. However, for a deliberation that wishes to arrive not only at fair but also at good results, the banning of experts and their expertise may prove undesirable. This problem and its solution will be discussed below.

Institutional prejudice and suasion by rhetoric or claimed superiority of judgment during the course of deliberation are not, however, the only distortions that deliberative practice has to worry about. In addition, there is the concern about the manipulation of opinion that has always already taken place before formal deliberations about the public good are inaugurated. The persuasive effects of authority, expertise, and rhetoric mentioned above can achieve this manipulation. Without the constraints of an institutional space designed to ensure fair deliberation, these effects may be amplified by the media, by public sentiment, and by group polarisation.[11] With this amplification, the number of options entertained in deliberation about what is good for the public is limited, and premature consensuses can be formed. To give an example of this narrowing which is again related to our original example, the major news media in the United States accepted and amplified the 'War on Terror' rhetoric of the Bush administration and used it as a 'shorthand device to summarize a wide range of complex issues and events'.[12] Synthesising and summarising the results of similar empirical studies on the impact of media coverage on political thought, Richard D. Anderson has concluded that 'the media's impact on the American citizen appears to be baleful for democratic deliberation. Media coverage of elections encourages citizens to think about ... personalities, not about issues, ... to focus on their feelings of intimacy with the candidate, not on reasoned considerations ... [and to] ... shift people's attention from issues they would otherwise consider important to the issues they see on the screen'.[13]

Thus far, this discussion has focused on those obstacles to deliberative democracy that hinder a citizen's ability to reason well and to decide fairly about political ends. It has not yet focused on those obstacles that, when deliberation is put into practice, compromise individual autonomy. By virtue of bypassing their reason entirely, these sorts of obstacles prevent citizens from

---

10   Dryzek 2002, p. 67.
11   Joslyn 1997; Talisse 2003, p. 109.
12   Lipschultz 2007.
13   Richard D. Anderson 1998, p. 481.

being 'authors as well as subjects of the law'.[14] There have been not a few social scientific studies on this subject, with some seeking specifically to explain how Bush maintained political support through the 2004 elections despite major domestic and foreign problems as well as turmoil internal to his administration. Based on experiments that showed a correlation between awareness of one's own mortality and support for charismatic and conservative leaders, one group of social psychologists hypothesised that Bush benefited from the frequent recollections of the terror of 9/11 made by candidates and by the media during the run-up to the election. When this specific hypothesis was tested, the test showed a correlation between reminders of mortality and of 9/11 and increased support for George W. Bush (while the opposite correlation was revealed for John Kerry).[15] Using different methodologies, recent studies in sociology and political science have also suggested that the emotions of fear and shame played a large part in shaping political conduct since 9/11.[16] If such correlations are confirmed, then there is more and more reason to suspect that passion and not reason plays a deciding factor in choices about the public good.

Another factor that compromises autonomy is ideology. This compromise is evident if one understands ideology as it has been classically formulated: that is, as the mystified consciousness of one's self, social relations, and world which is both produced by but also masks the real, 'material life process' of human beings.[17] Even if we reject the idea that there is a 'true consciousness' that can be found by social scientific research, critique, or revolutionary activity and, with Althusser, reformulate ideology as that necessary set of beliefs held by groups of individuals whose effect is to guarantee the reproduction of a given set of socioeconomic relations, there is still in this minimal definition a recognition of a compromise of autonomy.[18] This is true even if we go with the extremely thin definition offered by Adam Przeworski, who holds that to recognise ideology one does not need to attribute any economic causality for it but simply to recognise the empirical fact that 'individual beliefs are endogenous with regard to the distribution of income, [and] with regard to political institutions'.[19] This is the case because one of the features of ideology is that certain ends and certain reasons seem intuitively reasonable or unreasonable when

14   Cooke 2000, pp. 955–6.
15   Landau et al. 2004. Like many other findings in social psychology, this result has failed replication studies: Klein et al 2019.
16   Burkitt 2005; Lanning 2005.
17   Marx and Engels 1975, pp. 35–6.
18   Althusser 1972a, pp. 132–3; 1995d, p. 274.
19   Przeworski 1998, p. 155.

presented to a subject operating from within a specific ideology. In that they depend on the subject's own reason, decisions made on the basis of ideology are, in a certain sense, autonomous. However, the fact that this reason and the understanding of the world that this reason works with may serve ends other than that of the subject's or the public's good reflects, fundamentally, a compromise of autonomy. Therefore, though deliberations might seem to engage the faculty of reason and decisions might appear to the subject as freely made, what seems reasonable to a particular subject is always already somewhat or largely predetermined.

Though for the last few decades the psychological literature has, like the Anglo-American philosophical literature, been sceptical of the position that people are inclined by ideology rather than by self-interest, there have been a number of recent studies that support the points made above about ideology and its effect on reason.[20] This is the case even if the causal explanation for its existence is psychological rather than socioeconomic (the two explanations are not incompatible). For instance, a study that appeared in the *American Psychologist* shows that voters' self-identified traits and values are decisive in political choice, while another from *Social Psychology* registers a correlation between groups differentiated by their shared values and these groups' 'support for pro- and anti-war action'.[21] Most impressively, a series of studies conducted by John T. Jost and others have suggested that distinct sets of ideological belief systems can be empirically differentiated, that these belief systems are associated not only with political orientation but also with lifestyle and personality differences, and, finally, that 'people are motivated to engage in "system justification" – defined as the tendency to defend, bolster, and rationalise the societal status quo – even when social change would be preferable from the standpoint of self-interest'.[22]

The last obstacle to the practical success of deliberative democracy is that of the need for citizens to be informed about their world in order to make decisions about it. Because he is only concerned with establishing the basic principles of justice, in his now-classical formulation of the ideal deliberative space John Rawls specifies that all that is required for citizens to reason in public about the good is knowledge about the general features of the political world: that some people are rich and others are poor, some good and others bad, that some external goods are necessary for life and more goods make life

---

20   Jost 2006.
21   Bliuc et al. 2007; Caprara and Zimbardo 2004.
22   Jost, Nosek, and Gosling 2008; Jost 2006.

better, and so on.[23] However, when it comes to practical questions regarding what to do about a contemporary social problem, good deliberation seems to demand knowledge of the biological, psychological, social, economic, political, and juridical relations relevant to the question at hand. As Talisse summarises this problem of public ignorance, 'If [citizens] prove unable to understand the basic political facts from which inferences are to be drawn, they are unfit for deliberative democracy'.[24] In this instance, 'unfit' does not necessarily mean that these citizens are unable to deliberate. Rather, because they cannot gain the relevant information to make a rational and informed decision or because they do not care enough to gain it, such people are much more likely to arrive at conclusions that are motivated by appeal to emotions or that are due to suasion by elites or to merely fall back on ideological beliefs.[25]

3   Overcoming Obstacles

With all these obstacles to the practical implementation of deliberative democracy, the chance of its practical success looks bleak. However, along with noting the obstacles to deliberative democracy, many feasibility theorists have attempted to formulate a deliberative democracy that recognises and deals with these impediments. At this point in the debate, plausible solutions have already been provided for most of the hurdles just listed. Taking the problem of the necessity of a neutral space for discussion first, John Dryzek's argument that what is required for deliberation is not necessarily a neutral space but merely a pluralistic space that forbids coercive discourse and which permits and facilitates communication among a variety of discursive strategies, while ceding discursive privilege to none, seems about right. In the forums that he envisions, rational arguments would have to compete with many other forms of discourse. For instance, reasoned arguments would have to contend with or ally against those telling stories about their experience, issuing rhetorical pleas, or seeking solidarity through greeting and recognition.[26] By prohibiting any form of discourse from achieving hegemony and by establishing a space in which different modes of discourse compete on equal terms to influence others' preferences, the requirement of institutional neutrality for deliberation can be roughly met.

---

23   Rawls 1999, p. 119.
24   Talisse 2005, p. 456.
25   Posner 2005, p. 151; Somin 1998.
26   Dryzek 2002, pp. 68–80.

Dealing with the fact that manipulation of opinion has always already taken place prior to deliberation and that, to some extent, it will always be a factor during deliberations is, however, trickier than the problem of the necessity of a neutral space. It is, however, mostly tractable. To second what Misak, Bohman, and Talisse have argued and to reassert a portion of the argument that this book makes in Chapter 4, the problem that the manipulation of opinion presents to democracy can be dealt with by reframing deliberation as a process of public inquiry.[27] Instead of envisioning the deliberative process as one where subjects make use of their existing knowledge in order to convince others that their idea of the good should be adopted, deliberation conceived as a process of public inquiry views deliberation as a process by which a plurality of investigators – using plural methods – inquire into various domains of human conduct.[28] Rather than being the *substance* of the deliberation, individual beliefs here become *subject* to investigation. The effects of elite opinion, rhetoric, and media bias can thereby be mitigated. This is the case because, in the process of inquiry and in the discussion of its results, these beliefs can be challenged, confirmed, disconfirmed, and altered by the practical reasoning of others about the world. If they are discovered to be unfounded, too narrow, or uninformed, they can then be rejected or modified.

These practical reasons and this practical reasoning may come not only from those that are directly affected by the problem at hand or by its solution (and thus have some relevant insight) but also by those who, in their capacity as social scientists, have investigated social and economic phenomena relevant to understanding the problem and proposing possible solutions. To give one example, if citizens of an economically depressed region believe that enticing large corporations to locate or remain in their area will create jobs, stability, and prosperity, then data from economists showing that, in general, such public subsidies have not brought about these results may encourage the public to reconsider its views.[29] This is not to say that social scientists will have the last word. To continue with this example, it may be the case that citizens retain local knowledge that suggests that a particular industry will have a better chance for success in this region than in others. In cases where local experience and knowledge conflict with those of the expert, it is conceivable and desirable that, during the course of the public inquiry, this experience comes to inform and possibly correct the understanding of the expert.[30] At the end of this process,

---

27   Bohman 1998; Misak 2004; Talisse 2005.
28   Bohman 1999b, p. 472.
29   Buss 1999.
30   Bohman 2008, p. 103.

a collective and informed conclusion about the public good and what is to be done to reach it can be achieved.

In this understanding of deliberation as collective inquiry, the conclusions that any deliberation reaches are understood to be hypothetical. If it is a good solution, then the political course of action decided upon will bring about the result that the deliberators identified as desirable. If these means do not bring about the desired end, then the decision was not good and another inquiry is needed. Treating deliberation as inquiry thereby solves not only the problem of manipulation but also the epistemological problem mentioned near the beginning of the chapter that plagues purely procedural deliberative democracy. With the pragmatic criterion for verification just outlined, there is now an independent standard by which to gauge whether or not reasons are good or bad, namely, whether they allow for the realisation of the goal that a specific deliberation decided upon.

Another benefit of deliberative democracy reconceived as a process of public inquiry is that it deals with the problem of public ignorance. In every version of deliberation – including the purely procedural – deliberation is understood to be transformative inasmuch as it results in a 'change of preferences on the bases of which people decide how to act' collectively.[31] However, when it is conceived of as a process of collective inquiry, the effect of deliberation is understood to be transformative not only of preferences but also of beliefs about the world and about what the good is. In this process, ignorance is overcome as existing beliefs are submitted to the critical examination that comes about when these attitudes are challenged in a public forum by different beliefs and values and by empirical data. In short, the transformation that deliberation as public inquiry brings about is not only political but also educational.

4   Insurmountable Obstacles?

Despite the promise that deliberation reconceived as pluralistic public inquiry holds to overcome the practical hurdles to successful and fair democratic deliberation, it is hard to see how this process can correct for and overcome those factors that compromise individual autonomy by virtue of their bypassing reason entirely. This is because ideology and emotional appeals are somewhat immune to the effects of corrective reason and contrary evidence. In cases like those where representations of terror or death directly affect the emotions and

---

31   Przeworski 1998, p. 140.

motivate specific types of reactions, perhaps the best that we can do is to adopt rules like those suggested above about coercion that require us to be suspicious of rhetoric that involves known or suspected triggers and to treat this form of discourse differently than we do other forms of speech.

As for correcting for ideology, a similar proposal might be made. However, as ideology is constructive of our basic or background beliefs about the world and is more subtle in its effects than propaganda (which mainly appeals to the emotions), any rule or rules could only be proposed after extensive study of the ways in which specific ideologies function to make certain judgments about the world seem reasonable and others not. A small portion of the work required to do this in the social practice of science is outlined in Chapter 6, a field which is particularly amenable to self-correction. In normatively structured social relations other than science, the excision is more difficult. If we figure out how particular ideologies inform certain classes of people in their everyday lives, we might be able to establish rules that correct for, say, the tendency of a certain class to believe that inequality is natural. However, another difficulty soon arises: it is impossible to prove that the diagnosis of an ideology (which then leads to the formulation of such a rule) is not itself the product of ideological thinking. This is because any diagnosis of a particular group's ideology is always going to be made by a subject (or subjects) embedded in a particular ideology. As Althusser argues, there is no extra-ideological or universal perspective from which to identify and correct procedurally for ideologies.[32] For instance, in the example given above, only a subject whose perspective has been produced such that he or she believes that political inequality is not natural would initiate a research project into why another group believes that it is so.

Even with the conclusion that there is a category of obstacles to successful deliberation that are somewhat or even totally ineliminable, there is little doubt that deliberative democracy reconceived as pluralistic public inquiry presents a practicable mode of political association superior to our existing elective democracy in terms of procedural fairness, epistemic results, the republican cultivation of citizens, and the formation of a general political will. Though it may never produce outcomes as fair as those hypothesised in theories of pure procedural deliberative democracy, it does present itself as capable of producing better much outcomes than our current system. Specifically, it will be superior in the sense that what results from public inquiry is not merely a decision upon which everyone can agree but also the generation of a 'community' in the sense John Dewey uses the word in *The Public and Its Problems*:

---

32   Althusser 2014a, p. 265; Amariglio 1987, p. 193; Althusser 2014a, pp. 174–6.

that is, a body politic who communicates sufficiently about the relations that constitute it such that it is able to realise the goods it identifies as desirable.[33]

4.1   Ideology as Insurmountable

This is all good news, of course, but what do we do with that obstacle to deliberative democracy, ideology, that seems so hard to compensate for or eliminate? One of the first things that we might do with ideology is to engage in the critique not of existing ideologies but of the concept of ideology itself. Understood as false consciousness which hides real social and economic relations, ideology obviously compromises any deliberative effort in that the political ends that present themselves to a citizen as public goods may, in fact, only be good for a certain group of people. However, and as the point made above about the difficulty of finding an extra-ideological position suggests, the definition of ideology as false has proven to be highly problematic.[34] If we abandon the idea of ideology as false consciousness, though, and instead understand ideology with Althusser as a 'lived and believed reality', which constitutes subjects as subjects and whose effect is the reproduction of definite socioeconomic relations between particular groups, then ideology might not be the obstacle to effective deliberation that it at first appears.[35] Under this revised definition, ideology always exists and cannot be overcome. However, it exists only in the specific beliefs held by individuals, beliefs produced through each person's interactions with the world and with each other in specific class formations.[36]

Even though these beliefs make themselves known only through the actions of individuals, they are for the most part not singular but particular. This is because most human activities are associative or are structured by our associations. Our shared interactions, institutions, practices, and conflicts tend to produce groups that conceive of the world in similar ways (hence the particularity). These conceptions are all evaluative, and each valuation has its effect on a specific group's practices. Because of this, parts of the world and certain persons are seen as foundational, important, valued, useful, or reasonable to a certain group while other parts and persons are left out, devalued, or seen as useless and unreasonable. Often one group's conceptions of the world (and the practices derivative of those beliefs) are opposed by other groups who have had

---

33   Dewey 1927, p. 208.
34   So much so that, since Gramsci, many serious Marxian thinkers on the subject have abandoned this conception of ideology. See Rehmann 2007, pp. 219–25; Rosen 2013.
35   Althusser 2014a, 260–61; Rehmann 2007, p. 224.
36   Althusser 2014a, pp. 253–4.

different associative experiences and therefore conceive of the world and work in the world differently. Chapter 5 further develops this phenomenon insofar as it results in class formation and class struggle.

If we accept this conception of ideology as those necessary sets of beliefs held by definite groups of individuals whose cumulative effect is to guarantee the reproduction of certain socioeconomic relations, then we might perhaps be moved to see ideology not as an obstacle to deliberative democratic practice but as its necessary precondition. As noted above, deliberative democracy conceived as public inquiry depends on a plurality of subjects or groups, each with a different perspective on the way in which the world works and about how to realise the good. It needs these perspectives if it is to subject these ideas to scrutiny and to critique in order to arrive at a better understanding of what the real public good is and how to realise it. To give two examples, that certain participants in deliberation about economic policy reflexively balk when they are told that capital gains relief for the wealthiest one percent of Americans will eventually benefit the quality of life for all Americans is a necessary starting point for effective deliberation about distribution. It is also a good thing that another group claims that less regulation for medical device makers and pharmaceutical companies will lead to better public health. As both claims are liable to be contested by groups with opposing ideologies, each provides a point at which collective inquiry can begin. Conflicting ideologies can thus be understood as a prerequisite for deliberation.

That ideology is a prerequisite for deliberative democracy may also be true in another sense. Surveying the literature of deliberative democracy, it is obvious that this project is – even in its most abstract and speculative form – a radically egalitarian one. At base, deliberative democracy is always presented as a more legitimate form of democracy because it corrects for the distortions that structural inequalities, uneven education advantages, entrenched bureaucracy, representative democracy, economic and media interests, and a public distracted from or disinterested in politics introduce into the expression of the democratic will. Those that benefit from these distortions are wont not to notice them or not to believe that they present a problem for democracy. This not noticing the contradiction between their democratic ideal and actual democratic practice is ideology at work. However, there is also another group of people who recognize these failings as pernicious and desire to ameliorate them. This latter ideology is expressed at the practical level by those who attempt to make political institutions fairer and more responsive to the demos and who also try to make the demos more active in political institutions. It is expressed at the theoretical level by those who attempt to convince others that deliberation is desirable, feasible, and necessary.

CHAPTER 8

Cosmopolitanism and Class Erasure

> ... we are confronted with a phenomenon that is international in
> scope, and with a diffuse ideology, which, though it has not yet been
> precisely defined, is capable of assuming a certain organisational
> form ... One senses, in these attempts, a mentality in search of itself,
> ... an ideology seeking to define itself, entrench itself, and also fur-
> nish itself with means of action. If this mentality is international,
> and in the process of taking institutional form, then a new 'Inter-
> national' is in the making. There is perhaps something to be gained
> from trying to discover what it conceals.[1]
>
> LOUIS ALTHUSSER, 'The International of Decent Feelings' (1946)

⁝

Fifteen years before he renewed philosophical Marxism with his re-readings of
Marx and Lenin, Louis Althusser authored a polemic titled 'The International
of Decent Feelings' (1946). The student philosopher who wrote this piece had
yet to renounce his Christianity and was heavily influenced by Catholic theology as well as by Hegelian interpretations of Marx. Though these interests do
not distinguish him from many of his philosophical peers who were looking to
Hegel to make Marxism more philosophically sophisticated or to reconcile it
with progressive theology, the scope of his critique of post-war Internationalism is startlingly original.

   In 'The International of Decent Feelings', Althusser argues that the post-
World War II claim made by Existentialists, Socialists, and progressive Christi-
ans that – after the death camps and under the threat of mass annihilation from
the Atom Bomb – we have all become 'proletarians of the human condition'
is a fallacious one and, further, that its adoption has pernicious political consequences. Against the contention of Malraux, Mauriac, Jaspers, Camus, and
other public intellectuals that fear of death is what we now all experience and
that this sentiment may form the basis for universal solidarity and universal

---

1 Althusser 1997a, pp. 22–3.

peace, Althusser points to the existence of a real, existing, proletariat. These persons are a class distinguishable from 'humanity as a whole'. Real social antagonisms exist for them and they are mostly aware that their interests are not those of capitalist states. Idealist and universalising myths of fear, Althusser argues, have the 'effect of tearing these [people] from the very reality of their existence, from their daily political and social struggles'.[2]

It is the contention of this chapter that the principal arguments for cosmopolitanism advanced by philosophers after the end of the Cold War and whose major impetuses have been post-Cold War political realignments, globalisation, resurgent nationalist and ethnic struggle, environmental crises, and the rise of global terrorism are analogous to those of certain post-World II French philosophers and their calls for universal solidarity in the face of atomic destruction. The two are comparable in their universalising tendencies and in their shared intention to provide moral and political order to a world historical situation that has undergone rapid change and where political and moral hegemony is ambiguous. Though the universalising tendency of fear is not always a constant (the sentiment of common suffering or the judgment of universal justice sometimes supplementing it, sometimes taking its place), this unhappy affect still plays a role in these arguments. Further, the cosmopolitan appeal to common ideals, to what we owe or can learn from each other, to our universal humanity, or to our deep attachments to others, often but not necessarily results in the forgetting of class differences and in the paving over of particular and existing class struggles. It does so by emphasising the importance of individual or government initiative in accord with a cosmopolitan normative framework.[3] Stopping at duty, it also erases the evidence of the ideological production of these universal ideals insofar as they can be understood as part of the class struggle. This is true of the moral theory of cosmopolitanism, as well as the political theory that follows from it, and these effects can also be seen in cultural cosmopolitanism.

Clearly, Althusser is not a common reference point for Appiah, Bohman, Held, Nussbaum, McKinnon, or other prominent theorists of cosmopolitanism. However, in the second half of the twentieth century, he was a perspicacious critic of the position that human values are universal or universalizable. In addition, Althusser developed a philosophical method by which the origin of a call for universal values could be identified and the effects of these values' adoption understood.[4] Though not a participant in last the few decades'

---

2 Althusser 1997a, p. 31.
3 Tsoneva 2016, p. 179.
4 Resch 1992, pp. 173–9.

debates on ethical and political cosmopolitanism, the critical framework that Althusser's developed provide us with insights into the origin and effects of contemporary theories that rely on notions of universal human values or characteristics.[5]

In order to make the point that cold war internationalism and contemporary cosmopolitanism are analogous in their universalising tendency and in their shared intention to provide moral and political order to a world historical situation that has undergone rapid change, the first section of this paper outlines Althusser's argument against a 'cosmopolitanism of fear'. The second section updates this argument by generalising it and by rendering it consistent with Althusser's mature understanding of 'humanity' and with the role that class struggle and the working class in particular play in human history. The critical framework that this updated argument provides will then be applied to two variants of cosmopolitan value theory: moral and cultural, as these two strands are represented in the works of Martha Nussbaum and Kwame Anthony Appiah. With this accomplished, this chapter concludes with the argument that both moral and cultural cosmopolitans fail to sufficiently recognise the global class struggles that are the responses of the masses to globalisation and to the cosmopolitanism institutions and practices that provide it with its juridical and political apparatuses. Further, it contends that this forgetting makes the ethical and political projects which are to follow from these normative theories less achievable.

1   Against a 'Cosmopolitanism of Fear'

The International of Decent Feelings, Althusser explains, is a growing but still somewhat inchoate political movement that has formed in response to the horrors of the war and through a vision of a future for humanity that now includes the immanent possibility of such horrors as show trials, death camps, and atomic bombs.[6] This movement is based on the recognition that 'humanity is threatened', that we are all equal under this fear, and that we have therefore become 'a proletariat of terror'.[7] The leaders of this movement, Camus, Koestler, Mauriac, Malraux, and Jaspers, are a diverse group of individuals – novelists, Christian theologians, journalists, politicians, and philosophers – and they come from many sides of the political spectrum. These men find themselves

---

5   Though his influence can be seen in É. Balibar 2018.
6   Althusser 1997a, p. 22.
7   Althusser 1997a, p. 23.

united rhetorically, sentimentally, and politically by a shared consciousness of man's destiny. This knowledge motivates them to make speeches and films, to write plays and novels, to analyse the human condition in academic journals, and to begin the organisation of international moral campaigns for peace and for human rights. They do these things because they abhor the 'peace' and the possibilities for violent and horrible ends with which the end of the war has left them. For these diverse thinkers, Althusser observes, it is the 'growing awareness that humanity is threatened' that motivates the "Internation" of humane protest' for which they call.[8]

A protest movement, yes, but also only a cosmopolitanism of good sentiments. It remains merely this, argues Althusser, because the unity that humans are encouraged to see themselves under and to act from – that of fear of our fate – is a psychological one. As he writes, '[T]his is a *de facto* equality, which governs all our acts in which we live and move ...'[9] The universal consciousness of this equality is that which motivates a good conscience and good political action: if we are all united by fears of the end of humanity then, conscientiously, we should all engage in a struggle to regain and secure our common humanity.

However, as Althusser points out, this is not a struggle for a new order – this is too risky – but for the preservation and securing of what we have. The war has taught us that we are mortal, that we all can die and that experiments with new social forms can lead to horrible consequences. For this movement, '[t]here can no longer be any question of inventing new customs; what is at stake for us today is maintaining the life which ... is the only one we have ...' Further, there is no need to invent new ways of living because the phenomenon is psychological; all that we have to do is 'convert the content of our fear into the tranquility of our soul'.[10] That is, according to those who champion this new International, all that we need do is to imagine the possibility of our non-existence and we will be motivated to do those things that will ensure the continuity of ourselves as human beings.

The motivation for these sentiments, the fact that all of us will cease to exist at some point is, as Althusser points out, a banality and no more defines us than does the fact that it will rain.[11] In addition, because 'the content of [this] fear is something imaginary, non-existent' those who are anxious cannot emancipate themselves from the object that they fear through any type of definite action.[12]

---

8   Althusser 1997a, p. 23.
9   Althusser 1997a, p. 23.
10   Althusser 1997a, p. 33.
11   Althusser 1997a, p. 24.
12   Althusser 1997a, p. 26.

If this fear is indeed irrational and its origin insurmountable, then why are so many people making these arguments for a New International and what interests do they serve? Althusser's answer to this question is that the International of Decent Feelings is a court of moral appeal that serves certain functions in the post-war social, economic, political, and psychical landscape.[13] First, it absolves the bad consciences of those who were the aggressors in the war and also of those who killed in defence. '"We are all murderers!" cries Camus. Our crimes make us equal because we have all killed'.[14] Those who gain from this acknowledgement, Althusser argues, are those who want to 'conceal real reason and present [contemporary] realities', who want to show all humanity as, once again, morally equal, and who want to 'buy mercenaries for the next war'.[15] Second, it serves the interests of those who want to 'conjure away social antagonisms' by invoking the immanent death of humanity and of those who want to achieve European unity and peace not through action, but by 'a verbal, moralising socialism' that maintains 'the essential positions of capitalism'.[16] In short, the International of Decent Feelings is an ideology, one which serves those who desire a 'Western' socialism and are dismayed by the possibility for Europe of domination by American industry or Soviet totalitarianism.[17]

Not only are the fears that motivate this International irrational and the political effects that it engenders conservative, mystifying, and exculpatory – Althusser asserts that the phenomenon is unchristian as well. In these post-war analyses of the human condition, the Christian recognition of our equality before God is replaced by our equality before the fear of death.[18]

In addition to the sin of idolatry, where death becomes identical with God and the promise of an afterlife is forgotten, the International of Decent Feelings homogenises humanity. It neglects the existence of proletarians, a particular class that does not have to merely suffer in anguish and who is actually capable of delivering the emancipation from fear by re-appropriating the products of human production, including the atomic bomb. Unlike the universal 'proletariat of terror', this class does not have as its object something outside itself. As Althusser points out, 'poverty for the proletariat is not the fear of poverty, it is an actual present that never disappears, it is on the walls, on the table, [etc.] ...'[19]

13   Althusser 1997a, p. 28.
14   Althusser 1997a, p. 29.
15   Althusser 1997a, p. 30.
16   Althusser 1997a, p. 23.
17   Althusser 1997a, p. 30.
18   Althusser 1997a, p. 27.
19   Althusser 1997a, p. 25.

Because the oppression of the proletariat is real, concrete oppression, the proletariat has the possibility of transforming its condition, of 'converting concrete
servitude into concrete freedom'.[20] It can do so by harnessing and directing
technology, by re-appropriating the products of its labours, and by instantiating
a true fraternity of men. Thereby, it may lead 'the whole of humanity towards
its emancipation'.[21]

2   Reconstruction of Althusser's Anti-Cosmopolitan Argument

In 1946, Althusser's Catholic theology was much better developed than his
Marxism, which was of the type to be gained from Communist Party pamphlets.
Further, as Roland Boer has pointed out, Althusser's Hegelian-Marxist eschatology does not rest easily with his theology. If the International of Decent Feelings can be critiqued for the idolatry of mistaking the universal fear of death
for the universal human condition under God, then Althusser himself can be
critiqued for his youthful faith in the proletariat as the agent that will usher in
the universal destiny of the human race.[22]

   In his mature philosophy, Althusser abandoned the classical Marxist idea
of the proletariat as a universal subject and the telic view of history which
motivated it. However, from his theological argument, he retained something
resembling the notion of the 'ontological reserve', of the idea that there always
exists something in the universe that exceeds any conception we may have
of it.[23] This concept appears in his later work as the notion of the 'void', or
that background condition in which any and all historical events may occur.[24]
Though to do so is to embrace anachronism in intellectual history in order to
make a philosophical argument, the principle features of Althusser's mature
philosophy – contradiction, ateleology, structural causality, uneven development, anti-humanism, overdetermination, etc. – are consistent with the notion
of the void and with Althusser's critique of the International of Decent Feelings.[25] Accordingly, even if only implicitly, this chapter makes use of these of
these concepts and positions from Althusser's mature philosophy in its cri-

---

20   Althusser 1997a, p. 26.
21   Althusser 1997a, pp. 26, 31.
22   Boer 2007, pp. 471–2.
23   Boer 2007, p. 471.
24   François Matheron 1998.
25   Moten 2002, p. 194 argues that Althusser's anti-humanism is compatible with Althusser's
      1946 theological anthropology.

tique. However, one can only make use of these ideas if one abandons his early work's Hegelian-Marxist teleology while recognising the theological argument from the 'International of Decent Feelings' as consistent with his mature work. This done, one no longer takes the proletariat or 'workers' as the universal subject of history in the process of its becoming.

If one discards the notion of history as the progressive realisation of humanity in its full freedom and if one adopts Althusser's mature position that history is a series of socio-economic-political-ideological orders that coalesce or 'take' within a void, then his critique of the International of Decent Feelings still holds.[26] Most importantly, the inconsistency between this early essay's critique of idolatry and his idolisation of the proletariat can be avoided. From this perspective, the two essential aspects of his critique can be distilled. The first is that an internationalism or cosmopolitanism based upon a universal feature that all human beings share is philosophically and politically suspect. Such cosmopolitanisms are suspect first because they identify one or more features as essential to our common humanity and demand solidarity based upon these features. That these essential features change over time and differ from political perspective to political perspective makes 'humanity' an ideological rather than a metaphysical or scientific concept. To say that it is ideological is to note that the concept has a history, that it has been defined differently, at different times, by different peoples, for different uses, and that the reasons for these various definitions can be understood by looking at how each meaning functions politically and at what motivates their adoption.[27] Second, when the concept of humanity is used universally, it tends to occlude or ignore the fact of real, existing, concrete antagonisms among people that are the result not of disregard for our common humanity but of peoples' differing roles in the production, ownership, and distribution of capital. In short, it is used to erase the reality of class and class struggle.[28]

3   Contemporary Cosmopolitanisms

With the critical framework distilled from Althusser's critique of post-World War II Internationalism defined, this chapter will engage two contemporary

---

26   Goshgarian 2019.
27   Althusser 2007, pp. 4–11.
28   Manne 2016 makes a complementary point about humanisation and dehumanisation; when this concept is used to explain genocide, it renders the actual motivations of those doing the killing opaque as well as rendering invisible particular acts of resistance.

variants of cosmopolitan value theory: moral and cultural. These two types of cosmopolitanism have been widely disseminated and discussed in the literature. With the exception of economic and political cosmopolitanism, they also represent the main areas of research into philosophical cosmopolitan.[29] After a brief summary of the two variants, it will be shown that both moral and cultural cosmopolitanism fail to sufficiently recognise the class struggles that are the responses of the masses to exploitation and globalisation and that this forgetting makes the ethical or political projects which are to follow from these theories unrealisable.

3.1   Nussbaum's Moral Cosmopolitanism

Beginning in the early 1990s and continuing with a series of popular and academic articles that blended scholarship in the history of philosophy with contemporary moral philosophy, Martha Nussbaum formulated her moral cosmopolitanism in response to philosophical appeals for a reconstructed patriotism and to her own engagement with 'international quality-of-life issues'.[30] In these articles, cosmopolitanism is presented as a possible solution to humanity's problems inasmuch as these are caused, at least in part, by local loyalties, to family, tribe, nation, class, ethnicity, or race.[31] Examples of the problems that Nussbaum believes cosmopolitanism can address include the unequal distribution of the world's resources, war, racism, sexism, international cooperation, and environmental justice.[32] In addition, she argues that this principle can provide guidance as to the proper political form for human society.[33]

Nussbaum presents the solution to these problems in the guise of a reconstructed cosmopolitanism that borrows arguments from Greek and Roman philosophers about the loyalties humans owe to one another and about the virtues inherent in self and civic cultivation. Added to this Greco-Roman mix are Kantian ideas about human nature and the obligations that this essence entails. In this hybrid cosmopolitanism, Nussbaum starts with Diogenes' radical idea that he was not loyal to any particular group, be it family, local origin, or class, but to the world.[34] Approvingly, she recognises Diogenes' still heterodox position as a choice to be 'an exile from the comfort of patriot-

---

29   Kleingeld and Brown 2019.
30   Nussbaum 1994.
31   Nussbaum 1994.
32   Nussbaum 2001; 1997, p. 22; 1994.
33   Nussbaum 2001, p. 205.
34   Nussbaum 1994.

ism and its easy sentiments, to see our own ways of life from the point of view of justice and the good'.[35]

However, in order to see our own lives in this way, it is necessary to posit that there is: (a) some ontological unity that binds all humans together in some morally significant way; (b) that there is some recognisable good or goods that we all share; and (c) that we have the capacity to discern and deliberate about these goods. In support of these positions, Nussbaum basically reiterates Kant's political philosophy as it is presented in 'Idea for a Universal History with a Cosmopolitan Intent' and the 'Perpetual Peace' essays, minus his historiography. The larger unity we all share is our common humanity, she maintains. This common humanity fulfils each of these three conditions because its contents include the fact that we are all created equal, that we are endowed with reason, that we have the capacity for moral choice, and that we share certain fundamental moral norms.[36] It is these qualities and capacities that, Nussbaum argues, allow us to see ourselves as 'citizens of the world' and to feel that we owe duties to one another. They also permit us to deliberate with one another rationally about ways to achieve human goods globally.[37] Thus can we be motivated to deliver material aid to those who are not part of our immediate community or to engage in discussion with one other about whether it is right to cause environmental devastation in areas of the globe that are not where we presently live.[38]

Though the moral and political framework that Nussbaum embraces is that of Kantian cosmopolitanism, she does not believe that we are endowed with an innate, universal moral sense that allows us to know immediately what is right and wrong. Instead, she presents her ideal cosmopolitan individual as one who comes to practical knowledge through a rich process of stoic self-cultivation and the study of other cultures. She therefore proposes as salutary for all a passionate and cerebral education whereby individuals and particular groups come to know themselves in relation to the common humanity that they share with others 'as similarly human, as bearers of an equal moral dignity, as members of a single body and a set of purposes ...'[39] Through these and similar experiences, Nussbaum argues that we can transform our evaluative capacities such that we become capable of thinking first about what we owe

---

35   Nussbaum 1994.

36   Nussbaum 1994.

37   Nussbaum 1994.

38   Nussbaum 2001, p. 178.

39   Nussbaum 1997, p. 22.

to others, about that which we share with them, and, eventually, about what is best for us all as human beings.

3.2   *Appiah's Cultural Cosmopolitanism*

In his 2007 book *Cosmopolitanism, Ethics in a World of Strangers*, Appiah shares Nussbaum's appreciation for diverse cultures and also notes the morally beneficial effects that may result from exposure to them. However, he does not fully endorse her argument that there are universal moral principles which result from our common humanity, and that brook no exceptions.[40] Instead, Appiah outlines a cosmopolitanism that incorporates aspects of both moral cosmopolitanism and cultural parochialism but which modifies both from their strong forms.[41] Thus, in regard to moral cosmopolitanism, Appiah strongly tempers the moral universalism found in such philosophers as Singer, Unger, or Nussbaum and replaces it with the argument that, though universal human values exist, they are not sufficient on their own for overcoming disagreements about values and practices between individuals and groups. Similarly, in regard to cultural parochialism, Appiah challenges the argument that ethnic or national cultures have a right to exist and to preserve their culture while still endorsing the claim that cultural differences can be useful for discovering best how to live.

Appiah's endorsement of parochialism is a limited endorsement. It is based, fundamentally, on a respect for cultural difference both for its own sake and for the sake of the human good. Though he does not provide a strictly functionalist definition of norms, Appiah notes that a culture's particular system of value is the result of and adapted to its own unique experience in the world. As these values reflect upon and mediate this experience, they are good for the specific culture that developed them.[42] This is Appiah's intrinsic justification of the preservation of difference. Further, because specific values are human responses to their lived environments and, as such, represent solutions to general human problems, it is reasonable to believe that we can learn about what to value and how to value from other cultures.[43] This is Appiah's extrinsic justification for the preservation and respect of difference. It is also one of the factors that limit his cosmopolitanism: one cannot simultaneously respect difference and expect everyone to become a cosmopolitan.

Though learning about other cultures may be salutary and teach us about what we should or might value, it is not the case for Appiah that learning about

---

40   Appiah 2007, p. 162.
41   Appiah 2007, p. xvii.
42   Appiah 2007, p. 4.
43   Appiah 2007, pp. 41, 43.

or even experiencing diverse cultures will make one a good person concerned with the welfare of all humanity. In this regard, he cites the example of Sir Richard Burton who, despite travelling extensively and modifying his language, appearance, and gesture such that he could pass as a native in many places, retained many of the prejudices of Victorian culture.[44] Therefore, Appiah concludes, familiarity with and learning about diverse human cultures is insufficient to generate tolerance of human difference, an understanding of the common qualities that unite us all, and compassion for humanity. If any progress is to be made in this regard, it must be achieved by other means. The principle methods that Appiah cites for this transformation are living with and engaging in conversation with people who hold different values from us.[45]

But why is learning about other cultures insufficient to generate tolerance, understanding, and compassion? Appiah claims that this insufficiency is due to the nature of moral value and to our moral psychology. In terms of the metaphysics of morals, he rejects the 'positivist' argument which holds that values are merely beliefs or opinions about states of things and that these values cannot, therefore, be subjected to rational scrutiny or empirical demonstration as to their veracity.[46] On the contrary, moral concepts are understood psychologically by Appiah as primarily action guiding. They are thus subject to empirical scrutiny.[47] Further, inasmuch as values are shared among individuals, they are objective and represent a social consensus.[48] The meanings and import of values are communicated, he believes, in conversations and stories. In the latter, values are shown 'at work', guiding specific actions and leading to specific consequences. In the former, they convey content about what the holder of that value thinks is the appropriate response to a situation or situations.

That moral values have an objective status within a culture does not mean that someone outside the culture from which they originate can understand them immediately. However, it is also not the case that we cannot communicate our values to others. By virtue of being human, we share certain experiences and certain features of the mind and these provide a basis for communication and understanding between different cultures.[49] In addition, we share many 'thin' values, such as politeness, good parenting, or piety, in which there is a shared notion of a certain obligation, but which becomes fleshed out or 'thick'

---

44   Appiah 2007, p. 8.
45   Appiah 2007, pp. 85, 95–9.
46   Appiah 2007, p. 25.
47   Appiah 2007, p. 26.
48   Althusser 2007, p. 28.
49   Appiah 2007, pp. 94–6.

when embedded in a particular culture.[50] Though we might disagree strenu-ously with what a certain culture believes it means to be a good parent, the thin value of good parenting is shared. We can move from these thin concepts to discussions of the thicker, culturally embedded values.[51]

Despite the possibility of this conversation, there are still many hurdles to a discussion that can result in a shared understanding and to having a dialogue that can help guide us to a shared approach to the decisions that face us all.[52] Just because we have had a discussion with someone with whom our values conflict and understand what value is at stake for both of us, does not mean that we come to any agreement about what is to be done.[53] In addition, people do not change their actions or beliefs because of discussion and agreement.[54] They do so, Appiah maintains, because, after prolonged exposure to different ways of life, they gradually come to a new way of seeing things.[55] Women, he argues, have increased their status and freedom in the developed West in the last few generations not because of argument, but because those in the global North got used to them exercising a different status and making different choices.[56]

This, then, is Appiah's strongest endorsement of cultural cosmopolitanism: we should take interest in what other people do because exposure to these actions tends to make us accept them and, therefore, renders us less likely to have conflicts with them.[57] Starting with those thin values and obligations we hold in common as humans, we need to have conversations across borders and to engage with the experience and ideas of others.[58] However, because there is no possibility of a final casuistry of values where we might be able to decide which values are the best and which should take precedence for all, Appiah argues that we need to be fallibilists in regards to morals.[59] In addition, if it is the case that there is no way to adjudicate among values and potentially useful values can emerge from any culture, then we must also be pluralists.[60]

50   Appiah 2007, pp. 46–8.
51   Appiah 2007, p. 66.
52   Appiah 2007, pp. 43, 66.
53   Appiah 2007, pp. 59–60.
54   Appiah 2007, p. 73.
55   Appiah 2007, p. 78.
56   Appiah 2007, p. 76.
57   Appiah 2007, p. 78.
58   Appiah 2007, pp. 95, 134.
59   Appiah 2007, p. xxi.
60   Appiah 2007, p. 144.

4   Critique of Moral and Cultural Cosmopolitanisms

Nussbaum's and Appiah's cosmopolitanisms are tough to argue with. Who except for religious, racial, or ethnic fundamentalists could disagree with Appiah's conclusion and who but nationalist and extreme social conservatives would reject Nussbaum's? *Prima Facie*, the political and moral programme that each endorses as the outcome of the adoption of their version of cosmopolitanism is similarly unobjectionable. Live with others, talk to them, find common ground, avoid conflicts, come to a shared approach for how we will face our common problems, live morally, and think about helping those beyond your immediate community, says Appiah. Cultivate yourself, respect one another, do not discriminate, apply the same values globally that you do locally, establish internationalist institutions that promote justice, says Nussbaum. To the liberal mind, it seems intuitively obvious that, if we did any of these things, we would be making the world a healthier, saner, less violent, and, yes, more humane place.

Undoubtedly, if we adopted all or even some of the practices that Nussbaum and Appiah suggest, there would be, for some people, for some amount of time, less suffering in the world and more happiness. However, these practices cannot be a total solution to the problems that motivate them and, further, the philosophies that support these actions may actually work to justify liberal institutions and practices that prolong these problems' existence. These problems include environmental devastation, population displacement, increases in relative poverty, resurgent nationalist and ethnic struggles, xenophobia, human rights violations, and the rise of global and local terrorism.

Using the critical framework distilled from Althusser's work on the International of Decent Feelings, one may question the initial intuition that, by adopting Nussbaum's moral cosmopolitanism or Appiah's cultural cosmopolitanism, we could make the world a healthier, saner, less violent, and more humane place. Directed by Althusser's hermeneutic of suspicion, the first place that we should look is at these philosophies' idea of what is humane or 'human' and what values or possibilities for valuation this definition entails. Second, we should look at what is insufficiently recognised when that which all humans share is the primary (Nussbaum) or secondary (Appiah) justification for our global and local actions rather than some other force or loyalty.

As detailed above, the common humanity to which Nussbaum's cosmopolitanism appeals includes the notions that we are all created equal, that we are endowed with reason, that we have the capacity for moral choice, and that we share certain fundamental moral norms. These qualities, she argues, allows us to see ourselves as 'citizens of the world', to feel that we owe duties to one another, and to deliberate with one another rationally about ways to achieve human goods globally. Motivated by these duties, we should feel compelled to, for instance, feed those who are hungry, work to end persistent discrimination, and to mitigate environmental devastation. Further, we should erect and support institutions that take care of these needs, that prevent these wrongs, or that undo the damage which has been done.

What is missed in this discussion, however, is that many of these problems and wrongs cannot be traced to a lack of compassion for or duty towards our fellow man or insufficient institutions to realise these common ideals. Nor can they be permanently repaired by the individual adoption of this duty or by its institutionalisation. They can, however, be traced back directly to the impacts of the expansion of global capital and its interest in exploiting labour and land in support of increased profits. Focused on what all humanity shares and needs – equality, rationality, respect, the fulfilment of basic human needs – Nussbaum's cosmopolitanism misses that which cleaves people from one another most consequentially: whether or not and how they have power to direct their lives by virtue of the role that they play in the socio-economic system. By addressing what we may all share but forgetting that which we do not all share, a common class interest, Nussbaum's cosmopolitanism addresses the symptoms of discrimination but never its causes. Appealing to moral cosmopolitanism, a non-governmental organisation may recognise and seek to repair the harm done to the environment and to the humans who inhabit it. It may also address the immiseration of a local economy caused by the actions of a multinational agricultural enterprise. However, it cannot, by the same appeal, argue that the multinational has no right to buy up land, to plant a monoculture, to displace persons, to employ them at below living wage, and to benefit in this regard from the mass of the unwaged left in these actions' wake. To do so demands another normative-juridical regime. Cosmopolitanism, however, seeks moral and juridical solutions to problems that have been permitted and exacerbated by the very practical rules and systems that it wishes to universalise. Further, it ignores these systems' relations to the economic systems whose functioning they assure.

A priori, we may not be able to establish that capitalism tends to violate our common humanity. This is especially true if 'humanity' is always an ideological concept, an index for a particular normative conception of how we should be. On the contrary, cosmopolitanism, with its emphasis on the exchangeability of every person and place, allows some aspects of liberalism to be well expressed, at least for a certain class of people.[61] However, for another class of

---

61   Stuhr 2017, p. 293.

people, those negatively affected by the role they play in the capitalist system, the appeal to our common humanity and to the institutions that may safeguard the 'humanity' we share in common is insufficient to address the ills that they suffer by it. Recognising that 'there but for the grace of God go I', as moral cosmopolitanism encourages us to do cannot, by itself, put an end to the reality that we inhabit a social and economic system which requires a part of the population to exploit, dominate, and oppress another of its component parts for its continued reproduction. Neither is the Golden Rule sufficient, which, formulated in a Kantian way, as 'Do unto others as you would universally wish that all would do unto you', could equally be one of moral cosmopolitan's maxims.

In his argument, Appiah notices this result, at least insofar as it involves the impossibility of putting oneself into an 'other's' shoes so that the Golden Rule might be put into effect. Given the difference between the norms that different cultures (and individual human beings) embrace, it is impossible to know what an 'other' would have done unto them. Appiah points out that even in what, to most people, would be clearly defined situations in which the rule should be applied, it is impossible to know that when you are doing for others what you would have done for yourself is going to be accepted as the right thing to do. One example that he gives is of a person who desperately needs a blood transfusion if they are not going to die and of a doctor who believes that, if she were in the situation, she would want to have that transfusion. However, the patient in this example is a Jehovah's Witness and believes that he will go to hell if the transfusion is performed.[62] In this situation, the particularity of each culture's norms makes applying this seemingly anodyne universal moral criterion impossible.

Looked at as a whole, one of the main themes of Appiah's book is that there are no universal moral values that have sufficient content to guide every action. However, he notes well and gives copious examples of particular moral values that allow individuals, in a particular group, in a particular situation and time, to act well. In short, Appiah gets particularity, whether it be religious, artistic, political, historical, or ethnic. He also notes well that it is the particular moral norms that a specific culture evolved over time to guide relations among its members which precipitate conflicts when we try to live together with people from different cultures. These situations are the motivation for his cultural cosmopolitanism: it is designed to provide us with a means to become comfortable with the diverse practices of others so that these conflicts do not lead to oppression and violence.

---

62   Appiah 2007, pp. 61–2.

Appiah's emphasis on particularity and pluralism also allows him to diagnose with acuity why and when it is that values clash such that oppression and violence occurs. This happens, he maintains, when the moral principles that were once evolved to support a particular way of life are stripped of the forms of life to which they gave sustenance and then are believed to be applicable to all humanity. In other words, local norms stripped of the lifeworld in which they were enmeshed are mistaken for universal moral cosmopolitan principles. He gives examples of religious fundamentalisms in this regard, but also of certain Marxisms.[63] Certainly, in the figure of Pol Pot that he cites and Pol's combination of dialectical materialist laws with certain tenets of Therevada Buddhism, this type of transformation is recognisable.[64]

But does this critique hold for all Marxisms? Is there just something that is always dangerous about taking a set of normative assumptions from a particular lifeworld and then universalising them? More specifically, is there a problem with taking a set of normative assumptions that originated with a mid-nineteenth century European intellectual and workers' movement as universal? Appiah would probably argue that there is. However, to see the claims of the working class as merely normative claims generated by a particular culture to serve its needs is to misdiagnose these claims' status and origin. It is not a clash of beliefs between capitalist and worker that motivates the worker's animus to the capitalist. Capitalist and worker are often, after all, from the same culture and the antagonism between worker and capitalist is built into economic as well as ideological structures. In addition, the deeper and further that capitalism extends its reach, the less endemic and more pandemic this antagonism becomes. What motivates this antagonism is that, daily, the un- or under-waged person's form of life is ordered, controlled, and threatened with extinction by capitalists' actions in pursuit of profits. The values that the worker or underemployed person expresses – that she would want more control over her own life and the freedom and power to experience different modes of life, just as the capitalist enjoys – are therefore not merely particular judgments but are universal sentiments expressed from a particular viewpoint.

Appiah would probably not see in this explanation how the values expressed by workers differ in their origins from other sorts of particular values. After all, these values originate from a particular form of life and come in conflict with the values of the capitalist, which themselves may be thought to originate from another form of life. However, one point of this chapter is that both values

63   Appiah 2007, 140–1.
64   Short 2006, 149–50.

COSMOPOLITANISM AND CLASS ERASURE   175

originate from the same form of life: capitalism, in which we are all, mostly, enmeshed. As such, they enjoy a different status. In addition, the emphasis that Appiah places on the particularity of cultural morals and how they must be respected does not equip his philosophy to deal well with demands made from those who are impoverished by capitalist expansion, whose environment is compromised, and certainly not from those who would argue that capitalism is a system of economics, values, policies, and institutions that must be overthrown or otherwise surpassed.

We can see this when Appiah tries to deal with what should be done for the terribly impoverished, for those who do not have enough to eat. Rightly, he says that we should not follow Singer and Unger in their directions to give away our fortunes and save the poor for a day when, the next day, the same structural problems that led to their impoverishment would still exists.[65] One would expect, at this point, that Appiah might endorse working to end or transform the socio-economic system that contributes to this impoverishment. However, he instead suggests that we should contribute to modest institutional reform.[66] If Appiah does not take the claims of those who are affected negatively by global capitalism as having any different status than the claims of those who, say, are offended by polygamous relationships, such is the limit of what he can argue. The conflicts that cultural cosmopolitanism is designed to overcome will keep occurring unless the particular structuring reality of the capitalist system is acknowledged.

With its survey of two representative contemporary cosmopolitanisms, this chapter has attempted to show how the appeal to common ideals, to what we can learn from each other, to our universal humanity, or to our deep attachments to others, often results in the forgetting of class differences and in the paving over of existing class struggles. This is true of the moral theory of cosmopolitanism as well as for cultural cosmopolitanism. Both variants, if adopted, would surely make the world a better place, for some people, and for some time. However, each variant not only fails to sufficiently recognise the global class struggles that are the responses of the masses to globalisation, but this occlusion and the endorsement of moral or cultural cosmopolitanism makes the ethical or political projects which are to follow from these theories unrealisable.

---

65   Appiah 2007, p. 168.
66   Appiah 2007, p. 170.

Works Cited

Abramson, Paul R., John H. Aldrich, Jill Rickershauser, and David W. Rohde 2007. 'Fear in the Voting Booth: The 2004 Presidential Election'. *Political Behavior* 29 (2):197–220.

Addis, Laird 1966. 'Freedom and the Marxist Philosophy of History'. *Philosophy of Science* 33 (1/2):101–17.

Adler, Laure 2011. 'Figures de Louis Althusser (1/5)'. France Culture. July 11, 2011. https://www.franceculture.fr/emissions/hors-champs/figures-de-louis-althusser-15.

Adorno, Theodor 1977. 'Sociology and Empirical Research'. In *The Positivist Dispute in German Sociology*, translated by Glyn Adey and David Frisby, 68–86. London: Heineman.

Alcoff, Linda 1999. 'Towards a Phenomenology of Racial Embodiment'. *Radical Philosophy*, June, 15–26.

Allen, Amy 2016. *The End of Progress: Decolonising the Normative Foundations of Critical Theory*. New York: Columbia University Press.

Al-Saji, Alia 2014. 'A Phenomenology of Hesitation: Interrupting Racialising Habits of Seeing'. In *Living Alterities: Phenomenology, Embodiment, and Race*, edited by Emily Lee, 133–172. State University of New York Press.

Althusser, Louis 1966a. 'ALT2. A7–01.09 «Théorie Marxiste et Parti Communiste» («Union théorie/pratique»). (1966–1967)'. Fonds Althusser. Institut Mémoires de l'Édition Contemporaine.

Althusser, Louis 1966b. 'Théorie Marxiste et Parti Communiste (Union théorie/pratique) (1966–1967)'. Fonds Althusser 20ALT/7/9–11. Institut Mémoires de l'Édition Contemporaine.

Althusser, Louis 1969a. 'Contradiction and Overdetermination'. In *For Marx*, 87–128. London: Allen Lane.

Althusser, Louis 1969b. *For Marx*. London: Allen Lane.

Althusser, Louis 1970. 'From Capital to Marx's Philosophy'. In *Reading 'Capital'*. London: NLB.

Althusser, Louis 1972a. 'Ideology and Ideological State Apparatuses'. In *Lenin and Philosophy, and Other Essays*, 127–86. New York: Monthly Review Press.

Althusser, Louis 1972b. *Lenin and Philosophy, and Other Essays*. New York: Monthly Review Press.

Althusser, Louis 1972c. 'Lenin and Philosphy (February 1968)'. In *Lenin and Philosophy, and Other Essays.*, 23–70. New York: Monthly Review Press.

Althusser, Louis 1972d. 'Philosophy as a Revolutionary Weapon (February 1968)'. In *Lenin and Philosophy, and Other Essays.*, 11–22. New York: Monthly Review Press.

Althusser, Louis 1973. *Réponse a John Lewis*. Paris: François Maspero.

Althusser, Louis 1974. *Philosophie et philosophie spontanée des savants, 1967*. Paris: F. Maspero.

Althusser, Louis 1975. 'Texte de Louis Althusser sur la philosophie marxiste'. Fonds Althusser 20ALT/22/2. Institut Mémoires de l'Édition Contemporaine.

Althusser, Louis 1976a. 'Elements of Self-Criticism'. In *Essays in Self-Criticism*, 105–50. London; Atlantic Highlands, N.J.: NLB; Humanities Press.

Althusser, Louis 1976b. *Essays in Self-Criticism*. London; Atlantic Highlands, N.J.: NLB; Humanities Press.

Althusser, Louis 1976c. 'Être marxiste en philosophie, chapters 1–12 (1976)'. Fonds Althusser. L'Institut Mémoires de l'Édition Contemporaine.

Althusser, Louis 1976d. 'Notes de Louis Althusser sur l'«Interview imaginaire»'. Fonds Althusser 20ALT/24/13. Institut Mémoires de l'Édition Contemporaine.

Althusser, Louis 1976e. 'Reply to John Lewis'. In *Essays in Self-Criticism*, 33–100. London; Atlantic Highlands, N.J.: NLB; Humanities Press.

Althusser, Louis 1977a. '«Initiation à la philosophie (pour les non-philosophes)»'. (suite)'. Fonds Althusser. Institut Mémoires de l'Édition Contemporaine.

Althusser, Louis 1977b. 'Introduction: Unfinished History'. In *Proletarian Science?: The Case of Lysenko*, 7–17 by Dominique Lecourt. London; Atlantic Highlands, N.J.: NLB; Humanities Press.

Althusser, Louis 1978a. *Ce Qui Ne Peut plus Durer Dans Le Parti Communiste*. https://gallica.bnf.fr/ark:/12148/bpt6k4800576k.

Althusser, Louis 1978b. 'Cours sur le mode d'exposition chez Marx'. Fonds Althusser 20ALT/28/5. Institut Mémoires de l'Édition Contemporaine.

Althusser, Louis 1978c. 'What Must Change in the Party'. *New Left Review*, I, no. 109 (June):19–45.

Althusser, Louis 1979. 'The Crisis of Marxism'. In *Power and Opposition in Post-Revolutionary Societies*, edited by Il Manifesto, 225–37. London: Ink Links Ltd.

Althusser, Louis 1980. 'Entretien avec Giorgio Fanti'. Fonds Althusser 20ALT/46/36. Institut Mémoires de l'Édition Contemporaine.

Althusser, Louis 1982a. 'La grande répétition de l'histoire'. Fonds Althusser 20ALT/29/1. Institut Mémoires de l'Édition Contemporaine.

Althusser, Louis 1982b. 'Ouvrage sans titre commençant par: «J'écris ce livre en octobre 1982»'. Fonds Althusser. Institut Mémoires de l'Édition Contemporaine.

Althusser, Louis 1982c. '«Sur le mode de production»'. Fonds Althusser 20ALT/29/2. Institut Mémoires de l'Édition Contemporaine.

Althusser, Louis 1985a. '«La philosophie c'est enfantin»'. Fonds Althusser 20ALT/29/20. Institut Mémoires de l'Édition Contemporaine.

Althusser, Louis 1985b. 'Qu'y faire? Que faire?' Fonds Althusser 20ALT/29/26. L'Institut Mémoires de l'Édition Contemporaine.

Althusser, Louis 1986a. 'Thèses de juin'. Fonds Althusser 20ALT/29/30. Institut Mémoires de l'Édition Contemporaine.

Althusser, Louis 1986b. 'Philosophie et marxisme. Entretiens avec Fernanda Navarro'. Fonds Althusser 20ALT/30/1. Institut Mémoires de l'Édition Contemporaine.

Althusser, Louis 1990a. 'Is It Simple to Be a Marxist in Philosophy?' In *Philosophy and the Spontaneous Philosophy of the Scientists & Other Essays*, edited by Gregory Elliott, 203–40. London; New York: Verso.

Althusser, Louis 1990b. 'Marxism Today'. In *Philosophy and the Spontaneous Philosophy of the Scientists & Other Essays*, edited by Gregory Elliott, 267–80. London; New York: Verso.

Althusser, Louis 1990c. 'Philosophy and the Spontaneous Philosophy of the Scientists'. In *Philosophy and the Spontaneous Philosophy of the Scientists & Other Essays*, translated by Gregory Elliott. London; New York: Verso.

Althusser, Louis 1990d. 'The Transformation of Philosophy (1976)'. In *Philosophy and the Spontaneous Philosophy of the Scientists & Other Essays*, edited by Gregory Elliott, 241–66. London; New York: Verso.

Althusser, Louis 1990e. 'Theory, Theoretical Practice and Theoretical Formation: Ideology and Ideological Struggle'. In *Philosophy and the Spontaneous Philosophy of the Scientists & Other Essays*, edited by Gregory Elliott, 1–41. London; New York: Verso.

Althusser, Louis 1994a. 'La transformation de la philosophie – Conférence de Grenade (1976)'. In *Sur la philosophie*, 139–78. L'infini. Paris: Gallimard.

Althusser, Louis 1994b. *Sur la philosophie*. L'infini. Paris: Gallimard.

Althusser, Louis 1995a. 'Cremonini, peintre de l'abstrait (1964–66)'. In *Ecrits philosophiques et politiques, Tome 2*, edited by François Matheron, 573–90. Ecrits philosophiques et politiques. Paris: Stock IMEC.

Althusser, Louis 1995b. *Ecrits philosophiques et politiques, Tome II*. Edited by François Matheron. Ecrits philosophiques et politiques. Paris: Stock IMEC.

Althusser, Louis 1995c. 'Sur Brecht et Marx (1968)'. In *Ecrits philosophiques et politiques, Tome 2*, edited by François Matheron, 541–58. Ecrits philosophiques et politiques. Paris: Stock IMEC.

Althusser, Louis 1995d. *Sur la reproduction*. Actuel Marx confrontation. Paris: Presses universitaires de France.

Althusser, Louis 1995e. *The Future Lasts Forever: A Memoir*. Edited by Olivier Corpet and Yann Moulier-Boutang. Translated by Richard Veasey. New York: New Press.

Althusser, Louis 1997a. 'The International of Decent Feelings'. In *The Spectre of Hegel: Early Writings*, edited by François Matheron, translated by G. M Goshgarian, 21–35. London; New York: Verso.

Althusser, Louis 1997b. 'The Only Materialist Tradition, Part I: Spinoza (1985)'. In *The New Spinoza*, edited by Ted Stolze and Warren Montag, 3–19. Theory out of Bounds 11. Minneapolis London: University of Minnesota press.

Althusser, Louis 1998a. 'Avant-Propos du livre de G. Duménil'. In *Solitude de Machiavel*, edited by Yves Syntomer. Paris: Presses Universitaire de France.

Althusser, Louis 1998b. *Lettres à Franca: 1961–1973*. Edited by François Matheron and Yann Moulier Boutang. Édition posthume d'oeuvres de Louis Althusser 6. Paris: Stock IMEC.

Althusser, Louis 1999. *Machiavelli and Us*. Edited by Gregory Elliot. London New York: Verso.

Althusser, Louis 2003a. 'On Levi-Strauss'. In *The Humanist Controversy and Other Writings, 1966–67*, edited by François Matheron, 19–33. London; New York: Verso.

Althusser, Louis 2003b. 'The Historical Task of Marxist Philosophy (1967)'. In *The Humanist Controversy and Other Writings, 1966–67*, edited by François Matheron, 155–220. London; New York: Verso.

Althusser, Louis 2003c. *The Humanist Controversy and Other Writings, 1966–67*. Edited by François Matheron. London; New York: Verso.

Althusser, Louis 2005a. 'Du Matérialisme Aléatoire (1986)'. *Multitudes*, no. 2:179–194.

Althusser, Louis 2005b. 'On the Young Marx: Theoretical Quetions (1961)'. In *For Marx*. London; New York: Verso.

Althusser, Louis 2006a. 'Marx in His Limits'. In *Philosophy of the Encounter: Later Writings, 1978–87*, 7–162. London New York: Verso.

Althusser, Louis 2006b. 'Philosophy and Marxism: Interviews with Fernanda Navarro (1984–87)'. In *Philosophy of the Encounter: Later Writings, 1978–87*, 251–89. Verso.

Althusser, Louis 2006c. *Philosophy of the Encounter: Later Writings, 1978–87*. London New York: Verso.

Althusser, Louis 2007. 'Letter to the Central Committee of the PCF, 18 March 1966'. *Historical Materialism* 15 (2):153–172.

Althusser, Louis 2011. *Lettres à Hélène: 1947–1980*. Edited by Olivier Corpet. 1 vols. Paris: B. Grasset IMEC.

Althusser, Louis 2013. *Initiation à la philosophie pour les non-philosophes*. Edited by G.M. Goshgarian. [Paris]: Presses universitaires de France.

Althusser, Louis 2014a. *On the Reproduction of Capitalism: Ideology and Ideological State Apparatuses*. London New York: Verso.

Althusser, Louis 2014b. *On the Reproduction of Capitalism: Ideology and Ideological State Apparatuses*. Translated by G. M Goshgarian. London; New York: Verso.

Althusser, Louis 2015. *Être marxiste en philosophie*. Edited by G.M. Goshgarian. Perspectives critiques. Paris: Presses universitaires de France.

Althusser, Louis 2016. *Les vaches noires: interview imaginaire (le malaise du XXIIe congrès) ce qui ne va pas camarades!* Translated by G. M Goshgarian. Paris: Puf.

Althusser, Louis 2017. 'The Crisis of Marxism (1977)'. *Viewpoint Magazine* (blog). December 15, 2017. https://www.viewpointmag.com/2017/12/15/crisis-marxism-1977/.

Althusser, Louis 2018a. 'À propos de Marx et l'histoire (1975)'. In *Écrits sur l'histoire: 1963–1986*, edited by G. M Goshgarian, 261–78. Paris: Presses universitaires de France.

Althusser, Louis 2018b. *Écrits sur l'histoire: 1963–1986*. Edited by G. M Goshgarian. Paris: Presses universitaires de France.

Althusser, Louis 2018c. *Que faire?* Translated by G. M Goshgarian.

Althusser, Louis, and Etienne Balibar 1970. *Reading 'Capital'*. London: NLB.

Althusser, Louis, and Institut Mémoires de l'édition contemporaine 2015. *Des rêves d'angoisse sans fin: récits de rêves (1941–1967); suivi de, Un meurtre à deux (1985)*. Edited by Olivier Corpet and Yann Moulier Boutang.

Amariglio, Jack J. 1987. 'Marxism against Economic Science: Althusser's Legacy'. *Research in Political Economy* 10:159–94.

Anderson, Perry 2016. *Considerations on Western Marxism*. London: Verso.

Anderson, Richard D. 1998. 'The Place of the Media in Popular Democracy'. *Critical Review* 12 (4):481–500. https://doi.org/10.1080/08913819808443513.

Anomaly, Jonathan 2017. 'Race Research and the Ethics of Belief'. *Journal of Bioethical Inquiry* 14 (2):287–97. https://doi.org/10.1007/s11673-017-9774-0.

Anonymous, and Louis [attributed to] Althusser 2010. 'On the Cultural Revolution'. Translated by Jason E Smith. *Décalages* 1 (1). http://scholar.oxy.edu/decalages/vol1/iss1/9. Last accessed June 11, 2020.

Appiah, K. Anthony 2007. *Cosmopolitanism: Ethics in a World of Strangers*. New York: W.W. Norton.

Appiah, Kwame Anthony 2001. 'Soul Making'. In *The State and the Shaping of Identity*. Tanner Lectures. Cambridge, U.K.

Appiah, Kwame Anthony 2018. 'Why Social Class Matters, Even If We Don't Agree What It Means'. *The Chronicle of Higher Education*, August 19, 2018. https://www.chronicle.com/article/Why-Social-Class-Matters-Even/244290.

Ardill, Allan 2008. 'Sociobiology and Law'. Queensland, Australia.: Griffith University.

Arsenault, Amelia, and Manuel Castells 2006. 'Conquering the Minds, Conquering Iraq: The Social Production of Misinformation in the United States – a Case Study'. *Information, Communication & Society* 9 (3):284–307. https://doi.org/10.1080/1369118 0600751256.

Badiou, Alain 2011. 'Can Change Be Thought? (Interview)'. In *Badiou and Politics*, 289–317. Durham, NC: Duke University Press.

Baert, Patrick 2005. *Philosophy of the Social Sciences: Towards Pragmatism*. Cambridge, UK; Malden, MA: Polity.

Baggini, Julian 2018. 'Why Sexist and Racist Philosophers Might Still Be Admirable'. Aeon. November 7, 2018. https://aeon.co/ideas/why-sexist-and-racist-philosophers -might-still-be-admirable.

Bailey, Zinzi D., Nancy Krieger, Madina Agénor, Jasmine Graves, Natalia Linos, and Mary T. Bassett 2017. 'Structural Racism and Health Inequities in the USA: Evidence and Interventions'. *The Lancet* 389 (10077):1453–63. https://doi.org/10.1016/S0140-6736(17)30569-X.

Baldacchino, John 2018. *Post-Marxist Marxism: Questioning the Answer Difference and Realism after Lukács and Adorno*. Routledge.

Balfour, Lawrie 1998. ''A Most Disagreeable Mirror': Race Consciousness as Double Consciousness'. *Political Theory* 26 (3):346–69.

Balibar, Etienne 1991. 'Tais-toi, Althusser! (1988)'. In *Ecrits pour Althusser*, 59–89. Paris: Editions la Découverte.

Balibar, Étienne 2018. *Secularism and Cosmopolitanism: Critical Hypotheses on Religion and Politics.* Columbia University Press.

Balibar, Etienne, Margaret Cohen, and Bruce Robbins 1994. 'Althusser's Object'. *Social Text*, no. 39 (July):157–88. https://doi.org/10.2307/466368.

Balibar, Étienne, Michel 1976. 'Correspondance échangée autour du projet d' «Interview Imaginaire»/Vâches Noires'. Fonds Althusser 20ALT/24/18. Institut Mémoires de l'Édition Contemporaine.

Balibar, Étienne, and Immanuel Maurice Wallerstein 1991. *Race, nation, class: ambiguous identities.* London; New York: Verso.

Baltas, Aristides 1993. 'Critical Notice: Louis Althusser's Philosophy and the Spontaneous Philosophy of the Scientists and Other Essays'. *Philosophy of Science* 60 (4):647–658.

Baltas, Aristildes 1993. 'Critical Notice: Louis Althusser's 'Philosophy and The Spontaneous Philosophy of the Scientists''. *Philosophy of Science* 60 (4):647.

Barder, Alexander D. 2019. 'Scientific Racism, Race War and the Global Racial Imaginary'. *Third World Quarterly* 40 (2):207–23. https://doi.org/10.1080/01436597.2019.1575200.

Bargu, Banu 2012. 'In the Theater of Politics: Althusser's Aleatory Materialism and Aesthetics'. *Diacritics* 40 (3):86–113.

Basset, Mary, and Nancy Krieger 1986. 'The Health of Black Folk: Disease, Class and Ideology of Science'. *Monthly Review*, July, 74–85. https://doi.org/10.14452/MR-038-03-1986-07_8.

Baumol, William J. 1983. 'Marx and the Iron Law of Wages'. *The American Economic Review* 73 (2):303–8.

Bayne, Tim, and Cecilia Heyes 2019. 'What Is Cognition?' *Current Biology* 29 (13):R608–15. https://doi.org/10.1016/j.cub.2019.05.044.

Beaulieu, Alain 2003. 'La politique de Gilles Deleuze et le matérialisme aléatoire du dernier Althusser'. *Actuel Marx* n° 34 (2):161–74. https://doi.org/10.3917/amx.034.0161.

Benedjaïzo 2015. 'Louis Althusser, un marxiste imaginaire'. *France Culture.* https://www.franceculture.fr/emissions/une-vie-une-oeuvre/louis-althusser-un-marxiste-imaginaire.

Bensaïd, Daniel 1999. 'Un univers de pensée aboli'. In *Contre Althusser: Pour Marx. Nouvelle édition, augmentée*, 229–63.

Bettcher, Talia 2012. 'Trans Women and the Meaning of 'Woman''. In *Philosophy of Sex: Contemporary Readings 6th Ed.*, edited by Nicholas Power, Raja Halwani, and Alan

Soble, 233–50. Rowman & Littlefield. https://www.academia.edu/2593425/Trans_W omen_and_the_Meaning_of_Woman_.

Bhaskar, Roy 1989. *Reclaiming Reality: A Critical Approach to Contemporary Philosophy.* London; New York: Verso.

Billington, Michael 2002. 'After The Gods, Hampstead Theatre, London'. *The Guardian,* June 19, 2002, sec. Stage. https://www.theguardian.com/stage/2002/jun/19/theatre .artsfeatures1.

Bimber, Bruce 1990. 'Karl Marx and the Three Faces of Technological Determinism'. *Social Studies of Science* 20 (2):333–51.

Bliuc, Ana-Maria, Craig McGarty, Katherine Reynolds, and Daniela Muntele 2007. 'Opinion-Based Group Membership as a Predictor of Commitment to Political Action'. *European Journal of Social Psychology* 37 (1):19–32. https://doi.org/10.1002/ ejsp.334.

Boer, Roland 2007. 'Althusser's Catholic Marxism'. *Rethinking Marxism* 19 (4):469– 486,557.

Bohman, James. 1998. 'Survey Article: The Coming of Age of Deliberative Democracy'. *Journal of Political Philosophy* 6 (4):400–425.

Bohman, James. 1999a. 'Democracy as Inquiry, Inquiry as Democratic: Pragmatism, Social Science, and the Cognitive Division of Labor'. *American Journal of Political Science* 43 (2):590–607. https://doi.org/10.2307/2991808.

Bohman, James. 1999b. 'Theories, Practices, and Pluralism A Pragmatic Interpretation of Critical Social Science'. *Philosophy of the Social Sciences* 29 (4):459–80. https://doi .org/10.1177/004839319902900401.

Bohman, James. 2002. 'How to Make a Social Science Practical: Pragmatism, Critical Social Science and Multiperspectival Theory'. *Millennium – Journal of International Studies* 31 (3):499–524. https://doi.org/10.1177/03058298020310030701.

Bohman, James. 2008. 'Critical Theory as Practical Knowledge: Participants, Observers, and Critics'. In *The Blackwell Guide to the Philosophy of the Social Sciences,* 89–109. John Wiley & Sons, Ltd. https://doi.org/10.1002/9780470756485.ch4.

Bohman, James. 2019. 'Critical Theory'. Edited by Edward N. Zalta. *The Stanford Encyclopedia of Philosophy.* Metaphysics Research Lab, Stanford University. https://plato .stanford.edu/archives/win2019/entries/critical-theory/.

Bohnert, Amy S.B., and Carl A. Latkin 2009. 'HIV Testing and Conspiracy Beliefs Regarding the Origins of HIV among African Americans'. *AIDS Patient Care and STDs* 23 (9):759–63. https://doi.org/10.1089/apc.2009.0061.

Bordo, Susan 2015. *The Male Body a New Look at Men in Public and in Private.* New York: Farrar, Straus and Giroux.

Bottomore, Tom 2002. *The Frankfurt School and Its Critics.* London: Routledge.

Bourdin, Jean-Claude 2010. 'The Uncertain Materialism of Louis Althusser'. *Graduate Faculty Philosophy Journal* 22 (1):271–287.

Bourdin, Jean-Claude 2012. 'Ce que fait la rencontre aléatoire au matérialisme (et à la philosophie)'. In *Autour d'Althusser: penser un matérialisme aléatoire: problèmes et perspectives*, edited by Annie Ibrahim, 54–82. Paris: Temps des cerises.

Boyer, Anne 2014. 'Kill the Philosopher in Your Head'. *The New Inquiry* (blog). February 11, 2014. https://thenewinquiry.com/kill-the-philosopher-in-your-head/.

Breckman, Warren 2013. *Adventures of the Symbolic: Post-Marxism and Radical Democracy*. New York: Columbia University Press.

Bruschi, Fabio 2018. 'Discours Scientifique, Formation Théorique et Parti Expérimentateur. Une Étude de La Politique Du Théoricisme'. *Décalages* 2 (2). https://scholar.oxy.edu/decalages/vol2/iss2/5. Last accessed June 11, 2020.

Bryant, Levi R, Nick Srnicek, and Graham Harman 2011. *The Speculative Turn: Continental Materialism and Realism*. Melbourne, [Victoria] Australia: re.press.

Bukharin, Nikolai 2012. *Historical Materialism: A System of Sociology*. London: Routledge.

Burkitt, Ian 2005. 'Powerful Emotions: Power, Government and Opposition in the 'War on Terror''. *Sociology* 39 (4):679–95.

Buss, Terry F. 1999. 'The Case Against Targeted Industry Strategies'. *Economic Development Quarterly* 13 (4):339–56. https://doi.org/10.1177/089124249901300406.

Butler, Judith 1997. *The Psychic Life of Power: Theories in Subjection*. Stanford, Calif.: Stanford University Press.

Cangiani, Michele 2013. 'Althusser and the Critique of Political Economy'. In *Encountering Althusser: Politics and Materialism in Contemporary Radical Thought*. New York: Bloomsbury Academic.

Caprara, Gian Vittorio, and Philip G. Zimbardo 2004. 'Personalising Politics: A Congruency Model of Political Preference'. *The American Psychologist* 59 (7):581–94. https://doi.org/10.1037/0003-066X.59.7.581.

Cardella, Sebastián 2014. 'Entre Maquiavelo y Adorno: Louis Althusser y las relaciones entre teoría y práctica política'. In *Proceedings of the VIII Jornadas de Sociología de la UNLP* (La Plata, 2014). http://sedici.unlp.edu.ar/handle/10915/47833.

Catanzaro, Gisela Mara 2013. 'Afinidades críticas: Consideraciones sobre la relación entre política y conocimiento en L. Althusser, en diálogo con los cuestionamientos de Th. Adorno al positivismo'. *REDES* 19 (36):105–28.

Catanzaro, Gisela Mara 2015. 'Emancipación y democracia: sus relaciones desde las reflexiones sobre autonomía y corte de Adorno y Althusser'. *Opción* 31 (76). https://produccioncientificaluz.org/index.php/opcion/article/view/19746.

Cavazzini, Andrea 2009. *Crise du marxisme et critique de l'État: le dernier combat d'Althusser; [suivi de L'État, le marxisme, le communisme: un débat entre Althusser et Poulantzas]*. Reims: le Clou dans le fer.

Chetcuti, Natacha 2009. 'De «On ne naît pas femme» à «On n'est pas femme». De Simone de Beauvoir à Monique Wittig'. *Genre, sexualité & société*, no. 1 (June). https://doi.org/10.4000/gss.477.

Cohen, G.A. 2000. *Karl Marx's Theory of History: A Defence*. Princeton: Princeton University Press.

Collier, A. 1996. *Scientific Realism and Socialist Thought*. Hemel Hemsptead: Harvester Wheatsheaf.

Cook, Deborah 2001. 'Adorno, Ideology and Ideology Critique'. *Philosophy and Social Criticism* 27 (1):1–20.

Cooke, Maeve 2000. 'Five Arguments for Deliberative Democracy'. *Political Studies* 48 (5):947–69. https://doi.org/10.1111/1467-9248.00289.

Dahms, Harry F. 2008. 'How Social Science Is Impossible without Critical Theory: The Immersion of Mainstream Approaches in Time and Space'. In *No Social Science without Critical Theory*, edited by F. Dahms Harry, 25:3–61. Current Perspectives in Social Theory. Emerald Group Publishing Limited. https://doi.org/10.1016/S0278-1204(08)00001-7.

Dahms, Harry F. 2017. 'Critical Theory as Radical Comparative–Historical Research'. In *The Palgrave Handbook of Critical Theory*, edited by Michael J. Thompson, 165–84. Political Philosophy and Public Purpose. New York: Palgrave Macmillan US. https://doi.org/10.1057/978-1-137-55801-5_8.

D'Arcy, Stephen 2014. 'An Exploited, Dominated, and Oppressed Class?' *The Public Autonomy Project* (blog). November 24, 2014. https://publicautonomy.org/2014/11/24/exploitation-domination-oppression/.

Davis, Mary 1995. 'Towards a Theory of Marxism and Oppression'. *Contemporary Politics* 1 (2):102–13. https://doi.org/10.1080/13569779508449883.

Day, Ronald E. 2011. 'The Aleatory Encounter and the Common Name Reading Negri Reading Althusser'. *Journal of Communication Inquiry* 35 (4):362–369.

Del Lucchese Filippo 2010. 'On the Emptiness of an Encounter: Althusser's Reading of Machiavelli'. Translated by Warren Montag. *Décalages* 1 (1). http://scholar.oxy.edu/decalages/vol1/iss1/5. Last accessed June 11, 2020.

Demaitre, Edmund 1965. 'In Search of Humanism Marxism-Leninism'. *Problems of Communism* 14 (5):18–30.

Dennis, Rutledge M. 1995. 'Social Darwinism, Scientific Racism, and the Metaphysics of Race'. *The Journal of Negro Education* 64 (3):243–52. https://doi.org/10.2307/2967206.

Depetris-Chauvin, Emilio 2015. 'Fear of Obama: An Empirical Study of the Demand for Guns and the U.S. 2008 Presidential Election'. *Journal of Public Economics* 130 (October):66–79. https://doi.org/10.1016/j.jpubeco.2015.04.008.

Dewey, John 1939. 'Culture & Human Nature; The Problem of Frredom'. In *Freedom and Culture*. New York: G.P. Putnam's Sons.

Dewey, John 2000. *Liberalism and Social Action*. Amherst (New York): Prometheus Books.

Dewey, John 2008a. 'Freedom and Culture'. In *The Later Works, 1925–1953. Volume 13,*

Volume 13, edited by Jo Ann Boydston, 63–188. Carbondale (Ill.): Southern Illinois University Press.

Dewey, John 2008b. 'Why I Am Not a Communist'. In *The Later Works of John Dewey, 1925–1953*, edited by Jo Ann Boydston, 9: 1933–34:91–95. Carbondale: Southern Illinois University Press.

Diefenbach, Katja 2013. 'Althusser with Deleuze: How to Think Spinoza's Immanent Cause'. In *Encountering Althusser: Politics and Materialism in Contemporary Radical Thought*. New York: Bloomsbury Academic.

Dosse, Francois 1997. *History of Structuralism. Vol. 1: The Rising Sign: 1945–1966*. Minneapolis, Minn.: University of Minnesota Press.

'Dossier «Collège Hyppolite -Wolf» Concernant l'annulation Par Le Collège de France Du VIIème Congrès Hegel Prévu Les 8–12 Avril 1969 et Auquel Devaient Participer Louis Althusser et Herbert Marcuse'. 1969. Fonds Althusser 20ALT/34/16. Institut Mémoires de l'Édition Contemporaine.

Dotson, Kristie 2011. 'Tracking Epistemic Violence, Tracking Practices of Silencing'. *Hypatia* 26 (2):236–57. https://doi.org/10.1111/j.1527-2001.2011.01177.x.

Druelle, Fabrice 2018. '«Louis Althusser: L'énigme du philosophe meurtrier»'. *France Inter*. https://www.franceinter.fr/emissions/affaires-sensibles/affaires-sensibles-30-mars-2018.

Dryzek, John S. 2002. *Deliberative Democracy and Beyond: Liberals, Critics, Contestations*. Oxford University Press. https://www.oxfordscholarship.com/view/10.1093/019925043X.001.0001/acprof-9780199250431.

Dukes, Hunter 2016. 'Assembling the Mechanosphere: Monod, Althusser, Deleuze and Guattari'. *Deleuze Studies* 10 (4):514–30. https://doi.org/10.3366/dls.2016.0243.

Dumenil, Gérard 1977. *Le concept de loi économique dans 'Le Capital'*. Paris: F. Maspero.

Dupuis-Déri, Francis 2015. 'La banalité du mâle. Louis Althusser a tué sa conjointe, Hélène Rytmann-Legotien, qui voulait le quitter'. *Nouvelles Questions Féministes* Vol. 34 (1):84–101.

Dupuis-Déri, Francis 2016. 'Post-scriptum de l'article «La banalité du mâle: Louis Althusser a tué sa conjointe, Hélène Rytmann-Legotien, qui voulait le quitter»'. *Nouvelles Questions Féministes* 35 (1):131–35. https://doi.org/10.3917/nqf.351.0131.

Durkheim, Émile, and George Simpson 1933. *Émile Durkheim on The Division of Labor in Society*. New York: Macmillan.

Elliott, Gregory 1999. 'Introduction: In the Mirror of Machiavelli'. In *Machiavelli and Us*, edited by Gregory Elliott, xi–xxii. London New York: Verso.

Elliott, Gregory 2006a. *Althusser: The Detour of Theory*. Leiden; Boston: Brill.

Elliott, Gregory 2006b. 'Postscript: The Necessity of Contingency'. In *Althusser: The Detour of Theory*, 317–72. Historical Materialism Book Series. Leiden; Boston: Brill.

Engels, Frederick 1973. 'Socialism: Utopian and Scientific'. In *Karl Marx and Frederick Engels Selected Works in Three Volumes: Volume 3*, 95–151. Moscow: Progress Publishers.

Entman, Robert M. 2010. 'Media Framing Biases and Political Power: Explaining Slant in News of Campaign 2008:' *Journalism*, August. https://doi.org/10.1177/1464884910367587.

Fabula, Équipe de recherche 2018. 'Colloque: 'Louis Althusser: politique, philosophie' (Cerisy)'. Text. http://www.ccic-cerisy.asso.fr/althusser18.html. July 25, 2018. https://www.fabula.org/actualites/louis-althusser-politique-philosophie-dir-julia-christ-bertrand-ogilvie_84459.php.

Ferdinand, Keith C. 2008. 'Fixed-Dose Isosorbide Dinitrate-Hydralazine: Race-Based Cardiovascular Medicine Benefit or Mirage?' *The Journal of Law, Medicine & Ethics* 36 (3):458–63. https://doi.org/10.1111/j.1748-720X.2008.291.x.

Fernández Liria, Pedro 2002. 'Regreso al «Campo de Batalla»'. In *Para un materialismo aleatorio*, 73–125. Madrid: Arena Libros.

Fernandez, Mary Elizabeth, and Akke Tick 1994. 'Gender and Indigenous Knowledge'. *Indigenous Knowledge Monitor* 2 (August). https://doi.org/10.1215/97808223938 49-014.

Finkelstein, Gabriel 2001. 'Romanticism, Race, and Recapitulation'. *Science* 294 (5549): 2101–2. https://doi.org/10.1126/science.1066826.

Finn, Geraldine 1996. *Why Althusser Killed His Wife: Essays on Discourse and Violence*. Humanities Press.

Fraser, Nancy 2013. 'What's Critical about Critical Theory?' Feminists Read Habermas (RLE Feminist Theory). May 20, 2013. https://doi.org/10.4324/9780203094006 -8.

Freud, Sigmund, James Strachey, Anna Freud, Alix Strachey, and Alan Tyson 1964. *The Standard Edition of the Complete Psychological Works of Sigmund Freud. Volume XXII, 1932–1936, Volume XXII, 1932–1936*. London: The Hogarth Press: The Institute of Psycho-Analysis.

Frye, Marilyn 1983. *The Politics of Reality: Essays in Feminist Theory*.

Furner, James 2015. 'Marx with Kant on Exploitation'. *Contemporary Political Theory* 14 (1):23–44. https://doi.org/10.1057/cpt.2013.49.

Garo, Isabelle 2012. '«Il Pleut» – Matérialisme de la rencontre et politique du vide chez le dernier Althusser'. In *Autour d'Althusser: penser un matérialisme aléatoire: problèmes et perspectives*, edited by Annie Ibrahim, 164–86. Paris: Temps des cerises.

Garo, Isabelle 2013. 'The Impossible Break: Ideology in Movement between Philosophy and Politics'. In *Encountering Althusser: Politics and Materialism in Contemporary Radical Thought*. New York: Bloomsbury Academic.

Gary, Ian, and Terry Lynn Karl 2003. *Bottom of the Barrel: Africa's Oil Boom and the Poor*. Catholic Relief Services.

George, François 1971. 'Reading Althusser'. *Telos* 1971 (7):73–98. https://doi.org/10.3817/0371007073.

Gershberg, Zac 2017. 'Rhetoric in a Transmedia Storytelling Campaign: How Trump

Deployed the Paranoid Style in 2016'. The Presidency and Social Media. December 22, 2017. https://doi.org/10.4324/9781315112824-10.

Geuss, Raymond 2010. *The Idea of a Critical Theory: Habermas and the Frankfurt School.* Cambridge: Cambridge University Press.

Giardina, Michael D. 2010. 'Barack Obama, Islamophobia, and the 2008 U.S. Presidential Election Media Spectacle'. *Counterpoints* 346:135–57.

Gilbert, Dorie J. 2003. 'The Sociocultural Construction of AIDS among African American Women'. In *African American Women and HIV/AIDS: Critical Responses*, edited by Ednita M Wright, 5–27. Westport, Conn.: Praeger.

Gillot, Pascale 2012. 'Althusser, Wittgenstein, et la question du sujet'. In *Autour d'Althusser: penser un matérialisme aléatoire: problèmes et perspectives*, edited by Annie Ibrahim, 122–44. Paris: Temps des cerises.

Glazier, Rebecca A., and Amber E. Boydstun 2012. 'The President, the Press, and the War: A Tale of Two Framing Agendas'. *Political Communication* 29 (4):428–46. https://doi.org/10.1080/10584609.2012.721870.

Goldstein, Philip 2005. *Post-Marxist Theory: An Introduction.* State University of New York Press. https://muse.jhu.edu/book/4881.

Gorz, André 1964. *Stratégie ouvrière et néocapitalisme.* Paris: Éd. du seuil.

Goshgarian, G.M. 2003. 'Introduction to The Humanist Controversy and Other Writings, 1966–67'. In *The Humanist Controversy and Other Writings, 1966–67*, xi–lxi. London; New York: Verso.

Goshgarian, G.M. 2006. 'Translator's Introduction'. In *Louis Althusser, Philosophy of the Encounter: Later Writings, 1978–87*, xiii–l. Verso.

Goshgarian, G.M. 2013. 'The Very Essence of the Object, the Soul of Marxism and Other Singular Things: Spinoza in Althusser 1959–67'. In *Encountering Althusser: Politics and Materialism in Contemporary Radical Thought.* New York: Bloomsbury Academic.

Goshgarian, G.M. 2015. 'A Marxist in Philosophy'. *Diacritics* 43 (2):24–46.

Goshgarian, G.M. 2019. 'The Void of the Forms of Historicity as Such'. *Rethinking Marxism* 31 (3):243–72. https://doi.org/10.1080/08935696.2019.1623541.

Grollios, Vasilis 2013. 'Alex Callinicos's Marxism: Dialectics and Materialism in Althusser and Frankfurt School'. *Critique* 41 (1):55–75. https://doi.org/10.1080/03017605.2013.776231.

Guillaumin, Colette 1995. *Racism, sexism, power, and ideology.* London; New York: Routledge.

Haack, Susan 2012. 'Six Signs of Scientism'. *Logos & Episteme: An International Journal of Epistemology* 3 (1):75–95.

Habermas, Jürgen 2007. *The Philosophical Discourse of Modernity: Twelve Lectures.* Cambridge; Malden: Polity Press.

Haider, Asad, and Salar Mohandesi 2012. 'Underground Currents: Louis Althusser's 'On

Marxist Thought'.' *Viewpoint Magazine* (blog). September 12, 2012. http://viewpoint mag.com/2012/09/12/underground-currents-louis-althussers-on-marxist-thought/.

Haller, John S. 1997. *Outcasts from Evolution: Scientific Attitudes of Racial Inferiority, 1859–1900.* Carbondale: Southern Illinois University Press.

Harding, Sandra 1991a. " ... And Race'?: Toward the Science Question in Global Feminisms'. In *Whose Science? Whose Knowledge?*, 191–217. Thinking from Women's Lives. Cornell University Press. https://www.jstor.org/stable/10.7591/j.ctt1hhfnmg.11.

Harding, Sandra 1991b. ''Strong Objectivity' and Socially Situated Knowledge'. In *Whose Science? Whose Knowledge?*, 138–63. Thinking from Women's Lives. Cornell University Press. https://www.jstor.org/stable/10.7591/j.ctt1hhfnmg.9.

Hayes, Danny, and Matt Guardino 2010. 'Whose Views Made the News? Media Coverage and the March to War in Iraq'. *Political Communication* 27 (1):59–87. https://doi.org/ 10.1080/10584600903502615.

Heineman, Robert 1991. 'A Review of Evolutionary Jurisprudence: Prospects and Limitations on the Use of Modern Darwinism throughout the Legal Process'. *Politics and the Life Sciences* 9 (2):285–86. https://doi.org/10.1017/S0730938400010911.

Heisler, Ron 2001. 'Response to the Modern Ranters: A Layman's Naive Thoughts on the Cult of Roy Bhaskar'. *What Next?*, no. 18. http://www.whatnextjournal.org.uk/Pages/ Back/Wnext18/Bhaskar.html.

Henninger, Max 2007. 'Facticity and Contingency in Louis Althusser's Aleatory Materialism'. *Pli: The Warwick Journal of Philosophy* 18 (January):34–59.

Hillygus, D. Sunshine, and Todd G. Shields 2005. 'Moral Issues and Voter Decision Making in the 2004 Presidential Election'. *PS: Political Science & Politics* 38 (2):201–9. https://doi.org/10.1017/S1049096505056301.

Hochman, Adam 2013. 'Do We Need a Device to Acquire Ethnic Concepts?' *Philosophy of Science* 80 (5):994–1005. https://doi.org/10.1086/673896.

Hochman, Adam 2016. 'Race: Deflate or Pop?' *Studies in History and Philosophy of Biological and Biomedical Sciences* 57 (June):60–68. https://doi.org/10.1016/j.shpsc.2016 .03.003.

Hochman, Adam 2019. 'Race and Reference'. *Biology and Philosophy* 34 (2):32. https:// doi.org/10.1007/s10539-019-9685-z.

Hodges, Donald, and Ross Gandy 1980. 'Varieties of Economic Determinism'. Edited by William H. Shaw, Gerald A. Cohen, Frank Parkin, Ben Fine, and Laurence Harris. *The Journal of Economic History* 40 (2):373–76.

Holbert, R. Lance 2004. 'Political Talk Radio, Perceived Fairness, and the Establishment of President George W. Bush's Political Legitimacy'. *Harvard International Journal of Press/Politics* 9 (3):12–27. https://doi.org/10.1177/1081180X04265976.

Horkheimer, Max 1999. 'Traditional and Critical Theory'. In *Critical Theory: Selected Essays*, 188–243. New York: Continuum Press.

Hunley, J.D. 1991. *Life and Thought of Friedrich Engels.* Yale University Press. https://doi .org/10.2307/j.ctt211qx5f.

Ichida, Yoshihiko, and Francois Matheron 2005. 'Un, Deux, Trois, Quatre, Dix Mille Althusser?' *Multitudes*, no. 2:167–178.

Illas, Edgar 2013. 'The Procrustean Bed of Class Struggle'. *Décalages* 1 (3):2. https://scholar.oxy.edu/handle/20.500.12711/12964.

Irwin, Katherine 2001. 'Legitimating the First Tattoo: Moral Passage through Informal Interaction'. *Symbolic Interaction* 24 (1):49–73. https://doi.org/10.1525/si.2001.24.1.49.

Iyengar, Shanto 2005. 'Speaking of Values: The Framing of American Politics'. *The Forum* 3 (3). https://doi.org/10.2202/1540-8884.1093.

Jacoby, Russell 2010. *Dialectic of Defeat: Contours of Western Marxism*. Cambridge, GBR: Cambridge University Press.

Jaeggi, Rahel 2008. 'Qu'est-ce que la critique de l'idéologie?' *Actuel Marx* n° 43 (1):96–108.

Jaeggi, Rahel 2014. *Alienation*. Columbia University Press.

Jaeggi, Rahel 2016. 'What (If Anything) Is Wrong with Capitalism? Dysfunctionality, Exploitation and Alienation: Three Approaches to the Critique of Capitalism'. *The Southern Journal of Philosophy* 54 (S1):44–65. https://doi.org/10.1111/sjp.12188.

Jaeggi, Rahel 2017. 'Crisis, Contradiction, and the Task of a Critical Theory'. In *Feminism, Capitalism, and Critique: Essays in Honor of Nancy Fraser*, edited by Banu Bargu and Chiara Bottici, 209–24. Cham: Springer International Publishing. https://doi.org/10.1007/978-3-319-52386-6_12.

Jaggar, Alison M. 1989. 'Love and Knowledge: Emotion in Feminist Epistemology'. *Inquiry* 32 (2):151–76. https://doi.org/10.1080/00201748908602185.

Jay, Martin 1984. *Marxism and Totality: The Adventures of a Concept from Lukács to Habermas*. Berkeley: University of California Press.

Jennings, Carolyn Dicey 2016. 'Women in Philosophy 1930–1979: What Can It Tell Us about Diversity Today? (Updated Numbers, 5/29/16)'. New APPS: Art, Politics, Philosophy, Science. May 29, 2016. https://www.newappsblog.com/2016/05/women-in-philosophy-1930-1979-what-can-it-tell-us-about-diversity-today.html.

Jennings, Carolyn Dicey, and Eric Schwitzgebel 2015. 'An Empirical Look at Gender and Research Specialisation'. presented at the Hypatia, Philadelphia, Penn., May. http://faculty.ucmerced.edu/cjennings3/Hypatia.pdf.

Johnston, Adrian 2013. 'A Critique of Natural Economy: Quantum Physics with Zizek'. In *Zizek Now: Current Perspectives in Zizek Studies*, edited by Jamil Khader and Molly Anne Rothenberg, 103–20. John Wiley & Sons.

Jones, Claudia 1995. ' "An End to the Neglect of the Problems of Negro Women." In *Words of Fire: An Anthology of African-American Feminist Thought*, edited by Beverly Guy-Sheftall. New York: New Press: Distributed by W.W. Norton.

Joslyn, Mark R. 1997. 'The Public Nature of Personal Opinion: The Impact of Collective Sentiment on Individual Appraisal'. *Political Behavior* 19 (4):337–63.

Jost, John T. 2006. 'The End of the End of Ideology'. *The American Psychologist* 61 (7):651–70. https://doi.org/10.1037/0003-066X.61.7.651.

Jost, John T. 2017. 'Ideological Asymmetries and the Essence of Political Psychology'. *Political Psychology* 38 (2):167–208. https://doi.org/10.1111/pops.12407.

Jost, John T., Brian A. Nosek, and Samuel D. Gosling 2008. 'Ideology: Its Resurgence in Social, Personality, and Political Psychology'. *Perspectives on Psychological Science* 3 (2):126–36.

Judt, Tony 1992. *Past Imperfect: French Intellectuals, 1944–1956.* Berkeley: University of California press.

Kaidesoja, Tuukka 2005. 'The Trouble with Transcendental Arguments: Towards a Naturalisation of Roy Bhaskar's Early Realist Ontology'. *Journal of Critical Realism* 4 (1):28–61. https://doi.org/10.1558/jocr.v4i1.28.

Karol, David, and Edward Miguel 2007. 'The Electoral Cost of War: Iraq Casualties and the 2004 U.S. Presidential Election'. *The Journal of Politics* 69 (3):633–48. https://doi.org/10.1111/j.1468-2508.2007.00564.x.

Kelley, Donald R. 2002. 'Intellectual History and Cultural History: The inside and the Outside'. *History of the Human Sciences* 15 (2):1. https://doi.org/10.1177/0952695102015002123.

Kellner, Douglas 2007. 'Bushspeak and the Politics of Lying: Presidential Rhetoric in the 'War on Terror'.' *Presidential Studies Quarterly* 37 (4):622–45.

Kemp, Stephen 2005. 'Critical Realism and the Limits of Philosophy'. *European Journal of Social Theory* 8 (2):171–91. https://doi.org/10.1177/1368431005051762.

Khilnani, Sunil 1993. *Arguing Revolution: The Intellectual Left in Postwar France.* New Haven [etc.: Yale University Press.

Kirn, Gal 2013. 'Between the Tenth and Eleventh Theses on Feuerbach: Althusser's Return to the New Materialism'. In *Encountering Althusser: Politics and Materialism in Contemporary Radical Thought.* New York: Bloomsbury Academic.

Kitcher, Philip 1990. *Vaulting Ambition: Sociobiology and the Quest for Human Nature.* Cambridge, Mass.: MIT Press.

Kivinen, Osmo, and Tero Piiroinen 2004. 'The Relevance of Ontological Commitments in Social Sciences: Realist and Pragmatist Viewpoints'. *Journal for the Theory of Social Behaviour* 34 (3):231–48. https://doi.org/10.1111/j.0021-8308.2004.00246.x.

Kivinen, Osmo, and Tero Piiroinen 2006. 'Toward Pragmatist Methodological Relationalism: From Philosophising Sociology to Sociologising Philosophy'. *Philosophy of the Social Sciences* 36 (3):303–29. https://doi.org/10.1177/0048393106289794.

Klein, R.A., Cook, C.L., Ebersole, C.R., Vitiello, C.A., Nosek, B.A., Chartier, C.R., ... Ratliff, K.A. (2019, December 11). 'Many Labs 4: Failure to Replicate Mortality Salience Effect With and Without Original Author Involvement.' PsyArxiv Preprints https://doi.org/10.31234/osf.io/vef2

Kleingeld, Pauline, and Eric Brown 2019. 'Cosmopolitanism'. In *The Stanford Encyclopedia of Philosophy,* edited by Edward N. Zalta, Winter 2019. Metaphysics Research Lab, Stanford University. https://plato.stanford.edu/archives/win2019/entries/cosmopolitanism/.

Koechlin, Daniel 2015. 'The Critique of Alienated Labor: Marx, Marcuse and Counter-models of the 1960s'. *Revue Francaise Detudes Americaines* N° spécial 145 (4):183–95.

Koopman, Colin 2011. 'Genealogical Pragmatism: How History Matters for Foucault and Dewey'. *Journal of the Philosophy of History* 5 (3):533–61. https://doi.org/10.1163/187226311X599943.

Kuklin, Bailey 2004. 'Evolution, Politics and Law'. *Valparaiso Law Review* 38 (4):1129–1248.

Laclau, Ernesto, and Chantal Mouffe 2001. *Hegemony and Socialist Strategy: Towards a Radical Democratic Politics*. London; New York: Verso.

Lahtinen, Mikko 2009. *Politics and Philosophy: Niccolo Machiavelli and Louis Althusser's Aleatory Materialism*. Leiden; Boston: Brill. http://books.google.fr/books?hl=fr&lr=&id=fAKGR24Ua4wC&oi=fnd&pg=PR9&dq=althusser+aleatory+materialism&ots=aBHL2heydf&sig=ene9XOuqMp31hLzZvpRGrM9SjMk.

Landau, Mark J., Sheldon Solomon, Jeff Greenberg, Florette Cohen, Tom Pyszczynski, Jamie Arndt, Claude H. Miller, Daniel M. Ogilvie, and Alison Cook 2004. 'Deliver Us from Evil: The Effects of Mortality Salience and Reminders of 9/11 on Support for President George W. Bush'. *Personality and Social Psychology Bulletin* 30 (9):1136–50. https://doi.org/10.1177/0146167204267988.

Langevin, Michel 1966. 'L'Enrichissement Du Marxisme à Partir Des Resultats Du Developpement Des Sciences de La Nature: "la Dialectique de La Nature"'. In *Cahiers de l'Université Nouvelle. Esquisse d'une Histoire de La Pensée Scientifique*. Paris, Rue Navarin.

Lanning, Kevin 2005. 'The Social Psychology of the 2004 U.S. Presidential Election'. *Analyses of Social Issues and Public Policy* 5 (1):145–52. https://doi.org/10.1111/j.1530-2415.2005.00060.x.

Le Blanc, Paul 1990. *Lenin and the Revolutionary Party*. Atlantic Highlands, NJ: Humanities Press International.

'Le Caïman', "très proche" d'Althusser' 2006, February 2, *Le Monde*. https://www.lemonde.fr/culture/article/2006/02/02/theatre-le-caiman-tres-proche-d-althusser_737257_3246.html.

Lee, Emily S. 2014. *Living Alterities: Phenomenology, Embodiment, and Race*. State University of New York Press.

Leiter, Brian 2018. 'Academic Ethics: Should Scholars Avoid Citing the Work of Awful People?' *The Chronicle of Higher Education*, October 25, 2018. https://www.chronicle.com/article/Academic-Ethics-Should/244882.

Lenin, V.I. 1965. 'KOMMUNISMUS, Journal of the Communist International For the Countries of South-Eastern Europe (in German), Vienna (June 1920)'. In *Collected Work*, translated by Julius Katzer, 4th ed., 31:165–67. Moscow: Progress Publishers.

Lennon, Kathleen 1997. 'Feminist Epistemology as Local Epistemology: Kathleen Lennon'. *Aristotelian Society Supplementary Volume* 71 (1):37–54. https://doi.org/10.1111/1467-8349.00018.

Lewis, Paul 2000. 'Realism, Causality and the Problem of Social Structure'. *Journal for the Theory of Social Behaviour* 30 (3):249–68. https://doi.org/10.1111/1468-5914.00129.

Lewis, William S. 2005a. 'Knowledge versus 'Knowledge': Louis Althusser on the Autonomy of Science and Philosophy from Ideology'. *Rethinking Marxism* 17 (3):455–470.

Lewis, William S. 2005b. *Louis Althusser and the Traditions of French Marxism*. 1 vols. Lanham, Md: Lexington Books.

Lewis, William S. 2007a. ''Editorial Introduction to Louis Althusser's 'Letter to the Central Committee of the PCF, 18 March, 1966''.' *Historical Materialism* 15 (2):20.

Lewis, William S. 2007b. 'Concrete Analysis and Pragmatic Social Theory (Notes Towards an Althusserian Critical Theory)'. *International Studies in Philosophy* 39 (2):97–116.

Lewis, William S. 2013. 'Althusser on Laws Natural and Juridical'. In *Althusser and Law*, edited by Laurent Desutter, 33–48. Nomikoi Critical Legal Thinkers Series. Abingdon & New York: Routledge.

Lewis, William S. 2018. 'Sur Un Voyage En Grèce'. July 2018. https://www.imec-archives.com/papiers/william-lewis/.

Lewontin, R.C. 1979. 'Sociobiology as an Adaptationist Program'. *Behavioral Science* 24 (1):5–14. https://doi.org/10.1002/bs.3830240103.

Lindner, Urs 2011. 'Repenser la «coupure épistémologique». lire Marx avec et contre Althusser'. *Actuel Marx* n° 49 (1):121–39. https://doi.org/10.3917/amx.049.0121.

Lipschultz, Jeremy Harris 2007. 'Framing Terror: Violence, Social Conflict, and the 'War on Terror'.' *Electronic News* 1 (1):21–35. https://doi.org/10.1080/19312430709336902.

Longino, Helen E. 1990. *Science as Social Knowledge: Values and Objectivity in Scientific Inquiry*. Princeton, N.J.: Princeton University Press.

Macherey, Pierre 2008. 'Althusser et Le Concept de Philosophie Spontanée Des Savants'. Proceedings of the Groupe d'études 'La philosophie au sens large'. https://philolarge.hypotheses.org/files/2017/09/21-05-2008.pdf

Major, Brenda, Alison Blodorn, and Gregory Major Blascovich 2018. 'The Threat of Increasing Diversity: Why Many White Americans Support Trump in the 2016 Presidential Election'. *Group Processes & Intergroup Relations* 21 (6):931–40. https://doi.org/10.1177/1368430216677304.

Malkin, Catherine M., and Michael E. Lamb 1994. 'Child Maltreatment: A Test of Sociobiological Theory'. *Journal of Comparative Family Studies* 25 (1):121–33.

Mandel, Ernest 1964. 'The Economics Of Neo-Capitalism'. *Socialist Register* 1 (March): 56–67.

Mandel, Hadas, and Moshe Semyonov 2016. 'Going Back in Time? Gender Differences in Trends and Sources of the Racial Pay Gap, 1970 to 2010'. *American Sociological Review* 81 (5):1039–68. https://doi.org/10.1177/0003122416662958.

Manicas, Peter T. 1998. 'John Dewey and American Social Science'. In *Reading Dewey:*

Interpretations for a Postmodern Generation, edited by Larry A Hickman, 43–62. Bloomington: Indiana University Press.

Manicas, Peter T. 2015. *A Realist Philosophy of Social Science Explanation and Understanding*. Cambridge: Cambridge University Press.

Manne, Kate 2016. 'Humanism'. *Social Theory and Practice* 42 (2):389–415.

Manne, Kate 2017. *Down Girl: The Logic of Misogyny*. Oxford University Press.

Manstead, Antony S.R. 2018. 'The Psychology of Social Class: How Socioeconomic Status Impacts Thought, Feelings, and Behaviour'. *The British Journal of Social Psychology* 57 (2):267–91. https://doi.org/10.1111/bjso.12251.

Marcus, Judith, and Zoltán Tarr 1984. *Foundations of the Frankfurt School of Social Research*. New Brunswick, U.S.A.: Transaction Books.

Marks, Jonathan 2017. *Is Science Racist?* Malden, MA: Polity, 2017.

Maruzzella, David 2019. 'The Two Bachelards of Louis Althusser'. *Parrhesia* 31:174–206.

Marx, Karl 1992. *Early Writings of Karl Marx*. Translated by Rodney Livingstone and Gregor Benton. Harmondsworth: Penguin.

Marx, Karl, and Frederick Engels 1982. 'Letter from Marx to Arnold Ruge'. In *Collected Works. Vol. 3*, 141–45. London: Lawrence & Wishart.

Marx, Karl, and Frederick Engels 1987. *Marx & Engels Collected Works Vol 29: Marx:1857–1861*. Lawrence & Wishart.

Marx, Karl, and Frederick Engels 1989. *Marx & Engels Collected Works Vol 24: Marx and Engels:1874–1883*. Lawrence & Wishart. http://muse.jhu.edu/book/33048.

Marx, Karl, and Friedrich Engels 1975. 'The German Ideology'. In *Collected Works, Volume 5*. New York: International Publishers. https://www.marxists.org/archive/marx/works/1845/german-ideology/.

Marx, Karl, and Friedrich Engels 1976. *Collected Works [of] Karl Marx [and] Frederick Engels. [Vol. 6], [Vol. 6]*. Edited by Jack Cohen. London: Lawrence & Wishart.

Marx, Karl, Friedrich Engels, Karl Marx, Institut Marksizma-Leninizma (Moskva), and Institut für Marxismus-Leninismus (Berlin) (øst) 1976. *Karl Marx Friedrich Engels Gesamtausgabe (MEGA) Band 1*. Berlin: Dietz.

Marx, Karl, and Erich Fromm 1961. *Marx's Concept of Man*. New York: F. Ungar Pub. Co.

Matheron, Francois 1998. 'The Recurrence of the Void in Louis Althusser'. Translated by Erin A. Post. *Rethinking Marxism* 10 (3):22–37.

Matheron, François 1999. 'Editorial Note'. In *Machiavelli and Us*, vi–xi. London New York: Verso.

Matheron, François 2004. 'Louis Althusser, or the Impure Purity of the Concept'. *Critical Companion to Contemporary Marxism*, 503–27.

McDermott, Daniel 2008. 'Analytical Political Philosophy'. In *Political Theory: Methods and Approaches*, edited by David Leopold and Marc Stears. Oxford University Press.

McInnes, Neil 1972. *The Western Marxists*. New York: Library Press.

McLaughlin, Neil 2008. 'Collaborative Circles and Their Discontents. Revisiting Conflict and Creativity in Frankfurt School Critical Theory'. *Sociologica*, no. 2/2008. https://doi.org/10.2383/27714.

McWhorter, Ladelle 2004. 'Sex, Race, and Biopower: A Foucauldian Genealogy'. *Hypatia* 19 (3):38–62.

Meikle, Scott 1999. 'Marx and the Stalinist History Textbook'. *Critique* 27 (1):181–201. https://doi.org/10.1080/03017609908413436.

Mendelson, Jack 1979. 'On Engel's Metaphysical Dialectics: A Foundation of Orthodox "Marxism"'? *Dialectical Anthropology* 4 (1):65–73.

Méndez, Agustín 2014. 'Eine andere Schauplatz. Variaciones en torno a lo inconsciente en Adorno y Althusser'. *Nuevo Pensamiento* 4 (4):8.

Merleau-Ponty, Maurice 1993. *Adventures of the Dialectic*. Evanson [Ill.: Northwestern University Press.

'Meurtrier de sa Femme, M. Louis Althusser bénéficie d'un non-lieu et demeure interné' 1981, January 26. *Le Monde*. http://www.lemonde.fr/archives/article/1981/01/26/meurtrier-de-sa-femme-m-louis-althusser-beneficie-d-un-non-lieu-et-demeure-interne_3041332_1819218.html.

Mikkola, Mari 2011. 'Ontological Commitments, Sex and Gender'. In *Feminist Metaphysics*, edited by Charlotte Witt, 67–83. Dordrecht: Springer.

Mikkola, Mari 2016. *The Wrong of Injustice: Dehumanisation and Its Role in Feminist Philosophy*. Studies in Feminist Philosophy. New York, NY: Oxford University Press.

Misak, C.J. 2004. *Truth, Politics, Morality: Pragmatism and Deliberation*. London; New York: Routledge.

Montagu, Ashley, and M.F. 1941. 'The Concept of Racie in the Human Sciences In the Light of Genetics'. *Journal of Heredity* 32 (8):243–48. https://doi.org/10.1093/oxfordjournals.jhered.a105051.

Morfino, Vittorio 2005. 'An Althusserian Lexicon'. Translated by Jason Smith. *Borderlands* 4 (2). http://www.borderlands.net.au/vol4no2_2005/morfino_lexicon.htm.

Moten, Fred 2002. 'The New International of Decent Feelings'. *Social Text* 20 (3):189–99.

Moulier-Boutang, Yann 1992. *Louis Althusser, une biographie 1. 1918–1945, 1. 1918–1945*. Paris: Grasset.

Moulier-Boutang, Yann 1997. 'L'interdit Biographique et l'autorisation de l'oeuvre'. *Futur Antérieur/L'Harmattan*. Numéro Special: Lire Althusser aujourd'hui. http://www.multitudes.net/L-interdit-biographique-et-l/.

Moulier-Boutang, Yann 2005. 'Le Matérialisme Comme Politique Aléatoire'. *Multitudes*, no. 2:159–165.

Mudde, Anna. 2014. 'Embodied Disagreements'. *Phaenex* 9 (2):99–111.

Mulvey, Laura 1975. 'Visual Pleasure and Narrative Cinema'. *Screen* 16 (3):6–18. https://doi.org/10.1093/screen/16.3.6.

Nanay, Bence 2010. 'Three Ways of Resisting Racism'. *Monist: An International Quarterly Journal of General Philosophical Inquiry* 93 (2):255–80.

Nash, Kate 2001. 'The "Cultural Turn" in Social Theory: Towards a Theory of Cultural Politics'. *Sociology* 35 (1):77–92. https://doi.org/10.1017/S0038038501000050.

Navarro, Fernanda 1998. 'An Encounter with Althusser'. *Rethinking Marxism* 10 (3):93–98.

Negri, Antonio 1996. 'Notes on the Evolution of the Thought of Louis Althusser'. In *Postmodern Materialism and the Future of Marxist Theory: Essays in the Althusserian Tradition*, edited by Antonio Callari and David Ruccio, 51–68. Hanover: Wesleyan University Press.

Norman, Jim 2019. 'Healthcare Once Again Tops List of Americans' Worries'. Gallup. Com. April 1, 2019. https://news.gallup.com/poll/248159/healthcare-once-again-top s-list-americans-worries.aspx.

'Northwestern Mutual – Planning & Progress Study 2018'. 2018. 2018. https://news.north westernmutual.com/planning-and-progress-2018.

Nussbaum, Martha C. 1994. 'Patriotism and Cosmopolitanism'. *Boston Review*, October 1, 1994. http://bostonreview.net/martha-nussbaum-patriotism-and-cosmopolita nism.

Nussbaum, Martha C. 1997. 'Kant and Stoic Cosmopolitanism'. *Journal of Political Philosophy* 5 (1):1–25. https://doi.org/10.1111/1467-9760.00021.

Nussbaum, Martha C. 2001. 'Duties of Justice, Duties of Material Aid: Cicero's Problematic Legacy'. *Bulletin of the American Academy of Arts and Sciences* 54 (3):38–52. https://doi.org/10.2307/3824685.

Park, Hyun Woong 2013. 'Overdetermination: Althusser versus Resnick and Wolff'. *Rethinking Marxism* 25 (3):325–40.

Parra, Eduardo Barbosa 2014. 'Notas Criticas sobre Marcuse e Althusser'. *Kínesis – Revista de Estudos dos Pós-Graduandos em Filosofia* 6 (11). http://www2.marilia.unesp .br/revistas/index.php/kinesis/article/view/4561.

Peden, Knox 2014. *Spinoza Contra Phenomenology: French Rationalism from Cavaillès to Deleuze.*

Persily, Nathaniel 2017. 'The 2016 U.S. Election: Can Democracy Survive the Internet?' *Journal of Democracy* 28 (2):63–76. https://doi.org/10.1353/jod.2017.0025.

Pfeifer, Geoff 2015. *The New Materialism: Althusser, Badiou, and Žižek*. Routledge.

Pigliucci, Massimo 2013. 'What Are We to Make of the Concept of Race?: Thoughts of a Philosopher–Scientist'. *Studies in History and Philosophy of Science Part C: Studies in History and Philosophy of Biological and Biomedical Sciences* 44 (3):272–77. https:// doi.org/10.1016/j.shpsc.2013.04.008.

Pigliucci, Massimo, and Jonathan Kaplan 2003. 'On the Concept of Biological Race and Its Applicability to Humans'. *Philosophy of Science* 70 (5):1161–72. https://doi.org/10 .1086/377397.

Plekhanov, Georgiï Valentinovich 1964. *The Materialist Conception of History*. New York: International Publishers. https://trove.nla.gov.au/version/26865200.

Pommier, Gérard 1998. *Louis du Néant: la mélancolie d'Althusser*. Paris: Aubier.

Pommier, Gérard 2009. *La mélancolie: vie et oeuvre d'Althusser*. Paris: Flammarion.

Posner, Richard A. 2005. *Law, Pragmatism, and Democracy*. Cambridge, MA: Harvard University Press.

Przeworski, Adam 1998. 'Deliberation and Ideological Domination'. In *Deliberative Democracy*, edited by John Elster, 140–60. Cambridge, U.K: Cambridge University Press. https://doi.org/10.1017/CBO9781139175005.008.

Quinnipiac University 2008. 'QU Poll Release Detail'. QU Poll. May 8, 2008. https://poll .qu.edu/national/release-detail?ReleaseID=1177.

Rancière, Jacques 1973. 'Sur La Théorie de l'idéologie Politique d'Althusser'. *L Homme et La Société* 27 (1):31–61. https://doi.org/10.3406/homso.1973.1785.

Rasella D. 2018. 'Child Morbidity and Mortality Associated with Alternative Policy Responses to the Economic Crisis in Brazil: A Nationwide Microsimulation Study. – PubMed – NCBI'. 2018. https://www.ncbi.nlm.nih.gov/pubmed/29787574.

Ratner, Carl 2014. 'Psychology of Oppression'. In *Encyclopedia of Critical Psychology*, edited by Thomas Teo, 1557–70. New York, NY: Springer New York. https://doi.org/ 10.1007/978-1-4614-5583-7_571.

Rawls, John 1999. *A Theory of Justice*. Cambridge, Massachusetts: Belknap Press: Harvard University Press.

Read, Jason 2013. 'To Think the New in the Absence of Its Conditions: Althusser and Negri and the Philosophy of Primitive Accumulation'. In *Encountering Althusser: Politics and Materialism in Contemporary Radical Thought*. New York: Bloomsbury Academic.

Rehmann, Jan 2007. 'Ideology Theory'. *Historical Materialism* 15 (4):211–39. https://doi .org/10.1163/156920607X251529.

Rekret, Paul 2016. 'Generalised Antagonism and Political Ontology in the Debate between Laclau and Negri'. In *Radical Democracy and Collective Movements Today*, edited by Alexandros Kioupkiolis and Giorgos Katsambekis. https://doi.org/10.4324/ 9781315603469-9.

Rekret, Paul, and Simon Choat 2016. 'From Political Topographies to Political Logics: Post-Marxism and Historicity'. *Constellations* 23 (2):281–91. https://doi.org/10.1111/ 1467-8675.12199.

Resch, Robert Paul 1992. *Althusser and the Renewal of Marxist Social Theory*. Berkeley (Calif.): University of California Press.

Robles, Gustavo Matías 2018. 'Sobre la constitución ideológica del sujeto: Theodor Adorno y Louis Althusser'. *Revista de Filosofía (Madrid, 1942)* 43 (1):85–02.

Rockmore, Tom 2014. 'Marx and the Transition Problem'. *Frontiers of Philosophy in China* 9 (3):342–49.

Rosen, Michael 2013. *On Voluntary Servitude: False Consciousness and the Theory of Ideology*. Polity.

Rosenfeld, Diane L. 2018. 'Does the Law Hear Women?' CNN. September 29, 2018. https://www.cnn.com/2018/09/29/opinions/metoo-laws-rosenfeld/index.html.

Rousseau, Jean-Jacques, Donald A Cress, and Peter Gay 1987. 'On the Social Contract'. In *Jean-Jacques Rousseau: The Basic Political Writings*, 141–227. Indianapolis, Ind.: Hackett Publishing.

Rousseau, Jean-Jacques, Christopher Kelly, and Allan Bloom 2010. *Emile, or, On Education: Includes Emile and Sophie, or, The Solitaries*. Hanover, N.H.: University Press of New England.

Rushton, J. Philippe, and Glayde Whitney 2002. 'Cross-National Variation in Violent Crime Rates: Race, r-K Theory, and Income'. *Population and Environment* 23 (6):501–11. https://doi.org/10.1023/A:1016335501805.

'Sami Frey lit: Lettres d' Althusser à Hélène 1/9' 2014. *France Culture*. https://www.franceculture.fr/emissions/denis-podalydes-lit/sami-frey-lit-lettres-dalthusser-helene-19.

Sanders, Lynn M. 1997. 'Against Deliberation'. *Political Theory* 25 (3):347–76.

Savage, Mike, Fiona Devine, Niall Cunningham, Mark Taylor, Yaojun Li, Johs Hjellbrekke, Brigitte Le Roux, Sam Friedman, and Andrew Miles 2013. 'A New Model of Social Class? Findings from the BBC's Great British Class Survey Experiment'. *Sociology* 47 (2):219–50. https://doi.org/10.1177/0038038513481128.

Schaff, Adam 1970. *Marxism and the Human Individual*. Translated by Olgierd Wojtasiewicz. New York: McGraw-Hill.

Schmidt, James 2007. 'The 'Eclipse of Reason' and the End of the Frankfurt School in America'. *New German Critique*, no. 100:47–76.

Schöttler, Peter 2013. 'Scientisme Sur l' histoire d' un Concept Difficile'. *Revue Synthèse* 134 (1):89–113.

Schriber, Roberta A., Joanne M. Chung, Katherine S. Sorensen, and Richard W. Robins 2017. 'Dispositional Contempt: A First Look at the Contemptuous Person. [Miscellaneous Article]'. *Journal of Personality* 113 (2):280–309. https://doi.org/10.1037/psppooooo101.

Schwitzgebel, Eric 2017. 'What Proportion of Philosophy Majors Are Women?' Daily Nous. December 9, 2017. http://dailynous.com/2017/12/09/women-majoring-philosophy-schwitzgebel/.

Sesardic, Neven 1985. *Marxian Utopia*. London, UK: CRCE.

Seymour, Richard 2017. 'The Murder of Hélène Rytman'. Versobooks.Com. July 24, 2017. https://www.versobooks.com/blogs/3324-the-murder-of-helene-rytman.

Shandro, Alan 2014. *Marxism, Lenin and the Logic of Hegemony: Spontaneity and Consciousness in the Class Struggle*. Brill. https://doi.org/10.1163/9789004271067_005.

Shapiro, Robert Y. 1998. 'Public Opinion, Elites, and Democracy'. *Critical Review* 12 (4):501–528. https://doi.org/10.1080/08913819808443514.

Sharp, Hasana 2000. ''Is It Simple to Be a Feminist in Philosophy?': Althusser and Feminist Theoretical Practice'. *Rethinking Marxism* 12 (2):18–34. https://doi.org/10.1080/08935690009358999.

Shelby, Tommie 2007. *We Who Are Dark: The Philosophical Foundations of Black Solidarity*. Cambridge, Mass.; London, England: The Belknap Press of the Harvard University Press.

Shettleworth, Sara J. 2010. *Cognition, Evolution, and Behavior*. Oxford; New York: Oxford University Press.

Short, Philip 2006. *Pol Pot: Anatomy of a Nightmare*.

Sim, Stuart 2013. *Post-Marxism: An Intellectual History*. London: Routledge.

Simmons, William Paul, and Sharon Parsons 2005. 'Beliefs in Conspiracy Theories Among African Americans: A Comparison of Elites and Masses'. *Social Science Quarterly* 86 (3):582–98.

Sinard, Alisonne 2017. 'Repas de famille ou folie d' Althusser: état(s) de crise(s) en scène'. France Culture. July 24, 2017. https://www.franceculture.fr/theatre/repas-de-famille -ou-folie-dalthusser-etats-de-crises-en-scene.

Smith, Linda Tuhiwai 2012. *Decolonising Methodologies*. 2nd ed. London: Zed Books. https://www.zedbooks.net/shop/book/decolonising-methodologies/.

Solomon, Miriam 1992. 'Scientific Rationality and Human Reasoning'. *Philosophy of Science* 59 (3):439–455. https://doi.org/10.1086/289680.

Solomon, Samuel 2012. 'L'espacement de La Lecture: Althusser, Derrida, and the Theory of Reading'. *Décalages* 1 (2). http://scholar.oxy.edu/decalages/vol1/iss2/4. Last accessed June 11, 2020.

Somin, Ilya 1998. 'Voter Ignorance and the Democratic Ideal'. *Critical Review* 12 (4):413–58. https://doi.org/10.1080/08913819808443511.

Sotiris, Panagiotis 2006. 'Contradictions of Aleatory Materialism: On Louis Althusser's Later Writings'. http://www.after1968.org/app/webroot/uploads/Article-Sotiris.pdf.

Sotiris, Panagiotis 2008. 'Philosophy of the Encounter: Later Writings, 1978–1987'. *Historical Materialism* 16 (3):147–78. https://doi.org/10.1163/156920608X315284.

Sotiris, Panagiotis 2019. 'Is a 'Left Populism' Possible?' *Historical Materialism* 27 (2):3–39. https://doi.org/10.1163/1569206X-00001832.

Spencer, Quayshawn 2015. 'Philosophy of Race Meets Population Genetics'. *Studies in History and Philosophy of Science Part C: Studies in History and Philosophy of Biological and Biomedical Sciences*, Genomics and Philosophy of Race, 52 (August):46–55. https://doi.org/10.1016/j.shpsc.2015.04.003.

Stalin, Iosif 1949. *History of the Communist Party of the Soviet Union: Bolsheviks: Short Course*. Moscow: Foreign languages publishing house.

Stalin, Joseph 1951. *Marxism and Linguistics*. New York: International Publishers.

Stepan, Nancy 1987. *The Idea of Race in Science: Great Britain, 1800–1960*. Houndmills, Basingstoke: Macmillan Press.

Stillman, Peter G. 2005. 'The Myth of Marx's Economic Determinism'. Marx Myths and

Legend. April 2005. https://www.marxists.org/subject/marxmyths/peter-stillman/ article.htm.

Streeck, Wolfgang 2015. 'Epilogue: Comparative-Historical Analysis: Past, Present, Future'. In *Advances in Comparative-Historical Analysis*, edited by James Mahoney and Kathleen Thelen. Cambridge [U.K.]: Cambridge University Press. https://doi .org/10.1017/CBO9781316273104.011.

Stuckey, Mary E., and Joshua R. Ritter 2007. 'George Bush, and American Democracy'. *Presidential Studies Quarterly* 37 (4):646–66.

Stuhr, John J. 2017. 'Somewhere, Dreaming of Cosmopolitanism'. In *Cosmopolitanism and Place*, edited by José M. Medina and Jessica Wahman, 280–95. Indiana University Press. https://muse.jhu.edu/chapter/2017310.

Sturrock, John 1999. *The Word from Paris: Essays on Modern French Thinkers and Writers*. London New York: Verso.

Suchting, Wal 2004. 'Althusser's Late Thinking about Materialism'. *Historical Materialism* 12 (1):3–70.

Talisse, Robert B. 2003. 'John Dewey's Liberalism: Individual, Community, and Self-Development (Book)'. *Transactions of the Charles S. Peirce Society* 39 (1):134.

Talisse, Robert B. 2005. *Democracy after Liberalism: Pragmatism and Deliberative Politics*. New York: Routledge.

Taylor, Paul C. 2000. 'Appiah's Uncompleted Argument: W.E.B. Du Bois and the Reality of Race'. *Social Theory and Practice* 26 (1):103–28.

Taylor, Paul C. 2014. *Race: A Philosophical Introduction*.

'The Distinguishing Features of Leninist Political Practice'. 1977. *Communist Practice* 1. https://www.marxists.org/history/erol/uk.hightide/distinguishingfeatures.htm.

Therborn, Göran. 2008. *From Marxism to Post-Marxism?* London; New York: Verso.

Thomas, Peter D. 2013. 'Althusser's Last Encounter: Gramsci'. In *Encountering Althusser: Politics and Materialism in Contemporary Radical Thought*. New York: Bloomsbury Academic.

Tooley, Greg A., Mari Karakis, Mark Stokes, and Joan Ozanne-Smith. 2006. 'Generalising the Cinderella Effect to Unintentional Childhood Fatalities'. *Evolution and Human Behavior* 27 (3):224–30. https://doi.org/10.1016/j.evolhumbehav.2005.10.001.

Toscano, Alberto. 2004. 'Aleatory Rationalism'. In *Badiou: Theoretical Writings*, edited by Alain Badiou, Ray Brassier, and Alberto Toscano, 260–74. London: Continuum. http://research.gold.ac.uk/2240/.

Tosel, André. 2005. 'Les Aléas Du Matérialisme Aléatoire Dans La Dernière Philosophie de Louis Althusser'. *Kouvélakis and Charbonier (Eds.)*.

Tosel, André. 2013. 'The Hazards of Aleatory Materialism in the Late Philosophy of Louis Althusser'. In *Encountering Althusser: Politics and Materialism in Contemporary Radical Thought*. New York: Bloomsbury Academic.

Trom, Danny. 2008. 'La crise de la critique sociale, vue de Paris et de Francfort'. *Esprit* Juillet (7):108–26.

Tsoneva, Jana. 2016. 'From the 'International of Decent Feelings' to the International of Decent Actions: Althusser's Relevance for the Environmental Conjuncture of Late Capitalism'. *Althusser and Theology*, January, 168–81. https://doi.org/10.1163/9789004291553_013.

Tucker, William H. 2003. 'A Closer Look at the Pioneer Fund: Response to Rushton'. Albany Law Review. June 22, 2003. https://link.galegroup.com/apps/doc/A109029836/AONE?sid=lms.

Turner, Ben. 2019. 'Affinity and Antagonism: Structuralism, Comparison and Transformation in Pluralist Political Ontology'. *Philosophy & Social Criticism* 45 (1):27–49. https://doi.org/10.1177/0191453718797985.

Van Reeth, Adèle. 2018. 'La vie secrète des philosophes (1/5): Le procès Althusser'. *France Culture*. https://www.franceculture.fr/emissions/les-chemins-de-la-philosophie/la-vie-secrete-des-philosophes-15-le-proces-althusser.

Vatter, Miguel. 2003. 'Althusser et Machiavel'. *Multitudes* n° 13 (3):151–63. https://doi.org/10.3917/mult.013.0151.

Verret, Michel. 1976. 'Correspondance échangée autour du projet d' « Interview Imaginaire »/Vâches Noires'. Fonds Althusser 20ALT/24/18. Institut Mémoires de l'Édition Contemporaine.

Vultee, Fred. 2010. 'Securitisation'. *Journalism Practice* 4 (1):33–47. https://doi.org/10.1080/17512780903172049.

Waal, Frans B.M. de. 1999. 'The End of Nature versus Nurture'. *Scientific American* 281 (6):94–99.

Weeks, Brian E., and R. Kelly Garrett. 2014. 'Electoral Consequences of Political Rumors: Motivated Reasoning, Candidate Rumors, and Vote Choice during the 2008 U.S. Presidential Election'. *International Journal of Public Opinion Research* 26 (4):401–22. https://doi.org/10.1093/ijpor/edu005.

West, Cornel 1982. *Prophesy Deliverance!: An Afro-American Revolutionary Christianity*. Philadelphia, P.A.: The Westminster Press.

Whitehall, Deborah 2016. 'A Rival History of Self-Determination'. *European Journal of International Law* 27 (3):719–43. https://doi.org/10.1093/ejil/chw042.

Willett, Cynthia 2008. 'False Consciousness and Moral Objectivity in Kansas'. *The Journal of Speculative Philosophy* 22 (4):290–99.

Williams, Caroline 2013. 'Althusser and Spinoza: The Enigma of the Subject'. In *Encountering Althusser: Politics and Materialism in Contemporary Radical Thought*. New York: Bloomsbury Academic.

Wilson, Sarah 2010. *The Visual World of French Theory: Figurations*. New Haven [Conn.]: Yale university press.

Wingfield, Adia Harvey, and Joe Feagin 2009. *Yes We Can?: White Racial Framing and the 2008 Presidential Campaign*. 1 edition. New York: Routledge.

Wolin, Richard 2012. *The Wind from the East: French Intellectuals, the Cultural Revolution, and the Legacy of the 1960s*. Princeton University Press.

Wood, Ellen Meiksins 1998. *The Retreat from Class: A New 'True' Socialism*. London; New York: Verso.

Woolley, S.C., and D. Guilbeault 2017. 'Computational Propaganda in the United States of America: Manufacturing Consensus Online'. https://ora.ox.ac.uk/objects/uuid:62 oce18f-69ed-4294-aa85-184af2b5052e.

Wright, Erik Olin 1979. *Class Structure and Income Determination*. New York: Academic Press.

Wright, Erik Olin 1997. *Class Counts: Comparative Studies in Class Analysis*. Cambridge; Paris: Cambridge University Press; Maison des Sciences de l'homme.

Wright, Erik Olin 2009. 'Understanding Class'. *New Left Review*, II, no. 60:101–16.

Wright, Erik Olin 2015. *Understanding Class*.

Wuisman, Jan 2005. 'The Logic of Scientific Discovery in Critical Realist Social Scientific Research'. *Journal of Critical Realism* 4 (2):366–94. https://doi.org/10.1558/jocr.v4i2 .366.

Wylie, Alison 2012. 'Feminist Philosophy of Science: Standpoint Matters'. *Proceedings and Addresses of the American Philosophical Association* 86 (2):47–76.

Wylie, Alison 2015. 'A Plurality of Pluralisms: Collaborative Practice in Archaeology'. In *Objectivity in Science: New Perspectives from Science and Technology Studies.*, edited by Flavia Padovani, Alan Richardson, and Jonathan Y. Tsou, 189–210. Cham: Springer. https://doi.org/10.1007/978-3-319-14349-1_10.

Yhuel, Isabelle 2018. 'Les lettres de Louis Althusser à Hélène'. *France Culture*. https:// www.franceculture.fr/emissions/latelier-fiction/les-lettres-de-louis-althusser-a-hel ene.

Young, Iris Marion 1996. ''Communication and the Other: Beyond Deliberative Democracy' in Democracy and Difference: Contesting the Boundaries of the Political'. In *Democracy and Difference: Contesting the Boundaries of the Political*, edited by Seyla Benhabib. Princeton, N.J.: Princeton Univeristy Press.

Yudell, Michael, and Rob Desalle 2000. 'Essay Review: Sociobiology: Twenty-Five Years Later'. *Journal of the History of Biology; Dordrecht* 33 (3):577–84. http://dx.doi.org.lib -proxy01.skidmore.edu:2048/10.1023/A:1004845822189.

Zaloom, Caitlin 2018. 'How Will We Pay? Projective Fictions and Regimes of Foresight in US College Finance'. *HAU: Journal of Ethnographic Theory* 8 (1–2):239–51. https:// doi.org/10.1086/698220.

Zuberi, Tukufu, and Eduardo Bonilla-Silva 2008. *White Logic, White Methods Racism and Methodology*. Lanham: Rowman & Littlefield Publishers.

Zurbriggen, Eileen L. 2005. 'Lies in a Time of Threat: Betrayal Blindness and the 2004 U.S. Presidential Election'. *Analyses of Social Issues and Public Policy* 5 (1):189–96. https://doi.org/10.1111/j.1530-2415.2005.00064.x.

Index

CPSIA information can be obtained
at www.ICGtesting.com
Printed in the USA
JSHW081540021122
32459JS00005B/8

9 781642 597899